The End of Poverty and the Taming of Inequality

"This book by one of China's foremost thinkers and campaigning scholars on rural poverty is a must-read. Deeply engrained in practical experience on the ground in China and beyond, its core message is universal: fighting poverty involves empowering poor people to take charge of their own future through better opportunities and through thoughtful, appropriate support by state and society."

—Stefan Dercon, *Professor of Economic Policy at the Blavatnik School of Government and the Economics Department, University of Oxford*

"This is a powerful book on poverty and inequality in China. By weaving personal stories and research findings, Professor Li Xiaoyun illustrates the multifaceted nature of poverty and the systemic approaches required to eliminate poverty and reduce inequality. The rigor and depth of the analyses presented throughout this book represent policy research at its best. This book provides timely insights for China and the world to gain much-needed understanding of poverty and devise effective solutions to end it."

—Qin Gao, *Professor of Social Policy and Social Work and Director of the China Center for Social Policy at Columbia University*

"In this stimulating book one of China's leading development scholars and practitioners explores the idea and prospects of fighting poverty by weaving together academic insights and philosophical reflections with decades of his practical experience striving to reduce poverty in rural China and in other parts of the world. Ending poverty is a global challenge and this book helps readers think through the ideas and hopefully sharpen their practical action. By building on sources as diverse as classic Western moral philosophy to the micro-level actions of villagers in Hebian, the author makes a unique contribution to the literature on ending poverty."

—David Hulme, *Professor of Development Studies and Executive Director of the Global Development Institute, University of Manchester*

"A pioneer in exploring innovative approaches to poverty reduction in China, Professor Li Xiaoyun has devoted his life to advancing the country's poverty alleviation efforts. Drawing from his extensive practical experience, this book compiles his profound reflections on poverty theories and his insights into the implementation of poverty alleviation strategies in China. It vividly recounts his personal experiences in designing and executing experimental poverty alleviation initiatives in underdeveloped rural areas, making it an essential and thought-provoking read."

—Li Shi, *Professor of Development Economics at Zhejiang University*

Xiaoyun Li

The End of Poverty and the Taming of Inequality

A Manifesto for Personal and Social Action

palgrave
macmillan

Xiaoyun Li
College of International Development
and Global Agriculture, College
of Humanities and Development Studies
China Agricultural University
Beijing, China

Translated by
Jin Xu
China Agricultural University,
Beijing, China

Jing Gu
Institute of Development Studies
Sussex, UK

Sam Huckstep
Center for Global Development
London, UK

ISBN 978-981-96-0683-2 ISBN 978-981-96-0684-9 (eBook)
https://doi.org/10.1007/978-981-96-0684-9

Jointly published with CITIC Press Corporation
The print edition is not for sale in China (Mainland). Customers from China (Mainland) please order the print book from: CITIC Press Corporation.

ISBN of the Chinese edition: 9787521729467
This work was supported by 中华社会科学基金 (Chinese Fund for Humanities and Social Science) 资助

This Palgrave Macmillan imprint is published by the registered company Springer Nature Singapore Pte Ltd.
The registered company address is: 152 Beach Road, #21-01/04 Gateway East, Singapore 189721, Singapore

Foreword

In this stimulating book Professor Xiaoyun Li of the China Agricultural University explores the idea and prospects of ending poverty by weaving together academic thinking and philosophy with decades of his practical experience striving to reduce poverty in rural China and in other parts of the world. For Li, poverty is not something that is about other people. In the book he takes the reader into his family's history and the problems his grandparents faced when trying to improve their lives by migrating to another rural area, Shaanxi Province in the 1960s, and of their having to beg for food as they relocated. China may have 'emerged' in the twenty-first century but for many, perhaps most, Chinese citizens' poverty and hunger (and even famine) were parts of their parents or grandparents' day-to-day life. Only in recent times has mass poverty been overcome and many rural parts of China still have living standards below the country's 'prosperity for all' ambitions.

The book starts with a chapter that establishes its analytical framework drawing on philosophy from Henri Rousseau to Karl Marx to Oscar Lewis. It contrasts examples of the experience of poverty from villages in Hebian to regions of the USA. While this reveals a deep concern with the poorest who cannot even meet basic subsistence needs it also identifies the roots of poverty as lying in the 'meta problem' of inequality. Hundreds of millions of families across the world may have become middle-class since 1990 but hundreds of millions are only one sickness/one health problem away from sliding back into destitution. These disadvantaged households work very hard and spend their incomes wisely (they are not lazy) but even their best efforts cannot overcome the economic and social structural challenges they face. Li compares outsiders' ideas of 'objective' poverty measurement with the varied 'subjective' accounts of people who have or are personally experiencing poverty and disadvantage. The second chapter examines poverty from an ethical perspective and concludes that there is a moral imperative for those who are rich or doing well, or even just a little better-off, to support poorer people in their efforts to escape poverty. Through his work on specific case studies, such as Mr Yong and Mr You, we are persuaded that poverty in China and beyond is not about 'them'...it is about 'us': what is increasingly conceptualised as 'relational poverty'.

The book then moves to a more applied and practical focus, building on Li's vast experience of poverty alleviation and eradication programmes, with a chapter analysing 'what needs to be done'? A comparison of the very differing strategies and policies about poverty reduction in Europe and the USA helps the reader integrate philosophical ideas with practical action. Building on this Chapter 4 poses the question 'why is it so difficult to eradicate poverty?'. It reinforces the argument in Chapter 2 that structural factors, the way rich and better-off people relate to those experiencing poverty, explain why poverty is so hard to tackle. If poverty is to be eradicated it requires action by the 'rich' and non-poor as well as action by poor people.

The final two chapters explore policies and programmes to overcome poverty. In Chapter 5 the 'big' policy solutions are discussed: industrialisation, urbanisation, social protection and broader pro-poor asset-building strategies. The conclusion, Chapter 6, takes us into the village and reflects on the lessons learned by Li and his team over the last 10 years in rural Hebian. It looks in detail at their action-research programmes and projects to diversify the local economy by establishing guesthouses to generate tourist and visitor income flows, alongside changes in agricultural practises. We find out what the villagers learned, as they sought to improve their incomes and prospects, and what Li and colleagues learned as they strove to be effective intermediaries integrating the villagers into the economic opportunities created by China's amazing economic growth. Some detailed examples of the ways in which life has changed, and often improved, are presented: from villagers setting up coffee shops to others producing walnut oil. These case studies help to make the reader more optimistic about poverty reduction and they put real flesh onto questions that are dealt with only theoretically in other books.

In this fascinating book Li brings together his ideas and learning from papers, articles and reports written over the last decade. The book is one of the paradoxical 'COVID-19 bonuses': faced with a period of inaction because of lockdowns Professor Li rolled up his sleeves to craft his thinking into a more integrated output. The reader of this book will be well-rewarded but, unless they know rural China in depth, I recommend that they start with the 'view from the village' provided in Chapter 6. This personal experience has profoundly shaped Professor Li's thinking and is extensively referred to in earlier chapters. Ending poverty is a global challenge and this book helps the reader think through the ideas and hopefully sharpen their practical action. By building on sources as diverse as classic Western moral philosophy to the micro-level actions of villagers in Hebian, Professor Li makes a unique contribution to the literature on ending poverty…many thanks.

David Hulme OBE, FASS, FAEA
Professor of Development Studies
Global Development Institute
University of Manchester
Manchester, UK

Preface

I was first exposed to the issue of poverty around the mid-1990s. When I was in Stuttgart, Germany, in 1993, a friend took me to visit a local NGO, 'Bread for the World', where I met Peter Rottach[1], a project officer of the organisation. He introduced me to their global poverty reduction projects and mentioned that their peer organisations also ran poverty projects in China. He hoped I would cooperate with them in China.

Later, with Peter's support, I started to work on a poverty project in Yanqing County, Beijing. This was the first poverty project I engaged in. In the 1990s, the mountainous areas on the outskirts of Beijing were very poor. During our visit to a village, Peter and I met two wide-eyed little girls. The older one greeted us in English, which surprised me. Later, villagers told us that the girls grew up in a very poor family and dropped out of school. It was the first time I was brought face-to-face with poverty.

At the time I didn't know much about poverty, I only had some work experience on rural microcredit. In early 1990s, very few Chinese experts could speak foreign langua ges and work with people from international organisations, and I was one of them. That was why the China International Centre for Economic and Technical Exchange (CICETE) of the Ministry of Commerce asked me to join their rural pro-poor microfinance

[1] It was a slip of the pen by the author in the original book. After checking with him, 'Feed the World' and 'Peter Rotch' are replaced by 'Bread for the World' (a German organisation Brot für die Welt) and 'Peter Rottach' in this English version.

project in the Jinping and Malipo counties of Yunnan Province. As I said, I was a development broker. I was working as an intermediary between the national government and international organisations, helping international NGOs design and implement their foreign aid projects in China. But in the early years, I could only 'copy' international development practises, including the participatory approach to poverty and empowering women.

At around the same time, I gave a lecture to participants of a training programme at the Central Academy of Agricultural Management for Public Officials. A burly man came to me during a break. He said, 'Xiaoyun, do you still remember me? I was looking for you'. After talking to him, I remembered I had often seen this young man in the courtyard of the Yinnan District Administrative Office in Ningxia when I was a child. In front of my family's house was the office of the local Youth League committee, where this young man, then an official, worked. He was called Yang, and at that point served as the secretary of the local Youth League executive committee. He was now participating in this training programme as the deputy agriculture commissioner at the Yinnan District Administrative Office of Ningxia. He came to my house the night of the lecture and said he wanted to visit my father, who had already retired and was helping me take care of my child. He also invited me to Ningxia to make some contributions to my hometown. I agreed to go back and have a look. Later, at his formal invitation, a few colleagues and I visited the region where I once lived.

My father used to work in Yanchi County in Ningxia, and I lived there for two years. During my visit to Yanchi, I asked Deputy Commissioner Yang whether I could visit Dingbian County, a neighbouring county that belongs to Shaanxi Province. After talking with the leaders of Dingbian, Yang took me to Dingbian. What he didn't know was that Dingbian County was my birthplace. It's where I spent my childhood, and even now I still miss it terribly.

When I was a child, the county was coated by blinding dust storms from spring to early summer. We lived in a small earthen house in the county town. It was a very simple house. When guests entered my home, they would see a *tukang* (a heatable brick bed usually seen in northern China); a single table; and a few small benches. We lived there with my maternal grandmother, and in the summer I would go to a small mountain valley where my paternal grandparents and uncle lived. My paternal grandparents were from Gansu. When a famine hit the province in the

1960s, my paternal grandparents and my uncle left Gansu for Dingbian County to seek help from my father. They found my maternal grandmother's house in a cold winter following the address given in a letter sent by my father. On their way to Dingbian County, they had to beg for food and money to survive. With the help of acquaintances, my maternal grandmother helped them settle in a small valley called Yingliangzi in Hongliugou Township, Dingbian County. This was similar to today's efforts to relocate populations for the purposes of helping the poor.

I last went to the small valley when I was seven or eight years old. I hadn't set foot there for more than two decades. It was a windy day when I, accompanied by local officials, visited the village, and I could not keep my eyes open for the dust. This experience brought me right back to my time there as a child. The car stopped in front of a few houses. I got out of the car. Everything in the village was still familiar, from the low and dilapidated earthen houses to the chimneys of cave homes in the valley. I walked to the hollow where the cave home of my paternal grandparents was located. Next to my grandparents' home was that of my uncle. My uncle had planned to get married and start a family in the valley. But he didn't return after he graduated from high school and worked in the country. The cave dwellings had been sitting vacant for a long time.

On my return from the valley, a group of villagers came over. The local officials and the villagers were full of curiosity. They wondered why a professor from Beijing was so familiar with their village.

What they didn't know was that I spent three summer vacations here in my childhood, eating at the villagers' houses. On dust storm days, my mouth would be filled with fine gritty sand when eating, an extremely uncomfortable experience I can feel now as I write. More than two decades had passed, and the village remained in poverty.

During that period, I often travelled back and forth between China and Europe. Returning to this poor and backward village that time made me incredibly emotional. I put together the cash my colleagues and I had brought with us and gave it to a village official. He recognised me and remembered my visits to this place as a child. I thanked him for taking care of my grandparents in the past and asked him to give the money to the villagers as a thank-you gift. My grandparents were from outside the region, but the villagers hadn't discriminated against them and had let them settle down here.

In August 2020, my colleagues and I visited this village again. The concerted national campaign against extreme poverty had brought about remarkable changes to this impoverished village. Though the landscape was very much the same, with its distinctive yellow valleys and caves, families who were still there all lived in good and big brick houses.

One's career choice is often greatly affected by one's experiences in life. Although I have not personally experienced the ordeal of poverty, I could never forget the suffering of the poor villagers I saw in Yanqing County in Beijing and Dingbian County in Shaanxi. For a long time, I was haunted by the memory of standing in the village during a dust storm, surrounded by villagers. Their expressions, their questions about me and my family—who lived a life quite far removed from their own, and their helpless sighs touched my heart.

For nearly a decade now, I have been helping people trapped in poverty in Hebian Village. Like villages in Yanqing and Dingbian, this was a place where when I first visited, I was moved by the hardship I encountered. Many colleagues and friends, including acquaintances working in media circles, have asked me why I worked in this village for so long. Some of them have been quite incredulous. At the same time, many reports have put me on a pedestal as a role model with a strong political consciousness. In fact I do not have a high level of political consciousness; nor am I a role model. My concern for poverty has always been directly connected with my family's experience and the ordeal of the poor people I have met.

Why does poverty remain a stubborn fact of life in the world? What is the root cause of poverty? Why are some countries rich while others are trapped in poverty for a long time? Why do some people get rich while others remain poor? These questions continuously circle in my mind, and despite long thought I do not have answers I trust. This is mainly—and I must say this now, at the start of the book—because I have always been more focused on the operational challenges of solving real-life problems than in undertaking research. To understand the 'meta-questions' of poverty I turn to Rousseau, who offers theoretical perspectives on how differences between 'natural' men have evolved into social differences, and how private property can cause such differences to evolve into inequality and poverty. I have captured some clues about the meta-question of poverty from his works. Conversely Marx attributes inequality to the institutions of capitalism and to root causes at the social level.

Today, overcoming poverty remains a complex challenge. When discussing pervasive poverty in regions such as Africa, we tend to examine development issues from a comparative perspective. I call this kind of poverty underdevelopment. Underdevelopment is a relative concept which implies a lack of development and is a critical concern of research today. The poverty we discuss here is a macro-level relative concept. We need to point out that the comparison between development and underdevelopment is mainly derived from the critical development perspectives underpinned by Eurocentric values. In other words, underdeveloped groups do not necessarily consider themselves to be in poverty. Instead, they are in poverty in the eyes of developed groups. Many socio-culturalist scholars criticise those engaged in poverty reduction for considering these areas' cultural values and livelihood issues from an outsider's point of view. They imply that economically and socially developed outsider groups always measure the values of so-called backward areas against their own values. From this perspective, poverty reduction mainly refers to the process of promoting economic growth and advancing economic and social modernisation.

For over two decades, we have been helping the poor in China. In particular, we prioritise areas in 'deep' poverty. We consider deep poverty a relative concept derived from comparisons across all areas in China. So, when I talk about the meta-question of poverty in the book, I mention modernity. My point is that the poverty we are talking about today is a problem of modernity gaps between different groups. This view is not a value judgement in itself.

The widening gap between rich and poor, which we might find within a county, a township or even a village, is another poverty-related issue. The poverty we mention in this context is different from poverty in an underdeveloped country. This type of poverty is directly related to economic and social transformation, but is unlikely to be solved by achieving a 'developed' state. Therefore, throughout this book, I try to treat inequality as the meta-question of poverty. But no matter how we look at poverty, it is not easy to grasp the essence of it. To me, the sheer fact that China was able to eliminate absolute rural poverty in a very short period of time, was precisely due to a deep understanding of poverty in the country which was then followed by a targeted strategy to address it—an endeavour led by the Central Committee of the Communist Party of China with Xi Jinping at its core. This achievement would have been impossible without the great spirit of poverty alleviation, the leadership of the Party and the political advantages of the socialist system.

Understanding poverty is one thing, but alleviating and eliminating it is another. Absolute poverty, defined as the state by which an individual cannot meet basic life needs, including food, shelter and clothing, can be eliminated. Indeed, China was able to successfully declare domestic absolute poverty brought to an end in 2021. It is a moral obligation to end absolute poverty, not only for China but for the entire world. This is the foundation for the legitimacy of poverty reduction projects.

In the past few years, I have delivered speeches on poverty and poverty reduction at numerous events, and have published commentaries introducing poverty reduction policies in newspapers and other publications. Many of these were written at the invitation of official media outlets. When I was stuck at home during the COVID-19 pandemic, I sorted and organised these articles and commentaries and compiled them into a booklet entitled 'The End of Poverty' in the Chinese language. This book is now, with some changes and updates, edited and published in English. It should be noted that this is neither an academic work nor a work of thought. It is largely composed of very varying thoughts and essays, which do not always connect directly to each other. Some chapters also overlap with each other in terms of substance and argument. However, considering that these were some of my thoughts at the time, I did not make many changes to the articles. I am personally liable for any improprieties and illogicality that remain. I want to mention that, for international readers who may be interested in the similarities and differences of Chinese and Western poverty reduction policies and practices, some clues may be found in Chapters 4 and 5; for those who are keen on sustainability issues, go through the final four articles in Chapter 6 which, newly added in this English version, mainly introduce what happened in China's post-poverty reduction era (after 2020), for example, policies and actions aimed at sustaining achievements made in the previous fight against poverty, and advancing rural revitalisation. Hereby I would like to thank my PhD students at the time: Xiaoli Lin, Lanlan Ji and Jin Xu for helping me organise this collection in Chinese. I know some of my arguments in the original version were not well thought out or clarified, this adds to the difficulties of the translation. The team has corrected many existing errors and supplemented with necessary information and clarifications to make the script in English more clear and readable, but still unclarity may remain, of which I will take most of the responsibilities. Acknowledging this, my thanks now are extended to Jin Xu, Jing Gu and Sam Huckstep for their translation and editing work that helps bring this book to the English-speaking audience, and to Tianlu Zheng, Jiayu Li, Pengfei Li and Mingzhu Wang, graduate students at China Agricultural University, who assisted in different ways in the process. I would also like to express my sincere gratitude to Professor David Hulme at University of Manchester, Professor James Putzel at London School of Economics and Political Study, Professor Chang Shuan Li at Beijing Foreign Studies University and my colleague Professor Gubo Qi for their invaluable suggestions which helped enhance the quality of this translation.

Beijing, China Xiaoyun Li

Contents

CHAPTER 1

Origins of Poverty

Poverty is one of the most familiar and enduring conditions known to humanity. For almost as long as we have records of writing, it has been an object of consideration. However, the significance of poverty has changed over time. In non-industrialised societies widespread poverty was accepted as inevitable, while in modern times, especially with increased economic productivity ever since the industrialisation, this ceased to be the case. Three broad schools of thought attempt to explain the roots of poverty. The first attributes poverty to the particular qualities of the poor, such as laziness, low moral integrity, insufficient education and lack of skills. In general, it blames individuals. In a succession of nineteenth-century novels,[1] American writer Horatio Alger described hundreds of stories of the ascent from poverty to affluence. No matter how impoverished his protagonists are initially, all eventually manage to surmount their poverty through inner strength and persistent effort. The 'Alger hero' stories were meant to illustrate that all, including the poor, were masters of their own fate, an early rendition of the achievement model of income determination [1] still widely influential today. Economists generally believe that in a perfectly competitive economy, within free and democratic systems, individuals and groups can be supported to gradually converge economically. However, despite similar conditions now existing in many countries,

[1] Horatio Alger's most popular books were the *Ragged Dick*, *Luck and Pluck* and *Tattered Tom* series. Note by the translator.

X. Li, *The End of Poverty and the Taming of Inequality*,
https://doi.org/10.1007/978-981-96-0684-9_1

poverty stubbornly persists. This presents a factual challenge to this school of thought.

The second theoretical school holds that the environment of poverty generates a culture of poverty; groups caught in the culture of poverty have no means of overcoming poverty. The Five Families: Mexican Case Studies in the Culture of Poverty, by Oscar Lewis; The Moral Basis of a Backward Society, by Edward C. Banfield; and The Other America, by Michael Harrington, exemplify the 'culture of poverty' school, offering empirical information gathered from Mexico, Italy and the United States. The culture of poverty, once shaped, inevitably tends to perpetuate. Oscar Lewis suggested, that children growing up in poor families mostly have absorbed the basic values and norms of the sub-culture of poverty in the early days of their life, and are thus psychologically resistant to accepting the conditions of transformation or opportunities of improvement that will possibly change their life. The concept was criticised as blaming the victims of institutional racism and was almost universally shunned afterwards.

The third school believes poverty to be a structural issue, the result of constraining social, political and economic systems. Private property, and a series of consequent social and economic policies, has frequently been suggested to be at the heart of the perpetuation of poverty. Jean-Jacques Rousseau considered property the origin of inequality. Karl Marx systematically discussed the origin of poverty under capitalism, believing that, under capitalist private ownership, the owners of the means of production can impoverish workers by reaping the surplus value created by the workers. Mark Rank, one of the foremost American poverty scholars who provides the structural vulnerability framework argues that in the United States, the failure of the economic structure to provide all participants with sufficient opportunities is a central cause of poverty. His empirical analysis gives the lie to suggestions that poverty is largely the result of individual inadequacy. Alberto Alesina, a pioneer of modern political economist, further investigated the link between political systems and poverty, setting out to explain why the American welfare state is so small compared to its European counterparts.

Causes of poverty are undoubtedly complex, and mechanisms for poverty to perpetuate differ across societies and various social stages. In a transformational society, things get even more complex.

What Is the Origin of Poverty?[2]

Under the same cultural conditions the gap between individuals' well-being may result from differences in their 'abilities', it is more likely to be derived from a discrepancy in modern ethics under varied cultural conditions.

There are numerous questions about poverty that can be asked, but there is only one that no one could avoid asking. Those studying poverty or engaged in anti-poverty actions are frequently faced with this question: What is the origin of poverty. Take the impoverished Liangshan Yi Autonomous Prefecture in Sichuan Province, China, for example. Some say the Yi people are simply backward; some say they are 'spoiled' by poverty alleviation efforts; and there are various other discourses and explanations on its roots of poverty. In this case, as in many others, researchers and practitioners may easily be disoriented without a clear clue to this question. In this sense, this may be the meta-question of poverty.

From a depoliticised perspective, the origin of poverty and poverty reduction is associated with two lines of human behaviour, the first line is generating difference between people and the second is a counter-balance of the first.

The first line of human behaviour is driven by self-interest, based on the biological law, aiming to maximise individuals' interests for increasing their chances of survival. This has been underlying the socialisation process of primitive humankind all the way through to the development of modern societies.

In hunter-gatherer societies, the greatest hunter became the leader of the society. It was in this process that the difference of individuals' and the authority of some individuals' emerged. In *A Discourse upon the Origin and the Foundation of the Inequality among Mankind*, Jean-Jacques Rousseau proposed two kinds of inequalities, natural and artificial ones, the first arising from difference in strength and intelligence, the second from conventions of societies. He explained how the natural law-based competition resulted in 'difference' in original humans and how this

[2] The article was a speech by Prof. Li Xiaoyun at the 52nd session of Western Frontier Lectures of Sichuan University on June 29 and published at Narada Insights on July 6, 2017, at http://www.naradafoundation.org/content/5340.

difference was further socialised and politicised, leading to the formation of society and state.

Once political structures were established, groups and individuals at the top of political hierarchies tended to possess more material wealth, even when material scarcity was pervasive. Such cases can be observed among many remaining indigenous tribes today. Even in a relatively low-material equilibrium, tribal chiefs would display their difference from others through their material abundance, for example, more cows or leather compared to their tribe members. This difference would be extolled, rather than belittled by man, following the ethics of survival. This material superiority was merit-based. Today, we admire wealth as well. We resort to the explanation that great wealth comes from great abilities. Thus, admitting the difference of individuals' may be a starting point of inequality.

Meanwhile, another line of human behaviour exists to check and balance the difference induced from the survival competition, it is driven by the so-called altruism. In both animal kingdoms and human societies altruistic behaviour is common. It is natural for people to share things with his or her relatives, neighbours and friends. In primitive societies, people had many brothers and sisters that they would share their possessions with. When chatting with African friends today, we hear them frequently mention 'my brother' and 'my sister', but not all of these many 'brothers' and 'sisters' are biologically related. Their social network extends beyond families and kinship to broader communities. What they often say is: 'I am to share my possessions with my brothers and sisters if I have any'. Many current-day social forms involve sharing. Exactly what this means is a key subject of debates in anthropology: reciprocity. It was not until Marcel Mauss that most theories in the early twentieth century including those that survive to this day assumed people would only be motivated by self-interest [2]. Some scholars generally believe that self-interest remains a key aspect of gift-giving and reciprocity of community life. Mauss, however, presented its theory of gift as a theory of human solidarity, and in his eyes, gift is 'spontaneous, pure of ulterior motive'[3].

Beyond the non-institutional manifestations of the second line of human behaviour, there are also the institutional ones. With religion, mankind came to a stage of socialisation and organisation. From the beginning of Abrahamic faiths and Greek philosophy, religion has been closely intertwined with morality. Aristotle once said that citizens must not live a mechanic or a mercantile life for such a life is ignoble and inimical to virtue [4]. With one aim to cultivate virtue or morality, religion, has brought constraints on the self-interest-driven human behaviour. These two lines of human behaviour have thus formed a structural relationship.

Yet for quite a long time religion had suppressed human creativity until the Reformation led by Martin Luther. The Reformation advocated empowerment. It was followed by the Enlightenment, the formation of Protestantism and the emergence of capitalism when the world witnessed mankind's unprecedented pursuit of wealth. Max Weber once argued that protestant ethic, centred on hardwork and thrift, were important factors in the rising of capitalism [5]. Though many scholars [6] criticised Weber's argument, it is hard to deny that religion does play a role in fostering or motivating people's spiritual qualities, and in forging a new social mind towards wealth which is beyond the survival ethic found in primitive societies.

The United States was the first Western nation to be founded predominantly by Protestants. *The Mayflower Compact*, a document signed on the English ship Mayflower on November 21, 1620, prior to its landing at Plymouth, Massachusetts, was the first framework of government written and enacted in the territory of today's America. Yet the Compact presented a religious rational rather than an economic rational, to build a community with a disciplined protestant work ethic. America's unusual religiosity and generosity is closely linked. The country has a strong tradition of voluntary charitable giving. Measured by a fraction of people's income, Americans donate over two and a half times as much as Britons do, more than eight times as much as the Germans, and at twelve times the rate of the Japanese [10]. Statistics show that over 70% of America's charitable giving goes to organisations that are either religious by themselves or have a religious tie [11]. Some Chinese people may find it difficult to understand this kind of generosity. They would rather use their wealth to travel the world or enjoy themselves. They would not contribute to charity until they find other things boring.

To return to the two lines of behaviour mentioned above—the individual imperative to survive, and the collective impulse to support each other—we can see that the first is bound to lead to difference—including that between the rich and poor, while the second exists to balance the first one. These two constitute what I call the meta-questions of poverty and poverty reduction. In this sense, are the rich born great? Are the poor destined to be impoverished? This touches on the profound political and philosophical question explored by Rousseau in his *A Discourse upon the Origin and the Foundation of the Inequality among Mankind*, and I will discuss its insights in the following chapter.

But in practice, now that we can recognise these two impulses and the importance of working collectively for justice, why is it still so difficult to eliminate poverty? Eradication of poverty is indeed a difficult thing. The discourse between the rich and poor is unequal. The rich may attribute the poor's being poor to their 'uncivilisedness, laziness and sluggishness', but the rich seldom reveal the true story of how they become rich. The hidden truth is that to different degrees they take advantage of the 'difference' between the rich and poor. One can easily ask that does the difference between the rich and poor suffice to cause wide discrepancies in their well-beings. I don't want to deny the difference between people, but this cannot explain why in many societies poverty widely persists. This, to some extent, is an original sin, which can only be kept to oneself, and be put on a mystifying and moralising display. Usually, the rich say that 'I run fast and I work hard', and the poor refer to the rich as 'smart, hard-working, well-educated, widely-connected and skilful'. These are highly disguised discourses. The moral bearings of such discourse is that in modern society the rich are enchanted by it, while the poor are usually perplexed by it if not in the beginning then at the end of the day. Some may believe 'as long as I send my children to university, they will make money', while others feel that 'I've been working hard my whole life, but earn nothing'. The truth on poverty is often hard to see.

Now, let us turn to the discourse of 'people who help the poor'. We are neither rich nor poor but we help the poor. Socially we are not the 'have-nots' but economically we are not the 'haves', these identity mismatches often render discourse and behaviour inconsistencies. We tend to depict the poor from the perspective of the rich by saying they are poor because they always 'wait for, rely on and ask for assistance'.[3] We give the poor a myth, a promise of affluence, for them to develop the ambition to escape poverty despite the fact that again and again this same myth is shattered to pieces around us. What we really need is some self-criticism. We need to re-evaluate the effect of the poverty fight by rethinking our expectations and those of 'the poor'.

[3] '等靠要',deng kao yao, is a Chinese saying that describes the dependency of the poor that they usually wait for, rely on and ask for assistance from others. Note by the translator.

So, getting back to the meta-question 'what is the origin of poverty', let me try to put it this way. At first survival competition brings out people's difference in acquiring material possessions, gradually this difference is socialised that the strong and smart are honoured and the weak and witless are dishonoured, which intensifies the competition for survival. Out of the worship of material possession and the shame of material scarcity, morality emerges with an attempt to reduce the difference. But further socialisation of difference leads to the creation of society and state, class and stratification, which in turn solidifies the difference among people. With the global expansion of capitalism, the difference in acquiring material possessions goes beyond communities to populations and countries, producing a widening gap between the so-called rich and poor countries. It seems that the modern ethics tend to overcome this unintended consequence of capitalist expansion, but in essence, it serves to replicate itself in a wider non-capitalist world. In another word, under the same cultural conditions the gap between individuals' well-being may result from differences in their 'abilities', it is more likely to be derived from a discrepancy in modern ethics under varied cultural conditions.

What are the meta-solutions to poverty then? I mentioned that our discourses and behaviour concerning helping the poor are logically inconsistent. We need to base the solutions on the roots of poverty. The solutions to poverty constitute a metaphor for the ethics and moralities of modern states: to maintain the collective survival ethics, and assist people that are lagging behind in the modernisation process to approach and grasp the ethics of modern society.

Philosophically speaking, the meta-solution to poverty is to expand the ethics of modern society to people who haven't had it. The modern ethics is a set of basic knowledge of what is good and what is bad in modern society. In some pre-modern societies, for example, ethnic minority and impoverished areas, people may be comfortable with their 'natural' lifestyle, for example, meagre food and shabby house by modern standard. But for us who live in a modern world, it's absolutely not a decent life when children do not go to school, no medical care is available, and livestock and human living spaces merge—we tell them that this must be changed. It is challenging for them to accommodate these concepts since they live by their own ethics in a state of low-material equilibrium, which may be termed by themselves as 'a good life'. Thus we, as developmentalists, want to break their own ethics and bring in ours, just as some have suggested that to help the poor we ought to help them think outside their particular patterns.

'The poor in the context of modernisation' refers to people who are barely affected by modern ethics and those who do not think or act in a way underpinned by modern ethics. To enable them to approach or grasp modernity is quite challenging. For instance, it is very hard to establish a cooperative in a poor village. Once, a young man from Wenzhou, Zhejiang Province, visited the village I was working in and said to me, 'If this village were in Wenzhou, everything would have been much better'.[4] I was advised to set up cooperatives in the village, but for quite some time I felt it was naive to bring property rights and shareholding systems to an impoverished place, where egalitarianism prevailed. It was not easy to enable people who live in traditionalities to understand or master modern systems and concepts. Likewise, when conducting studies in Africa, we found that modernity is still a missing part there since colonialism.

Max Weber once argued that China failed to develop a modern capitalistic system [12]. This is not necessarily true, but he is to some extent right about the distinctiveness between a Chinese society and an European one that the former has not developed a rational system as the latter has. Varying levels of social anomie can still be found in China. For example, even in big metropolitan cities like Beijing, many people like to drive with a honk, and philanthropic ethics today never go beyond rules of traditional charities of old days.

The key of a meta-solution to poverty is the possibility to enable the change of ethics of the group living in traditionality. It may be easy to change one person, but difficult to change a group immersed in its own culture. In China we say areas in deep poverty is the hardest nut to crack in the fight against poverty. We use deep poverty to mean a severe lack of modernity. This is also termed as a 'development' issue that we often talk about. In theory, for many pre-modern groups, the difficulty of poverty reduction lies in how to get them to absorb the modern ethics. At least in economic terms, if people want to be rich, they have to align themselves to the market rules and values, while poverty results from failing to do so.

[4] Wenzhou, located near the middle of the East China Sea coastline, is the economic, cultural and transportation centre of southern Zhejiang Province. Part of the better-off areas in eastern China and centre of China's private economy, the city churns out many Chinese entrepreneurs. Note by the translator.

I hereby would like to share a small case of my work. I'm a development practitioner with a developmentalist mind, and my job is to enable more people to approach and grasp modern ethics to improve their well-being. I hope my development practise is not blind or without any framework, and that the development pathways could justify themselves. I worked on poverty reduction in a village in Yunnan province, which was not entirely isolated from the modern world, but whose survival ethics were quite different from the modern ethics. I was looking for a specific thing to connect the village to modernity, and after six months of search, I found it in the houses of the villagers'.

They use wood to build houses since no glass or bricks were available in this mountainous area. The traditional local stilt-style Yao home has no windows. It lets in beams of sunlight only through wood cracks in their house walls. Villagers had to go outside homes to bask in the sun. My idea is to build houses with glass windows that could on the one hand, let sunshine come in and on the other have Yao-style guest rooms which could generate cash flows from accommodating tourists or visitors. This is something that the villagers never foresee. In brief, I hope to illustrate with an experiment that we can make a difference by breaking through an old structure.

As to if it works or not, there is no answer yet.

Jean-Jacques Rousseau's Discourse on Inequality

Inequality and poverty go hand in hand. Poverty, says Rousseau, can be traced back to human self-prioritisation; escaping this self-serving conflict requires compassion.

Poverty is a concept that is both absolute and relative. People with no home to return to, no shelter to live in, and no food to eat are considered to experience absolute poverty. In this sense, poverty is an objective fact and easily recognisable. However, when a group, a country or a larger area is in a state of food shortage, one person lacking sufficient food is not necessarily poor when compared to his or her peers, and the political and economic significance of poverty becomes less salient. In other words, even if poverty is an objective reality as a lived experience, this objectiveness has its relativeness. And the definition of poverty can be fluid.

For instance, in 2012 the Chinese government set a new absolute poverty line for rural areas at RMB2,300 net annual income per capita (2011 constant price). The government reappraised its concept of poverty following economic growth, redrawing the line to 'free people from worries over food and clothing and give them access to compulsory education, basic medical services and safe housing'.[5] Raising the line meant also raising the minimum standard of acceptable living. In 1986, by contrast, the government's absolute rural poverty line was a mere RMB200 net annual income per capita (1985 constant price). Calculated by purchasing power parity, the purchasing power of RMB200 in 1986 was roughly 40% of the 2012 standard. The government's technical definitions of absolute poverty, as expressed in earnings, implied utterly different levels of well-being at different points. What is evident in this is that 'poverty' is a comparative concept and a relative one. If measured by the abundance of material production, individuals from many previous historical stages can be characterised as being 'in poverty' compared to modern society. In the eyes of the inhabitants of those historical societies, however, some of those whose living standards we would now consider poor were viewed as fortunate. We call those times 'poor' because we compare them with modern society.

This brings us to the meta-questions of poverty. The statement that poverty is a relative concept reflects the fact that human society is unequal. Inequality of opportunity leads to differences among groups or individuals, which result in gaps in access to well-being. What this means, where our responsibility for changing this lies, and what just distribution looks like in society, have long been subjects of debate. In his 1755 book *A Discourse upon the Origin and the Foundation of the Inequality among Mankind*, the French philosopher Jean-Jacques Rousseau explored the origin of human inequality. For Rousseau, real differences among people are not natural. Rowing against the current of his times, he argued that men had originally been equal but no longer were [13]. He sets out a thesis for how inequality takes place among people.

[5] In the *Outline for China's Rural Poverty Reduction and Development (2011–2020)*, the Chinese government first framed its new poverty reduction goals as 'liang bu chou, sanbaozhang (两不愁三保障)' literally 'two worry-frees and three guarantees', meaning freeing people from worries over food and clothing, and guaranteeing people their access to compulsory education, basic medical service and safe housing. Note by the translator.

Rousseau proposed that humankind is unequal in two ways. The first comprises differences that he perceives to be inherent to the individual, including differences in age, health, physical strength and intelligence. It is in the second that we have greater interest: spiritual or political inequality, derived from custom, privileges, wealth and power—culminating in control over others and the ability to force obedience. In the unregulated state of nature, Rousseau believed, the first form of inequality was inevitable, for obvious reasons: some people outperform others in physical strength, and without restraints they can impose their will. The question of human inequality beyond the state of nature lies in the second aspect of inequality, meaning that we need to explore how spiritual and political inequality is produced.

In fact, Rousseau's distinction between human inequality in a state of nature and inequality within politics, economy and society is flawed. Why is this the case? In his writings, Rousseau was firmly opposed to Thomas Hobbes' argument that people are naturally nasty and brutish. He instead insisted that in the state of nature—the state of, in his thinking, mankind before the corruption of society—humans were good and free [14], there is no fundamental difference between humans, thus no inequality. As for Nozick two centuries later, the moral problem of natural inequality therefore does not exist for Rousseau. However, economic and social inequality is indeed interconnected with natural inequality. Human inequality in political, economic and social dimensions is at least in part the result of evolution based on the natural attributes of humankind. In politics, for example, voters perceive tall people to be better suited to leadership.

Though Rousseau separated human differences in natural attributes from inequality in politics, economy and society, his discourse still acknowledged a connection between the two. Rousseau proposes that whoever first enclosed a plot of land and claimed it as their property, and secondly induced people to believe this claim, founded 'civilised' society [15]. This is a concept with which he takes issue, believing that society corrupts the purity of the state of nature. Rousseau argued that the first step taken towards unequal treatment—marked also the first step towards vice. For Rousseau, this occurs when, for example, those who are better-looking, or better at singing, are favoured over those less so in the competition for marriage. What this behaviour produced, he suggested, was comparison between people and obsession with one's own qualities, leading to vanity and contempt on the one hand, and shame and envy on the other. A society fermented with these new yeasts, he argued, is ultimately fatal to happiness and innocence. Here, he connected inequality with political trickery: inequality's origins lie, he argued, in our prioritisation of ourselves over others, the drive of amour propre—self-love. According to Rousseau, physically strong people can handle more work; smart people can benefit more from work; and creative people find ways of working more efficiently. People engaged in different jobs gain different levels of benefit from the work they do. Inequality in a state of nature is unobtrusively integrated into inequality between classes in the corrupt human society. From these roots of self-prioritisation, Rousseau argues, conflict emerges, leading to the recognition of the need for a central authority to keep peace. Despite his disagreements with Hobbes, Rousseau's hypothesis for the creation of the state is thus relatively similar to Hobbes' in Leviathan.

Where does this leave poverty? For Rousseau, the generation of property marked a further step towards inequality, which then created poverty. Property derives from the politico-evolutionary logic of the competition to survive. The possession of resources assists survival; by alienating property, however, those who are left with less have fewer opportunities to flourish, and less certainty of survival. As human society evolved, however, these simple survival-oriented imperatives become replaced by more complex structures. As society gradually became organised, various forms of social organisation—first a tribal chief system, and then a state system—strengthened norms of private property. Under such increasingly entrenched political and social systems, inequality evolved from being founded in individual differences to being institutionally embedded.

Regarding inequality as the root of poverty is of great significance. How we view poverty within 'nature' is affected by our basic perceptions of what is good, and beyond that by our social values and our views on the actions we should take to realise them. The most significant difference between humans and animals lies in civilisation, which is reflected not only by the level of material production but also by spirituality. Human society, both as a whole and as different individuals within a group, does not follow solely the principle of survival of the fittest; instead, it needs to run within a civilised moral framework, something we see in each civilisation at every stage of history. Rousseau believed that compassion is an important part of human nature: compassion is at the heart of human society, and the quality gives humankind its strength. Sociologically speaking, compassion greatly reduced the negative effects of the survival imperative; it directs humans to relieve the suffering of others, rather than prioritise solely the advance of oneself. Here, Rousseau and Hobbes again disagree. If Hobbes' state originates out of fear of each other, for Rousseau unification within human society comes from compassion, amour de soi displacing amour proper [16]. While the narrow prioritisation of individual survival trends largely towards inequality, compassion has a moral dimension which promotes the survival of those who are weaker. Thanks to compassion, behaviours that helped the weak were permitted, then cultivated. Although some other animals can to various extents help the weak among them, human compassion has resulted in mutual support which, more importantly, can develop into basic political and social systems which may first resist inequality between humans, and then create it within social structures.

In his book, Rousseau vividly presented the imagined human transition from 'natural attributes'—those that appear in the state of nature—to 'social attributes', which only appear with the development of society, and illustrated the relationship between poverty, property and the state. The trend that produced inequality and private property was an aspect of human evolution, but also harmed the healthy development of human society. Therefore, eliminating inequality and private property became a moral force in human evolution. Comprehending the nature of poverty itself is not difficult, but comprehending the nature of poverty from a perspective of eradicating poverty is very complicated. One increasingly widespread current trend in the world of work is a preoccupation with 'efficiency'. A focus on efficiency risks both depoliticising and demoralising poverty. Efficiency itself is unequal in a political or moral sense. There is no fundamental difference between accepting that capable people lead better lives in modern society and accepting that stronger people could cut more wood—and thus have more possession—in pre-modern society. Therefore, to regard inequality as the origin of poverty, private property as the root of inequality and social-political systems as the factor maintaining private property not only complicates perceptions of poverty but is itself a highly political perspective. Karl Marx went far beyond his predecessors in his reflections on human society and sharply identified eradicating private property as the solution for overcoming inequality.

In modern society, meta-questions of poverty are never singular but include a complex set of questions. They are not simply technocratic questions of the details of how much income the poor earn, but touch on the core issues of human social systems. Modern society must address inequality—a major issue that challenges the human origins of equality and confronts us today—in its rational pursuit of wealth and material abundance. Compassion, allowing people to step beyond amour propre to undertake collective action improving others' lives, is crucial.

Keith Payne and His Theory on Comparison and Inequality[6]

> Inequality is not primarily a matter of what people have or do not have. It is, rather, people's sense of where they stand in relation to others. Inequality affects our options, choices and self-perception; it will always be with us.

Poverty is inseparable from inequality. For this reason, we need to understand how inequality arises if we are to understand poverty. We have considered Jean-Jacques Rousseau's explanation of inequality's origins, but there are other theoretical explanations from different philosophical perspectives. As Kent Flannery and Joyce Marcus point out in *The Creation of Inequality*, Rousseau's account has errors, and we can pick them out without too much difficulty. Still, to do so is much like criticising Gregor Mendel for not knowing DNA [17]. Rousseau's analysis is foundational, even if it is flawed.

Philosophers and economists are not the only schools to have considered inequality. Psychologists have conducted intriguing research on its origins, and its effects. In his book The Broken Ladder: How Inequality Affects the Way We Think, Live and Die, Keith Payne explores how comparison between people affects inequality—and how inequality affects how people feel and act. His key idea is that poverty is not limited to poverty itself. Feeling poor matters, not just being poor. Whether somebody feels poor is more about how they perceive their standings in relation to others'. And when someone feels poor, they are more likely to act in ways that involve more risks and the possibility of self-destructive behaviour. Keith Payne, returning to the psychology of inequality, considers how our perceptions of ourselves are fundamentally based in comparison, which affects inequality. Humans instinctively want to consider ourselves better than others; most people believe they are better than most others at most things. Payne gives the example of a

[6] The Chinese edition was published by CITIC Press Group in 2019.

study of participants in car accidents. Almost all people involved in accidents, he notes, believe they drive better than most drivers. This is the case even when their driving does not differ from others' in any substantive way—and, of course, when it is in fact worse [18]. Another experiment surveying volunteers found that they almost all regarded themselves as kinder, more reliable and possessing higher moral standards than others [19]. In Keith Payne's view, when society places greater value on certain qualities, people are prone to exaggerating the quality in themselves. In the time of Aristotle, people rising up the social ladder tended to be lauded in theatre as heroes of one sort or another. Those with high social status were considered gentle and noble—the qualities generally admired in Greek society. We assume that those who have ascended to heights of wealth must have some qualities for being there, and we want to be there ourselves. Payne observes that this longing for high social positions is not particular to humankind. Similar phenomena have been observed among nonhuman primates. A study on monkeys found that their reactions to different fruits had little to do with the fruits themselves, but that they showed greater concern about comparing their social position with their counterparts. A monkey may be quite happy with cucumber, until they see that their peer is receiving a more desirable grape.

The reason why we generally want to see ourselves as holding admirable qualities may lie less in their symbolic meanings—their inherent good—but more in their connection with material and social benefits. John Rawls, a leading twentieth-century political philosopher, is widely regarded as a person of great intellect, but he proposes that his success was simply due to luck and coincidence: he had access to the right opportunities at the right time, often through circumstances beyond his control [20]. Rawls' clear-sightedness and humility are unusual. Historically, the most capable, intelligent and competitive individuals (or those who think they are) tend to advocate greater inequality in order to have greater scope to maximise these advantages; others without such advantages tend to seek fairer ways of distribution. This explains why, as we can often observe, the rich emphasise efficiency while the poor seek fairness.

In his magnum opus *A Theory of Justice*, Rawls argues that all people will favour equality once they abandon self-interest. He proposes a thought experiment to reveal this. He imagines a group of people behind a 'veil of ignorance'. They will enter a society which they must first design, but do not know where in the society they will be placed. They could be placed in a very advantageous position, or in a position of some difficulty. In this scenario, he suggests, participants would seek to create a fair society, minimising their own risk [18]. Such a taste for equality is somewhat alien to us. Qualities such as capability, creativity and competitiveness—married with opportunity—allow the accumulation of personal wealth and earn praise from others. This is very satisfying for those gaining, and they usually enjoy higher social status. In another word, such qualities are highly materialised. From an evolutionary perspective, this is understandable. The main challenge of humans as an animal has always been basic survival, which is now related to material wealth and possessions. In different stages of human development, material wealth and possessions may have different forms, but they are always associated with social positions which thus becomes a central theme for comparison. This is not to espouse some form of biological determinism, arguing that we are evolutionarily hardwired to prefer inequality. But when inquiring into socio-economic phenomena we must not neglect the basic perception of humans as living things, for whom comparison and a desire to gain greater security is natural.

Human society depends on love, harmony and solidarity—the goods for which we need security. However, individuals have never been free from the pursuit of and competition for material wealth, which leads to economic differences between individuals. This can be taken as a clue to the origins of inequality. In my view, many of the factors that Rousseau claimed as the source of human inequality, such as property, class and the state, only intensify inequality but are not its origin. Rawls' thought experiment is just that; and even societies which sought to put the collective first, found themselves terminally corroded by self-interest. We can make great efforts to reduce inequality and its effects, and can see some success—but it will always remain.

Is Poverty the Result of Laziness?[7]

> The poor are often told to 'pull themselves up by their bootstraps'. This is unfair: poverty is not the product of laziness or stupidity, but of structural barriers.

[7] Published at *Narada Insights* (March 14, 2019) at http://www.naradafoundation.org/content/6346.

Once, I was working to alleviate poverty in Hebian Village which is located in the China-Laos border areas and inhabited by Yao people. A visiting friend from Beijing saw the disorderly and messy public spaces there and said, 'They are poor because they are lazy'. I responded, 'I noticed many middle-class residential buildings in Beijing were as disorderly and messy. Would you call those people lazy?'.

If municipal services were unavailable and urban communities asked each household to clean their neighbourhoods each day, would this be a feasible, long-term solution? Rwanda offers the exception that proves the rule. One Saturday a month, all community members undertake umuganda, two hours of cleaning and improvement. This has made a big difference to community cleanliness, but even in this case it is only a two-hour-a-month commitment and accompanies state-led activities. Where this does not happen and places are messy, whose fault is it? Does it make sense to attribute cities' cleanliness to hardworking urban residents and the disorder and mess of villages to lazy rural residents? Where cities are clean, it is normally because of municipal services. Why not blame rural problems on a lack of support, in that case? Why should well-served urban residents condescendingly accuse villagers of being lazy?

When speaking of the work that needed to be done in the village, many people would say, 'The local villagers should be mobilised because this is their job'—something like Rwanda's umuganda. I thought so too when I first arrived in the village. At first, I set up the 'Hebian Development Team', hoping its members could serve the community as a backbone structure for improvement. As the workload became heavier over time, many people quit. Later, I made another attempt to organise a 'Hebian Startup Youth Team', hoping that young residents could organise to contribute to their village. During the development of Hebian Village, the villagers did mobilise for a lot of voluntary work. However, collective voluntary work faltered for one key reason: if one person stopped showing up, many others would follow suit. Such activities were not normal, and relied on motivated and charismatic leaders within the community. Paid activities are more reliable. Both the Development Team and the Youth Team ended with no definite results.

Poverty reduction has attracted wide attention in China in recent years.[8] Various slogans are often seen in rural areas, displaying the

[8] Since 2012, the Chinese government rolled out its targeted poverty alleviation strategy(精准扶贫, jing zhun fu pin), aiming to eliminating the remaining extreme poverty

government's determination to 'leave no one behind in targeted poverty reduction[9]'. Some slogans urge care and support: 'you and me together to aid those in need[10]', for example. Others encourage the poor to take action: 'never get short in ambition, never cease in hard work[11]' and 'do not wait for, rely on or ask for aid to overcome poverty[12]'. Instead, the argument goes, they should act for themselves. This presupposes that there are opportunities available, and that the poor have the necessary tools to seize them.

Are these slogans fair? Do they reflect the reality of what it is to be in poverty, and do they make reasonable demands of the poor? Imagine that I'm stuck in poverty, and somebody offers me help. Will I not want to escape poverty? Many want the poor to be more proactive, and blame them for not doing more to solve their own problems—like my friend accusing the Hebian villagers of laziness. Instead, the argument goes, they should seek out help and options to overcome their poverty, rather than wait to be asked to do so by other actors. What's the logic behind this? Are its assumptions sound?

I have been guilty of these same assumptions myself. When I first arrived in Hebian Village, I was advised by someone working in the local government that Hebian villagers could start a company raising indigenous pigs. I asked for the villagers' opinions; they were generally unenthusiastic. I felt frustrated by this, and wondered whether it really was true that they weren't energetic enough in wanting to escape their poverty. Later, I found out the reality of raising indigenous pigs. Each household only raises one or two such small-sized indigenous pigs, which would range freely on the hills and grow very slowly; this stage would be

in rural China, and in 2015 the strategy upgraded to a national war or battle on eradicating extreme poverty(脱贫攻坚战, tuo pin gong jian zhan).Various policy measures and programmes were introduced to lift the poor out of poverty until 2020 when the battle was won. The author mentioned poverty reduction has increasingly attracted ordinary people's attention in recent years. Recent years meant the period during which China were implementing the targeted strategy and advancing its national war on ending extreme poverty, specifically between 2012 to 2020. The article was written in 2019. Note by the translator.

[9] '精准脱贫,不拉一人',jing zhun tuo pin, bu la yi ren. Note by the translator.

[10] '扶贫济困,你我同行', fu pin ji kun, ni wo tong xing. Note by the translator.

[11] '人穷志不短,政策不养懒汉',ren qiong zhi bu duan, zheng ce bu yang lan han. Note by the translator.

[12] '扶贫不能等靠要',fu pin bu neng deng kao yao. Note by the translator.

relatively easy, but would still require effort. Once more pigs were raised, increasing the size of the herds, using pig feed would be unavoidable, and the risk of swine fever would inevitably grow. The villagers were aware of this before I was. A township-level official told me in a discussion of this project: 'It's not easy to press ahead with poverty alleviation among villagers. You offered them the means of raising pigs, only to get rejected. They were basically rejecting the chance to be lifted out of poverty'. I responded: 'Could pig-raising lift villagers out of poverty? With labour costs already rising, any hint of African swine fever would make the pigs impossible to sell'. Those in poverty may be more likely to take risks in some contexts; in others, they have less margin for error, and may shun high-risk enterprises.

We should not take poverty alleviation as a matter of course. Outsiders tend to interpret reluctance to adopt 'poverty reduction proposals' as 'numbness', assuming that the villagers don't want to get out of poverty. Don't you want to achieve prosperity? However, if someone tried to persuade you to buy stocks, many of you would have similar doubts. If urban residents lost their 'iron rice bowl [13]' of job security, many would find themselves in a more difficult position than their rural counterparts, not to mention making risky investment. How can we be so confident in instructing farmers how to overcome poverty? Investing time, money and effort in pig farming is as much a gamble for them as investing in stocks is for urban households in relative security.

Of course, we can't claim farmers don't need external support: they do. I've been engaged in poverty reduction for over two decades, and I've visited many places suffering from high poverty levels. I recently visited many poor villages, and the changes were profound, pointing to the achievements of targeted poverty alleviation. From 2012 to 2018, over 80 million people were lifted out of poverty in China.[14] This is quite phenomenal. Was this because all of them became impressively hard-working in a few years? In that case, it would be the most appealing

[13] '铁饭碗',tie fan wan, meaning a stable, life-long job. Note by the translator.

[14] The piece was written in 2019, so the author used statistics for the period between 2012 and 2018. If we look at the whole period of the battle on ending extreme poverty from 2012 to 2020, according to China's National Bureau of Statistics, a total of 98.99 million people were lifted out of poverty, using China's 2012 poverty line which is higher than the world bank's extreme poverty line. Note by the translator.

case for sociologists worldwide, and management experts should come flocking to Chinese villages to write motivational case studies.

Did they pull themselves up by their bootstraps? In the nineteenth century, American writer Horatio Alger described hundreds of stories of the ascent from poverty to affluence. No matter how impoverished his protagonists were initially, all eventually rose from poverty through inner strength and persistent effort. The stories were meant to illustrate that one was the master of one's own fate, a 'self-reliance model against poverty' that is still widely influential today. We have internalised this narrative, and still tend to hold the poor accountable for their poverty: they are 'lazy' or lacking in motivation.

The narrative is most strong in American media and culture, which has spread far beyond the United States. For those elsewhere, however, the particularities of the story's context have been forgotten. Before the founding of the United States, poverty-stricken people flooded into North America from England, Ireland and other areas. The 'new world' seemed void of state, society and, most importantly, differences in wealth, education and medical services. In such a context, affluence could be attained through individual efforts. And, in a context of limited governance in the Western regions, vast untapped natural resources, and enormous space, a rise in affluence was very possible. Many of the white people that immigrated to North America became relatively wealthy, living the so-called American Dream.

With equal foundations and opportunities, the individual effort was the key to wealth. Yet, the foundations and opportunities were not equal. Even now, black people in the United States are generally less affluent than white people, and the Native Americans who preceded either have the highest poverty rates of any racial group in the country. When the structures of governance are tilted against particular groups, more effort is required to obtain smaller results. Harvard University economist Alberto Alesina discussed the matter in the book, *Fighting Poverty in the U.S. and Europe: A World of Difference*, arguing that the U.S. Constitution explicitly protected the property rights and interests of the white and the rich [22]. This affected the story being told. White Americans acquired the belief that poverty results from individual failure, based on their own experience under particular conditions. Other American groups, many of whom were late-comers, did not achieve the same economic success, since, power, wealth and assets were already concentrated in the hands of the early-comers. By comparison, Latin America failed to realise general prosperity as the U.S. did. Does it make sense to claim that generation after generation of Latin American people were poor because they were lazy? Massive studies show that the unequal possession of assets during Latin America's early development in modern time resulted in local poverty. As Martin Ravallion argued in 2005, 'Inequality is bad for the poor [23]'.

Shortly after China adopted the policy for reform and opening up, relatively equal development conditions allowed the improvement of many farmers' living conditions. This happened across China. What does this tell us? It is unreasonable to claim that farmers were lazy before, and suddenly became hardworking due to state economic reform. Poverty is not caused by laziness: it is caused by structural access to opportunities.

Hebian Village is a mountainous village inhabited by the Yao ethnic group. In 2015 when I made my first visit there, it struck me that the village did not have a single brick or concrete structure; the road was lined with shabby wooden houses without windows. To access the village required driving forty minutes up a tortuous eight kilometres of earthen road, the sole road leading into the village. In the rainy season, the road would melt, making traffic impossible. Per capita, the villagers' yearly disposable income was RMB4,303. Forty-five percent of this income was sourced from agriculture, including twenty-seven percent from planting sugarcanes. Since the farms were located in a habitat for wild Asian elephants, the sugarcane harvest was often severely damaged. The compensation for this damage from the local nature reserve was only RMB700 per mu (under normal circumstances, the profit from sugarcane could reach over RMB2,000 per mu).[15]

Hebian is an ethnic minority village where few people speak Mandarin. Limited by language, few villagers travelled to work, instead mainly taking temporary jobs nearby. In 2015, each villager's earned income was RMB80-100 per day, but they didn't work every day. Their daily expenses accounted for up to forty-one percent of total expenses. For some households, children's school education could account for as much as twenty-five percent of their total income.[16] Despite their low incomes,

[15] A mu(亩) is a Chinese unit of land measurement. Its area varies, but it is most commonly approximately 807 square yards (0.165 acres, or 666.5 square metres), and 20 mu is one and a third hectares. Note by the translator.

[16] China implements a nine year compulsory education policy, which means basic education from grade one to grade nine is free. But since primary or middle school education

medical service, school boarding and traffic cost kept rising, pushing up their actual expenses and, consequently, many of them relied on debts to make ends meet. As a result, local farmers were stuck in a triple poverty trap: they had low income, high expenses and high debts. It is hard to see how to escape these traps with the tools available to them. If I were to remain in the village, I would probably have been its poorest resident; there are no easy answers. They needed outside help.

Once, while I was visiting another village, people asked, 'Why were you working against poverty in Hebian Village? Yao people there are just lazy'. But when we truly understood Hebian's conditions, how could we still believe its poverty was caused by laziness, stupidity or a lack of motivation?

I saw people in the village bustling about every day, stepping outside at six in the morning to feed pigs and cut sugarcane, then working late at night to tap rubber trees. For temporary jobs, workers bore the cost of food and traffic entirely on their own. Local women helped harvest watermelons in other villages, getting up at five in the morning, making their way by bike, and working till night in stuffy greenhouses to make RMB100 a day.

Local villagers often said that 'seeking money was a hard thing that they were not good at', a localised expression that accurately depicted their state. For them, making money was very hard and took great energy. They worked harder than many other people only for low pay.

Their low pay meant that necessary things consumed a higher proportion of their incomes. In Hebian Village, twenty-eight households had education-related expenses, accounting for an average of twenty percent of their household expenses in 2015. Only two of the ten households with the highest educational expenses retained a surplus after subtracting educational expenses from their net incomes. For the household with the highest negative balance, its net income was already negative because of heavy agricultural losses in 2015. In 2015, the average household medical costs amounted to RMB4,233—an average of RMB1,141 per person—while medical expenses consumed seventeen percent of total household

is mostly provided in township or city areas, many village kids have to go boarding on workdays, and their parents have to pay their living and traffic cost associated with a school boarding life. Note by the translator.

expenditure. Sixteen households (twenty-nine percent of total households) incurred disease and accident-related inpatient or surgical expenses, accounting for thirty-seven percent of the total medical expenditure.

The village did not contain a single affluent household. None of the physical dwellings could be described as decent. Were the villagers in this position because of laziness? No: their poverty was embedded in prevailing systems. 'The poor', like Hebian villagers, are unlikely to compete against others either in the job market or in income-generating activities. In a society of constantly intensified inequality, the poor and the rich are not on the same starting line. Some individuals escape poverty traps; Jack Ma,[17] for example, became an icon for his individual effort and tremendous success. However, it is becoming increasingly difficult for the poor to rely on individual efforts, and while the market may benefit the poor, it is not poor-friendly. The notion that 'poverty is the result of laziness' cannot be described as anything other than a lie.

While this is true, it is also the case that those in poverty can struggle to imagine a life of greater wealth. If the Hebian villagers faced a triple poverty trap (low wages, high expenses and high debt), there is a fourth one: the mental trap. The culture of poverty, once shaped, inevitably tends to perpetuate, as Oscar Lewis observes in *Five Families: Mexican Case Studies in the Culture of Poverty*. He suggests that children growing up in poor families mostly have absorbed the basic values and norms of the sub-culture of poverty in the early days of their life, and are thus psychologically resistant to accepting the conditions of transformation or opportunities of improvement that will possibly change their life [24] Many people simply transplanted this viewpoint to the study of poverty, holding individuals accountable for the culture of poverty and insisting that poverty resulted from laziness and stupidity. In the influential 1955 book *The Moral Basis of A Backward Society* by Edward C. Banfield, for example, cycles of poverty in a Southern Italian town are argued to be the result of an inability to cooperate; the poor of the village of 'Montegrano' are concluded to be self-destructively unable to help each other [25]. While the social actions of the villagers are proposed to contribute to ongoing poverty, however, it is still suggested that the environment that incentivises such actions is shaped by the area's land tenure arrangements, and the absence of institutions necessary for community trust.

[17] Jack Ma, co-founder of China's most successful tech empire Alibaba and billionaire entrepreneur. Note by the translator.

More widely, as the government slogan decries in Chinese villages, this perceived inability of the poor to do what's necessary to improve their situation has become pervasive. They are criticised for 'waiting for, relying on, and asking for aid'.

Individual failure happens in any society, and individual efforts are undoubtedly a prerequisite for gaining wealth. However, it is never a sufficient condition. Holding individuals accountable for a culture of poverty neglects the decisive influence of institutional and structural gaps in wealth, assets, education and opportunities. Such narratives have also weakened our sense of social responsibility and shifted our attention from institutional reforms. Achievements in the large-scale battle against poverty testify to the role of institutional factors in poverty reduction. Policies providing education, medical services and safe housing for poverty-stricken households offer specific examples of eliminating poverty institutionally. The battle against poverty must identify how to proceed with institutional reforms and establish fair economic and social systems.

Myths About Poverty Figures

'Official' poverty figures and 'objective' poverty don't always line up. This affects perceptions of poverty and government priorities.

Since 2012, the new Chinese administration has been working persistently towards the goal of building a moderately prosperous society[18] by 2020. It has begun to devote close attention to the issue of poverty, and has adopted a targeted poverty alleviation strategy. As a result, poverty alleviation has drawn the attention of the entire society. I'm often asked, 'Why are there still so many poor people after so many years of poverty alleviation efforts?' It is an easy question to ask but a tough one to answer. People have different views and thoughts on poverty and poverty alleviation. Some assume that public funds for poverty alleviation have been put to other uses. Others believe that the rich sustain their wealth by 'robbing' the poor. It can thus be difficult to give a single answer explaining why there are 'so many poor people'—or even, 'more and more poor people'.

[18] '小康社会', xiao kang she hui, Chinese president announced on 1 July 2021 that China has realised its first centenary goal—building a moderately prosperous society in all respects. Note by the translator.

But is it true, before continuing, that this is the case? Is the population of poor increasing despite the hard work put into poverty alleviation in China for so many years?

Poverty is an objective lived reality, but it does not occur in a vacuum. It is the product of combined political, economic and social factors. Before China adopted its reform and opening-up policy in 1978, material poverty was a pervasive problem in the country. In the mid-1980s, the government began its national poverty alleviation efforts. However, because there were so many poor people and not enough money, it could only focus on the poorest of the poor. This demanded the question: How can we identify the very poorest?

To assess poverty the central government established an income threshold, beneath which anyone is considered poor. In 1978, China's poverty threshold was an annual net income of RMB100 per capita.[19] I'm not sure of the contemporary equivalent to RMB100's purchasing power in 1978, but older generations know that at that time RMB10 per month was enough to meet one's basic needs. In 1978, 250 million people fell below the poverty threshold of RMB100 per capita in annual income. In 1985 this number was reduced to 125 million, and in 1990 to 85 million. The public thus had the impression that the number of people living in poverty in China had fallen below 100 million by the 1990s.

In 1993, the National Eight-Seven Poverty Alleviation Plan for 1994–2000[20] was rolled out to ensure that 80 million impoverished people would have access to adequate food and clothing by 2000. After 2000, China announced that its goal had been met. Due to this announcement, the general public believed that there were no longer any poor people in the country. To some extent, this general perception was rooted in reality because the problem of poverty was no longer as pervasive as it was before

[19] China specified its first income-based poverty line of RMB200 in 1986 which was based on a constant price of 1985.China's National Bureau of Statistics (NBS) thus estimated that in 1978 China's poverty threshold was standing at RMB100 per capita per year if factoring in inflation. Figures adopting China's poverty line in this article are sourced from NBS, and those adopting the World Bank lines are sourced from the World Bank. Note by the translator.

[20] '《国家八七扶贫攻坚计划》', guo jia ba qi fu pin gong jian ji hua, a strategy initiated by the Chinese government to combat poverty in rural areas. It was launched in 1994 with the goal of lifting 80 million people out of poverty by 2020, within a timeframe of severn years. Thus it was also called the National 8-7 Poverty Alleviation Plan. Note by the translator.

the reform. However, the general perception that China had eradicated poverty was also the result of a game played with the reporting numbers.

Following constant adjustment in the 1990s, the poverty line was established at an annual income of RMB625 per capita in 2000. Yet this adjustment resulted from a need to track rising prices. When measured by the sum's purchasing power, the poverty threshold had not significantly increased. In other words, China had been estimating the number of poor people according to an extremely low poverty threshold, meaning that the number of poor people seemed low and poverty reduction seemed easier. For example, in 1993, when the government's poverty threshold number was low, the poor population was estimated at 80 million. In 2000 the government, still using this threshold, announced that the country had ensured the basic needs of poor people. If the government had instead measured the number of poor using the current poverty line (of an annual income of RMB2,300 per capita),[21] there would have been more than 500 million people considered to be living in poverty and no chance for government to claim that poverty has been largely alleviated. In 2008, when the government raised the poverty threshold to RMB1,196, the size of the population in China officially recognised to be poverty-stricken increased to 40 million.

As we can see, the poverty threshold should be based on objective reality, such as how much money is needed to meet basic needs; on the other hand, it should consider different factors, including the government's financial capability and its poverty reduction goals.

Significantly, these figures are calculated by professional institutions and experts. Obscure data collection and calculations involving mathematical formulae keep the general public out of the loop. Thus, the objective reality of poverty has gradually evolved into a product of the combined influence of complex political, economic and social factors. The public is lost in the resulting maze of information and agendas. Moreover, the rural population can only find their place in the social structure based on income ranges set by the government. Since the poverty threshold was calculated at a low level for a long time, a gap emerged between public perception and government publicity. Due to an increase in media coverage, the public began to realise that many rural areas are still destitute. Data calculated according to a low poverty threshold suggested that

[21] In 2011, Chinese government raised its poverty line to RMB2300 which was based on a 2010 constant price. Note by the translator.

there were few poor people, but the fact is that many people whose net annual income was above the threshold were actually still in great poverty. There was thus a risk that people would lose faith in the government, especially if the poverty threshold remained unadjusted, the government continued to claim that a prosperous society had been completed, but a large number of people were still visibly living in poverty. Accordingly, the government decided to substantially raise the poverty threshold. In 2011, in accordance with rising costs of living, the poverty line was raised to RMB2,300, a sum that better aligned with the objective reality of poverty in China.

Due to the poverty threshold's sharp rise in 2011, the number of poor people in China soared to 122 million. This confused many Chinese. Hadn't the government announced that poverty was eliminated in the beginning of the twentieth century? Why were there still 122 million people living in poverty? The confusion stems from changes in the poverty threshold rather than changes in the actual number of poor people. The fate of the poor is largely affected by political and economic factors that influence how the poverty threshold is calculated and established. If your annual income is below the poverty threshold, you might receive government support while those above the poverty threshold may be excluded. However, if a person with an annual income of less than RMB2,300 is considered poor, why are those with an annual income of less than RMB2,800 not considered poor? Without accurate statistics or professional surveys, how can one know the income of farmers in the countryside? The numbers game not only leads to exclusion but also results in a power struggle over the question: Who is in poverty?

By saying that the calculation of poverty is a numbers game, I do not mean to deny our achievements in poverty reduction. Based on the World's Bank latest international poverty line (US$1.9 per person per day)[22], the incidence of poverty in China in 1981 was 88.3%; based on China's 2011 poverty threshold (RMB2,300 per capita annual income), the incidence of poverty in China in 1981 was 90%. The gap between these two numbers is not significantly large. In 2010, the incidence was greatly reduced, to 11.2% based on the World Bank's international standard of US$1.9, or 17.2% based on the RMB2,300 standard. In other

[22] The world bank has raised its extreme poverty line from US$1.9 per person per day to US$2.15 per person per day in 2022. The book is published in 2021, thus using the previous line. Note by the translator.

words, according to both international and national poverty line standards, the percentage of poverty-stricken people in China dropped from 80%–90% to only 11%–17% of the total population in thirty years. This is a remarkable achievement.

China's contributions to the reduction of global poverty are also exceptional. According to a global estimate based on the previous international poverty line of US$1.25 per person per day, from 1981 to 2005, 519 million people pulled themselves out of poverty. In other words, in 25 years, the income of 519 million people around the world increased to US$1.25 per day. However, if we exclude China, the global population of the impoverished would only have been reduced by 109 million. While the international community has always attributed achievements in global poverty reduction to their efforts, this data counters this conclusion. In general, China's achievements in fighting poverty result from Chinese people's hard work and have little to do with the international community and its aid. Of course, we could also say this argument is a number game.

So, how many people in China have pulled themselves out of poverty? It's a difficult question, despite those figures a moment ago. If measured by income alone, based on the World Bank's international poverty line and China's latest poverty threshold, the amount of the Chinese population living in poverty dropped by 600–700 million across four decades from 1978 to the present. It is estimated that there are still 50 to 100 million people living in poverty. This estimate, however, is based solely on income—but poverty is not just a matter of income. Even if someone has an annual net income of more than RMB2,300, they may still fall into poverty due to medical and educational costs and debts. We have not considered this situation when estimating the percentage of the population living in poverty.

Based on the current poverty threshold, China set the goal of eliminating poverty by 2020. Many people have asked me, 'There will be no poor people, right?' and I reply, 'It depends on the definition of poverty'. If the goal is to ensure that the income of all Chinese citizens will exceed RMB2,300 by 2020, and if that goal is met, I guess there will be no more poor people in China, at least in statistical terms. However, poverty is a relative concept. With the development of society and the continuous improvement of living standards, groups at the bottom of the social ladder will always be considered poor no matter how high their income is. In a transitional society like China, social classes are shifting. Groups that are living in poverty now may pull themselves out of poverty in a few years. Some rich people may become poor.

Poverty is relative and thus will not disappear. The indicators for measuring poverty will also change. In the past, those who didn't have enough to eat would be considered poor. Now, someone will be considered poor if he/she eats poor-quality food, wears low-quality clothes, or lives in a humble house. As long as social differentiation (which is hard to eliminate) remains, the concept of poverty will remain. The number of people living in poverty and the definition of poverty do not necessarily depend on the number of people who are 'truly' poor. To a large extent, it depends on how much moral responsibility the government is willing to assume, and on the country's political and economic situation. Generally speaking, when the current administration ends its term of office, it could declare that the country has eradicated poverty to present a positive image. The next administration can also declare poverty eradication as its goal and announce that the problem of poverty is still serious. So, in this sense, 'poverty' can be eradicated, alleviated or exacerbated without necessarily reflecting or affecting how many people are truly in poverty. The decision of how and whether the poor are categorised as poor belongs not to the poor themselves, but to decision-makers balancing multiple needs of their own.

The Trap of Poverty[23]

Even where absolute poverty is falling, relative poverty can remain a major problem. Efforts to reduce relative poverty have not always been successful; education, healthcare and infrastructure investment are likely to be our best bets.

Broadly, poverty reduction means reducing absolute poverty and limiting relative poverty (by narrowing inequality). Over the past three decades, absolute poverty in China has been alleviated significantly. This does not mean that all forms of poverty have been eliminated: in many

[23] Published at Farmers' Daily (2015-05-27) at http://szb.farmer.com.cn/nmrb/html/2015-05/27/nw.D110000nmrb_20150527_4-03.htm?div=-1.

places, relative poverty still remains. A village with bicycles, motorcycles and TV sets—which is now a common sight in China—may still impress us as poverty-stricken. Compared with urban populations, and rural populations in developed areas, the rural population in backward areas is at the bottom of society. Their relative poverty is not only determined by differences in income but also by a gap in overall living standards.

In my visit to a poor county in Yunnan, I found that many villages received support from government programmes, including poverty reduction and development programmes. My observation of one of the poor villages revealed that, although basic needs of food and clothing of the villagers had with state help been satisfied, those who were the poorest before the intervention remained poorer than their fellow villagers after the intervention. Even within the same county, the income gap between those with different geographical or stratification locations could be striking. Geographically privileged villages, those closer to markets or better connected to roads, were generally in a better financial position than those in mountainous areas. Within villages, disparities naturally also occur. The most affluent, were mostly those landed villagers, villagers with rich social connections or villagers holding official posts.

In the first decade of the new century, the welfare gap between the rich and poor has not narrowed, but instead has continued and widened. Consequently, as economic development slows, groups that earn less than the average income may be stuck in poverty for a prolonged period. Assuming that the poor are relatively deprived, it will take a long time to overcome poverty even if the economy is growing.

First, the continuing and widening of the welfare gap implies that the poor are seemingly caught in a poverty trap. This is a 'structural poverty trap' because the constraints on poverty reduction are relatively rigid. Opportunities and original conditions are not equal. Some groups are more able to continue growing their wealth because of their access to resources, technologies, relationships and information. While this seems fair—the market is free, and so long as these higher-opportunity groups follow the law they can reasonably pursue their own interest—it also leads to the monopolisation of opportunity by those already well-off, leaving those who are poor exploited and unable to progress.

Second, since the financial threshold for escaping poverty is constantly rising as the economy grows and costs increase, it is difficult for those in the poverty trap to overcome poverty on their own. An annual income of a few thousand yuan would have been considered affluence in the past but is small by today's standards. Currently, development-oriented poverty alleviation[24] is small in scope and weak in intensity, and it is hard for poor populations to sustainably increase their earnings enough to escape poverty traps. Also, even with high-intensity support available, poverty alleviation programmes have not always had their desired effects. For example, the drawbacks of farming households' scattered production gave birth to what is known as the 'company plus household' approach.[25] Still, company, instead of farming households, benefited most from the partnerships, seriously reducing the potential poverty reduction benefits of the approach.

Third, the direct or indirect capture of poverty reduction resources by actors for whom poverty reduction is not a major motivation inevitably makes it harder to reduce poverty. Again, this was the case for the 'company plus household' partnerships. Companies signed contracts with farmers in the name of centralised agricultural management; the benefits of poverty reduction programmes were thus largely leaked to companies, and the partnerships' poverty reduction effects were very limited.

[24] Development-oriented poverty alleviation is different from relief-based poverty alleviation. It has been China's core policy on poverty alleviation since mid-1980s. It highlights development as the essential means to end poverty, and regards the poor as the main actors. China aims to raise the living and production conditions of the poor, enhance their skills and capacities and integrate them into wider economic development process. Development-oriented poverty alleviation produces the basic conditions for rural economic development, and guides the poor to enlist in the effort. Note by the translator.

[25] The 'company plus household' model links individual farmers to companies in cases where cooperative-led approaches are less suitable. The approach requires stable and profitable companies in poor areas with secure markets for their products; raw materials and inputs which poor farmers can profitably provide; fair relationships between companies and households; and assistance to farmers by partners such as regional officials. These have often been used for the production of crops such as tea and sugarcane, but have not always been successful. Poor areas often do not have successful companies, and the relationships between companies and farmers may not be fairly managed. Input prices may also be volatile, potentially harming outcomes for farmers. Yunnan is one area where, according to World Bank assessments, the 'company + household' approach has largely failed. Note by the translator.

Poverty reduction systems thus need to adapt and be reformed. Direct and large-scale welfare transfer is neither feasible nor sustainable in China at the current stage. Direct welfare transfer generally works when the poor population is small and public funds are sufficient, but it carries high social and political costs.

To tackle current structural poverty, I suggest adjusting the development-oriented approach in two ways. First, development-oriented poverty alleviation is the main task, since the poor population remains large. However, some redistribution of wealth is needed to raise the poor's multidimensional starting point, narrow the initial economic gap, and lower the intensity of hardships which themselves reduce the income-earning ability of the poor. Social security, funding for education and infrastructure currently play important but inadequate roles. I suggest that, given we know their otherwise income-eclipsing role, public investment in medical services, education and rural infrastructure should be enhanced. This could allow the poor to invest their capital stock into activities that create a larger economic income. For example, we know that roads are vital to successful agriculture: without easy access to markets by road, agriculture is a sector offering low returns. In Hebian Village, however, the only road in 2015 had been made by the villagers themselves, and became impassable in poor weather. This is the kind of infrastructure investment that the state, and only the state, can make, and it has the potential to greatly contribute to poverty alleviation.

Second, the poor need increased asset stocks by some sort of redistribution. One way of measuring whether this is being achieved could be by assessing whether farmers are gaining shares in the 'company plus household' approach. However, companies in control of finance and information may falsify the accounts to claim lower profits, or even losses. Poverty alleviation authorities should audit these companies' accounts using independent accountants.

The poverty trap is structural, perpetuated by unequal opportunities. These suggestions have no prospect of transforming the lives of the poor in any short time frame. Only growth can do that. But where growth is not located in rural areas, outside assistance—normally from the state—is required.

Why Does Poverty Persist?[26]

Even where absolute poverty is reduced, relative poverty remains. Great strides have been made in China, but the poor need more support if poverty is to really be alleviated.

Even in developed countries, poverty remains. The problem is of course considerably greater in developing nations. But every country, rich or poor, has its bottom 10%. The poverty we discuss today involves its social reproduction and social construction; eliminating it is very difficult. In 1993 China proposed to lift 80 million people out of poverty by 2000. Today, there are still 80 million people in poverty; why is that the case, if 80 million people had been lifted out of poverty? This is a highly politicised issue.

To decide the number of the poor that the state could afford to support is a highly subjective process. In 1985, a poverty-stricken county was defined as one with a per capita annual income of less than RMB150. At the time, 258 countries were identified as poor. By 1993, the poverty line was adjusted to a per capita annual income of less than RMB300. A government sampling survey indicated that China had a poor population of 80 million, and 592 counties qualifying as poor. In 2006, the poverty threshold was raised to RMB600–700, and the size of the Chinese population defined as 'in poverty' decreased to 21.48 million. Later, in 2008, the threshold was further increased to RMB1,196; in 2011 China raised it again, to RMB2,300. This increased the size of the population defined as 'poor' up to 120 million. At the end of 2015, over 50 million people were defined as 'in poverty'.

The size of the Chinese population in poverty has fluctuated because the Chinese economy has been growing, and incomes have increased for the poor— requiring changes to the poverty threshold. The size of the population considered poor thus changes with changes to the poverty standard. The circumstances of China's poverty reduction efforts have also changed. At the end of the twentieth century, solving poverty was important in China's goal of building a moderately prosperous society.

[26] This chapter was originally a keynote speech made by Prof. Li Xiaoyun at the 'Ifeng DXW' salon and published at dxw.ifeng.com and WeChat official account 'ifengdxw' (2016–09–14) at https://mp.weixin.qq.com/s?-biz=MjM5Mjc5OTQ0MA==&mid=2652636540&idx=1&sn=105d3c3bc0019950667e00aa42764574.

Policies targeted counties identified as being in poverty. This could have undesirable effects: seeking funding, many counties tried to squeeze themselves into this category, undermining the reliability of the poverty standard and thus 'producing' more poverty.

The examples of the counties using a self-serving definition of poverty show at a more local level what is also true at the national level: the definition of poverty, and the resultant size of the population of 'poor', is not objective. Instead, the size of the poor population is the result of political and other considerations. While we may thus not be certain about the real number of poor, we can be sure that the bottom 10% in a country are in relative poverty. Without poverty alleviation efforts, this group will live a hard life, while with anti-poverty campaigns their lives can be improved. With help it is possible for them to lead a life of dignity, even if a luxurious lifestyle, with foreign vacations and suchlike, is impossible. In China this is possible in large part thanks to state interventions and programmes. In countries where the state does not have the capacity to intervene in such ways—such as in Malawi, a case which I will discuss later—the relatively poor have less access to social security provision, and a worse quality of life.

Two questions are raised here. First, why is there such a large number of poor? Because poverty does exist in absolute terms and many still suffer from it. That's why we see such a massive scale poverty reduction campaign in China in the 2010s. Second, why does this number always change, and sometimes even get bigger? Because the poverty line is being adjusted for political, social and economic considerations. Thus, while many are lifted out of poverty, many more enter it—or a newly defined version of poverty. This is the case globally as well as in China. The World Bank began using an extreme poverty line of roughly one dollar a day towards the end of the twentieth century; they now set the threshold at USD2.15 per day. Living standards will continue to improve, and thus the issue of poverty will always persist. In the OECD, poverty is defined as earning 50% of the median income.

If measured by the World Bank's poverty line of USD1, China's general poverty incidence was 84% in the late 1970s and early 1980s but dropped to 45% by 1986. At the time, this fact did not attract much attention. In the first seven or eight years of China's reform and opening-up era, China realised historical anti-poverty progress (in both scope and significance), lifting nearly half of its poor population, hundreds of millions of people, out of poverty (beyond the USD1 per day threshold).

Two lessons deserve to be highlighted. First, why were so many people lifted out of poverty at this early stage of China's reform and opening-up period? Our anti-poverty efforts were based on two initial conditions. The first was that the poverty reduction efforts started in a highly equal context. China's Gini coefficient at the time was less than 0.2, making China a fairly economically equal society.[27] This gave China a structural advantage in addressing poverty, and it was able to do so rapidly upon beginning the reform and opening-up period. Its rapidity in alleviating poverty during this period made it a source of inspiration for other developing countries watching its trajectory. The second was that, at this stage, without poverty alleviation authorities or dedicated programmes, China relied on a growth mechanism that benefited people relatively equally-a pro-poor growth pattern in another word. This was the key condition for sustainable and inclusive social development, and has become a difficult point in current anti-poverty efforts. Structural problems soon limited the poor's ability to escape poverty. The time when a poor household could gain affluence through individual actions—such as entering pig farmings—long past.

Second, why did China achieve a significant decrease in the incidence of poverty in the later stage, roughly from the mid-1980s to mid-1990s? The answer lies firstly in labour transfer: Township and Village Enterprises[28] employment allowed rural populations to access markets where wages were better. So, the considerable rise of agricultural income at the earlier stage (early 1980s) of the reform period and the increase in non-agricultural income (i.e. wage income from factory work) were the driving forces behind the greatest transformation in China's history. Secondly, the loosening of state controls on rural–urban mobility also contributed: people can move freely to seek opportunities in the market. Urbanisation,

[27] The Gini coefficient measures the level of income inequality within a population. A coefficient of 0 represents perfect equality, in which all population members have the same wealth values; a coefficient of 1 represents maximal inequality. In the late twentieth century, the Gini coefficient ranged between 0.24 and 0.49 in OECD countries. Note by the translator.

[28] Township and Village Enterprises (TVEs) are market-oriented public enterprises under the purview of local governments based in townships and villages in China. Most TVEs emerged during the Reform period in the 1980s and they expanded in the 1980s and early 1990s.As private ownership became less politically-controversial after the mid-1990s, the TVEs' proportionate share of the national economy declined. Note by the translator.

thus constituted another key driving force behind China's poverty reduction process. Since 2000, the stimulus of urbanisation has further reduced poverty.

Some points can be drawn from China's economic transformation. First, the fact that one billion Chinese people were lifted out of poverty is of great significance globally: the global poverty rate collapsed, in large part thanks to China's success. Second, of the many developing countries that started major transformation programmes in the 1980s, China was the only one to reduce poverty and grow on a massive scale. The fact that China reduced poverty by relying on agricultural development means that it also offers—in some ways—a successful model of transformation for other developing, agricultural-based countries. In 1978–1986, China registered an agricultural growth rate of 7%, an economic growth rate of 13%, and a halving of poverty incidence from 84 to 42%. World Bank economists attribute a large part of China's progress in poverty reduction in this period to agricultural growth [26]. This is a phenomenal, almost unbelievable, success. The massive poverty alleviation was the result of an increase in income originating from social changes—including the shift from an agricultural, rural economy to an industrialised, urban economy—but also from political and economic reform, especially the introduction of greater choice.

China faces two issues regarding poverty reduction today. The first is the challenge of the demographic transition, in which the number of workers will decrease dramatically while the number of elderly requiring support will go up. The fast transformation has left many behind in rural areas, who lack protection in employment, education, healthcare and even subsistence. This has generated a transitional population. If economic growth remains at 7 or 8% per year, and social security systems are continuously refined, the problems of the demographic transition can be mitigated. This will however almost certainly pose major difficulties.

The second challenge is that there are areas in China where the poor are relatively more concentrated. These areas are mostly remote and economically underdeveloped areas, and poverty there is more in absolute terms. This is a complex, structural problem. With low skill levels, these poor, rural groups cannot compete with others. Higher-paying jobs often require cultural literacy and education levels which these rural inhabitants do not possess. Even in targeted programmes, impoverished populations' lack of education and skills harms their ability to gather capital and increase their security. Say for example that a poverty reduction programme is initiated, and the government grants an RMB2,000 subsidy for raising cows. If the target population is not qualified to raise a cow, and lacks the human capital necessary for development through this path, such assistance is unlikely to reach them. Accompanying measures are needed. Comprehensive governance, including basic education—such as vocational training—and assistance in asset acquisition, are needed so that poor populations can compete with other groups.

The poor's assets are an important yet untapped capital for their livelihood improvement. In cities people could make money from selling or renting their house to others, while in rural areas it's hard to do so due to policy constraints we should still examine how the rural poor's assets can be used to improve their welfare and living standards. Asset management should be promoted in targeted poverty alleviation without undermining fairness or overly risking large-scope bankruptcy or other problems. Many people have explored this issue and believe China will encounter such problems. Empirical experience indicates that asset systems are directly related to a country's level of development (although we should note that the direction of causality goes both ways). For the sake of the poor and for China's wider development, it is important to identify how, stopping short of privatisation, we can improve the poor's asset management under the current social and political systems.

Language and Poverty[29]

Policies directed against 'poverty' are shaped by our language choices. Those without access to broadly spoken languages can face a structural barrier to development, yet standardisation of a single uniform language may risk harming cultural diversity, which can also be a source for development.

How do language and poverty interact? They might not seem the most obvious concepts to place alongside each other. In the researchers'

[29] Published at WeChat official account 'hanyutang' (2019–04-08) at https://mp.weixin.qq.com/s?__biz=MzA3OTI3MjEzNg==&mid=2650872931&idx=3&sn=8028356d6d3b36b59a23a70e99520960&chksm=8443bdc4b33434d24626928f4e07e84feb522b95bbfcc6beeb4a621cc31acc31f5023bbf35ad&mpshare=1&scene=1&srcid=0411BlOkdwOjVmK7lDU5UIGt#rd.

office or an impoverished village, however, they can be of crucial importance. The first interaction lies in how we define poverty. When we define poverty as loss of welfare in modern times, we identify it as a state of life measured against a broader standard of material welfare. We must then also define 'welfare'. Extreme poverty can be defined against the most basic aspects of welfare: intakes of calories and nutrition. Relative poverty can be defined against less basic aspects of welfare: standards in education, health and shelters. In the context of development, or modernisation, the pathway for improving welfare is thus conditional: one can improve its welfare through one's own personal efforts, unless one is entirely disabled, or a society do not provide any access to welfare. This conditionality is directly connected with language.

Language shapes the structures of policy and poverty. In the programme offices and policy headquarters, language choices determine who is prioritised, and when assistance ceases. In the wider populations, language affects access to opportunities. Globally, English is a prime example of this. A key reason for India's rapid development in software lies in the widespread English proficiency on the sub-continent. Proficiency in English also allows excellent Indian lawyers and doctors to immigrate to Europe and the United States and succeed.

In China's battle against poverty, language can also represent a structural obstacle for impoverished minority populations. Enabling children in poverty-stricken areas to speak Mandarin is important; populations that cannot speak it struggle to access the wider economy as migrants or traders. Most challengingly, this barrier to overcoming poverty is passed down from generation to generation. Helping disadvantaged populations to speak the national, standardised language is an important step in helping them more easily both engage in economic activities and access social services. It's impossible to imagine how a person that doesn't understand or speak Mandarin or even doesn't speak Chinese can integrate into the Chinese economic and social mainstream.

This was brought home to me when working on poverty alleviation in a Yao village in Mengla, where few local villagers spoke Mandarin. When I asked why they didn't travel for migrant work—an option which is often very profitable—they answered that they didn't speak Mandarin and that many employers didn't understand Yao. Popularising Mandarin amongst ethnic minority groups in secluded and remote areas at the preschool stage allows local people to attend higher education and have more options in society and the economy. Language is an important factor affecting the development of remote areas and regions inhabited by ethnic minority groups; lack of a shared language is a structural barrier to escaping poverty, and expanding language access opens up positive new opportunities.

In a similar way, there are also connections between cultural diversity and development. In modernisation, a single language improves the efficiency of economic activities: less time is required for interactions and transactions, and there are fewer risks of potentially costly misunderstandings. One vivid example is the use of computers in China. Compared to Western countries, Chinese people were slower in using computers for communication, mainly because of the difficulty of spelling and input in traditional Chinese characters, which are language problems inherent. However, because of the importance of digital literacy for economic development, Pinyin (a romanised system for Chinese hieroglyphs) was developed as a simplified substitute for traditional Chinese characters.

However, many scholars criticising development attribute loss of diversity in language and culture to modernisation. A single uniform language conflicts with cultural diversity and, though Pinyin and Mandarin are promoted for efficient economic activity, their ubiquity risks harming the welfare of groups speaking minority languages by gradually pushing these smaller languages out of use. Many scholars view standardising and unifying languages to promote development as a cultural tragedy. In fact, similar to non-verbal cultural patterns, the cultural pattern of diverse languages can also fuel development. Ethnic minorities' verbal patterns, such as songs and ceremonial rituals, are culturally significant but relatively scarce. Still, they have great economic value and make an important resource for development and poverty elimination. Therefore, we should understand the importance of a single standardised language in driving modern development, but also review the economic value of multiple languages and the importance of preserving diverse cultures.

Is Hunger and Poverty Synonymous?

Hunger and poverty are not synonymous. Enabling the poor to get rid of hunger is an essential part of poverty reduction policies, yet it does not provide sufficient impetus for the poor to get out of poverty.

To many the idea that poverty does not equal hunger—or even necessarily involve it—may sound strange. News reports and the basic facts of life mean that most of us have the impression that poverty is at least partially related to hunger. This was certainly the case for me. In the early 1990s I went on a field study in Mwanza one of Tanzania's lake zone regions. I was under the impression that hunger prevailed in Africa. However, during my weekly door-to-door interviews with farmers, I didn't spot any real issues with hunger. In 2011, I returned to Tanzania with Mr Zheng Wenkai, then the deputy director of the State Council Leading Group Office of Poverty Alleviation and Development and currently the president of the China Foundation for Poverty Alleviation.[30] When we were conducting a programme in a village in Morogoro, Tanzania, Mr Zheng wondered why there was no sight of hunger or poverty there.

We tend to equate poverty with hunger, but real hunger—famines—have more to do with governance than poverty (as Amartya Sen has observed). In fact, the poor are normally not starving. The 2019 Nobel Prize in Economics—won by Abhijit Banerjee and Esther Duflo—was won for research into just this: Banerjee and Duflo found that most people living under 99 cents per day were not starving. In a survey of the poor in 18 countries, the two researchers showed that food consumption only accounted for between 45 and 77% of impoverished, rural populations' total expenditure. Banerjee and Duflo also found that the poor, including the 'hungry' as classified by Food and Agriculture Organisation (FAO), wouldn't want to eat more even if they can. In fact, they were eating little [27]. This is an interesting phenomenon in the study of modern poverty. The poverty we are talking about today occurs amid rapid economic and social transformation. This makes it quite different from poverty in the past where hunger was the result of real scarcity. As Sen argues, hunger is now more about governance and less about wealth, and poverty and hunger are no longer synonymous [28].

Banerjee and Duflo concluded that absolute food shortages do not exist and that most people, even the majority of the poor, can make a

[30] The State Council Leading Group Office of Poverty Alleviation and Development was the senior body responsible for poverty reduction policy making and programming in China. It was superseded in 2021 by the National Rural Revitalisation Administration as China declared its victory on the war on rural extreme poverty. In 2023 the NRRA was absorbed by China's Ministry of Agriculture and Rural Affairs. Note by the translator.

living. This was because food for meeting calorie needs is low-cost under normal circumstances. In the Philippines, for example, they find that 21 cents are sufficient to buy food containing 2,400 kilocalories (the recommended average intake) [29]. In this case, if one lived on one dollar a day, they spent barely a fifth of their income on food. The sole problem in this example is that this cheap high-calorie diet consists of solely bananas and eggs—hardly food that most people would be enthusiastic about eating day after day. However, it is available and affordable. In many cases, hunger is not directly related to cash income. My research on the relationship between African agricultural development and food security supports Banerjee and Duflo's findings. In many tropical areas, food is quite adequately available at a low cost, giving most people access to basic food.

If this is the case, why are we discussing food supply in poverty-stricken countries? There has long been a perception in development circles, and more widely, of a poverty trap originating in hunger. The very poor, the argument goes, can't afford adequate nutrition. This leaves them very weak. Because they are weak, they are unable to find low-skilled work, for example as labourers. This leaves them unable to afford food, and to escape their poverty-induced weakness. This is a vicious cycle, but Banerjee and Duflo's research suggests it does not exist. In much of both Africa and rural China, it costs very little to have a homemade meal, but the thing is the poor are more willing to spend money on things other than food. In this sense, hunger is not normally related to poverty traps. Currently, although many developing areas seem poor, they are free from famine. This is very good news, and allows us to target other elements of poverty.

In another scenario of the relationship between hunger and poverty, when the poor migrate to cities for work, they can no longer harvest food to meet their daily energy demands as they did in the countryside. Instead, they must buy food with their salaries. Sadly, urban food prices are more expensive because they are raised to accord with average urban purchasing power. The urban food supply is no longer a process of directly harvesting and consuming raw materials but a commercial process integrating processing and sales, constrained by the minimum cost. Once rural migrants arrive in cities, their poverty is exacerbated because their income is below the average urban level, and they have to live on a strict budget. In this case, hunger becomes connected with poverty. Making no or little money in cities will cause hunger. Here, the hunger-based poverty trap risks again becoming a vicious cycle, in which migrant workers are too weak to work and thus cannot afford food.

Where hunger exists, it is the result of two causes. First, the poor do not have the means to obtain even the cheapest optimal food supply. This is most likely to be the case when they are unemployed with no income. In rural areas, this may occur when rural families without land of their own can no longer work on others' farms (such as if the cost of fertiliser goes up, reducing farmers' money for hiring workers). In urban areas, this may occur if migrants cannot find work. Migrants can return to their village, where they can be supported to avoid hunger even if they are jobless. Rural inhabitants unable to support themselves may need state help. This brings us to the second cause of hunger: institutional distribution of the food that is available. Amartya Sen's observation that recent famines were not caused by food shortages but by inadequate food distribution is again central.

The relationship between food and poverty also involves nutrition. The poor may be less hungry than we expect, but they do risk being malnourished, not receiving the nutrients they need. People's perceptions of nutrition may be inaccurate. During our struggle against COVID-19 in China, Dr Zhang Wenhong at Huashan Hospital Fudan University became an 'influencer', and was criticised online for advising people to avoid porridge for breakfast in favour of a high-protein diet. Porridge is however not inherently bad. Physiologically speaking, human nutrition refers to the balance of carbohydrates, proteins, fats and vitamins; certain amounts are needed for (especially in childhood) the development and maintenance of a healthy immune system, adequate energy levels, brain functioning and so on. We generally evaluate nutrition in connection with human height and weight. For instance, we use BMI as a standard of health and generally regard a BMI value of 18.5–25 as normal (WHO standard). These standards are not universally identical; by the standard of 'normalcy', India contributes a third of the world's undernutrition[31]. The public generally believes that with 'sufficient nutrition', children will grow taller, stronger and smarter. It is not quite so simple as this idea suggests; quite evidently, many short people are also smart, and nutrition plays a relatively limited role in such things.

[31] Data source: WHO, https://www.who.int/india/health-topics/nutrition. Note by the translator.

The connections between nutrition and poverty are extremely complicated. An iodine deficiency during pregnancy, for example, is known to have significant and irreversible effects on the cognitive development of the fetus. In 1995, David Barker found that the children of Tanzanian mothers who took iodine capsules during pregnancy went to school for four to six months longer than children of mothers who did not take iodine capsules. The 'Barker Hypothesis' led to an intermittent government programme that provided iodine capsules for pregnant women. Evaluations of the programme a decade later suggest that distributing iodine to pregnant mothers had a big impact on their child's education. If malnutrition affects the cognitive development of a child, it can also affect the broader development of a community or population. As a Chinese saying goes, 'the child is the father of the man'. If a child receives education for four to six months longer, they learn more, become more employable, and have better prospects.

Hunger and poverty involve diet and nutrition. In their book Poor Economics, Banerjee and Duflo drew a large sample from India and South Asia to examine consumption practices. Their theory was that the primary consideration for the poor's food purchases was neither price nor nutrition but taste. Rich people also pay attention to food's taste, but it has been observed that lower-income people attach greater importance to this aspect. Sometimes, issues of hunger, poverty and nutrition go beyond our concept of rationality. For example, in many cases, the poor are more likely to buy cigarettes and alcohol than milk or vitamins. This doesn't maximise their interests, if we set them out coldly; but is it irrational to want a small pleasure in a difficult life? During holidays, some poor people spend heavily on giving feasts and presenting gifts, far above their spending on nutritious food. Again, this is on the face of it an unproductive investment, but at the same time, community-building and meaning-making are also crucial parts of sustaining life and hope. Banerjee and Duflo suggest that some things are more important to the poor than nutrition; they prefer fun and enjoyment. I agreed with this perspective during my stay in Hebian Village. My colleagues bluntly criticised local villagers for buying fancy motorcycles, alcohol and clothes when they improved financially—'conspicuous consumption' rather than rational investment—but I believed it to be normal. Such consumption was not a spur-of-the-moment decision but their pursuit in life. The poor wish to be free from poverty not to maximise their nutrition scores, but to pursue a life they deem better. This brings us again back to Amartya

Sen, who famously argued that 'development is freedom'—including the freedom to buy and ride a fast bike if you do manage to escape poverty.

We often conflate poverty with subsistence. This is not wrong, because poverty alleviation efforts are intended to meet the most basic needs, and subsistence is the most basic. 'To free people from worries on food and clothing' is the basic living standard, but it may not be the poor's ultimate or even proximate goal. Poverty reduction does not equal prosperity, and the purpose of reducing poverty is not to achieve prosperity. In other words, the goal of poverty alleviation is not to enable the poor to afford motorcycles or cars. Of course, our poverty alleviation campaigns will be a great success if they enable the poor to afford cars, but they are more about ensuring the satisfaction of basic needs. In this sense, the assistance target must be an extremely small group that cannot meet basic needs with their own efforts. In my opinion, a large proportion of the poor people in Banerjee and Duflo's discussion can be better characterised as a 'less-developed' group: they meet a definition of relative poverty, but may not meet that of absolute poverty.

Poverty in the United States?

Poverty is not confined to developing countries. Richer countries may contain less absolute poverty, but relative poverty remains. Measuring this, and comparing poverty levels to other countries, is the subject of debate.

The United States is the richest country in the world. It has the largest GDP of any country, is viewed by prospective migrants as one of the most desirable destinations, and sends vast amounts of aid elsewhere. It is a highly developed country. This does not mean that poverty cannot be a serious problem there. Indeed, anyone who has visited or lived in the United States may well have observed that poverty can be quite severe in some areas. In some places, the presence of poverty is jarring in its proximity to great wealth. In Los Angeles, for instance, there are dangerous slums not far from Hollywood Boulevard. But is this the same sort of poverty as elsewhere? If we measure basic needs by the same standard across the world (for example, using the World Bank's income line of USD2.15 per day for extreme poverty), the poverty levels in the United States do not seem serious. Very few meet the global definition of absolute poverty. In the United States, relative poverty is a much more useful concept than absolute poverty: poverty in the United States has to be measured against the rest of US society. The US poverty incidence was 22% in 1955, dropped to 11% in 1973 and then increased to 15% in 2010. From 1973 to 2010, US per capita GDP grew by over 60%, but economic growth failed to positively influence poverty. By 2010, about 46 million people in the country lived in poverty.

As I mentioned earlier, China experienced a miracle of simultaneous rapid economic growth and poverty reduction over the past four decades. Some African countries also achieved substantial economic growth in the past decades but failed to make noticeable progress in the fight against poverty. If these countries offer an example of economic growth that does not reliably translate into poverty reduction, China, by contrast, was a model of pro-poor growth.

Of course, the decoupling of economic growth and poverty reduction in the United States and Africa are different in terms of either material production or social security. Consider, though, how the US measures poverty. In the early 1960s the economist Mollie Orshansky, working at the US Social Security Administration, studied US families' income and consumption. (As a statistical economist, her work was similar to that of Ms Wang Pingping from the National Bureau of Statistics of China—to give a parallel with the Chinese efforts in poverty alleviation.) Orshansky didn't expect her statistical research into food consumption to impact US poverty at the time, but her study was in fact important, and ended up being the nudge that created the national poverty line. Orshansky studied the daily food expenses of American families with three or more members and concluded that in order to maintain a nutritionally adequate diet, families generally needed to spend 30% of their after-tax income on food. According to Orshansky's estimate, the US poverty line in 1963 should be an annual income of USD3,165. In August 1969, the country officially adopted this figure as the national poverty line. Afterwards, except for adjustments to prices, the line stayed basically unchanged. In 2012, it was updated to an annual income of USD23,283. Angus Deaton criticised the United States for its failure to adjust the poverty line after many years [30].

When Orshansky drew her line, taking basic nutrition needs as a starting point, it was considered acceptable. At that point, the Johnson administration's economists needed a poverty line as a basis for the 'War on Poverty' initiative. Orshansky's estimate of USD3,000 was reasonable. A higher line, with a more generous version of the 'basic diet', was explored but abandoned: Orshansky first preferred the US Department of Agriculture's 'Low-cost Food Plan' as the basis, but this would have seen the poverty line set at a family annual income of USD4,000, considerably higher than the threshold eventually adopted. The process seemed to have politicised the establishment of the poverty line. Deaton, in his critique, is careful not to criticise the economists of the Johnson Administration or to belittle Orshansky's work; it was an important step, and furthermore the USD3,000 poverty line was acknowledged to be reasonable by a majority of US citizens. Deaton's intention in discussing the US poverty line was to illustrate that poverty was about far more than basic food nutrition [31].

As I've discussed, poverty and hunger are often made synonymous, but poverty is really about more than basic food shortages. After proposing the poverty line, Orshansky kept calling for its adjustment mainly because she found that the line insufficiently reflected the reality of poverty in the United States. Deaton was right, but perhaps overlooks the politics of the poverty line. If the US government had adjusted the threshold, it would have meant that greater poverty existed in the country and that the nation's economic growth had failed to wholly eliminate poverty. Deaton held that drawing such an absolute poverty line was feasible in developing countries in Africa or South Asia but unreasonable in the United States. Even in 1963, not all basic needs could be met with an annual income of USD3,165. The reality in the United States (as elsewhere) is that without enough income to fully participate in social activities and lead a life similar in key ways to peers, a family would be considered to be poor: social inclusion often has rigid costs, which the poor are less able to afford. Measuring such poverty required a standard of relative poverty.

It follows that poverty in the Untied States cannot be directly equated with poverty in Africa and Asia. Discussing US poverty in terms of absolute income does not reflect the real state of absolute poverty levels. Based on observations of US income distribution, the existence of relative poverty in the United States cannot be denied. The US Gini coefficient only changed slightly from the end of the Second World War to the mid-1970s. In 1966, the average income of the top 5% of American families was 11 times that of the bottom 20% of families; by 2010, this gap widened to 21 times. The bottom quintile of families made an annual average income of USD14,000 in 1966 and only USD15,000 by 2010, while in the same period, the average annual income of the highest-earning 5% of families' rose from USD154,000 to USD313,000. The data tell us that absolute income cannot measure US poverty, which is mainly about inequality.

The United States is a wealthy country, and a relatively small proportion of the population suffer material shortages. It is also generally perceived as a just and fair society. In a 2014 opinion poll, a third of Americans said that they believed that the American poor were poor due to a lack of effort [32]. Steinbeck is supposed to have suggested that the poor in America 'see themselves not as an exploited proletariat, but as temporarily embarrassed millionaires'; the presumption that there are opportunities to advance open to those willing to make an effort is at the centre of the 'American Dream'. Education and medical services are relatively easily accessible, making it harder to sense inequality of opportunity. However, America is not the unique country free from inequality. Inequality is everywhere in daily life, present in politics, employment, and social and cultural exclusion.

The establishment of a minimum wage in the United States is an important factor for income distribution. The federal government adjusts the minimum wage per inflation and market wages, and Congress has a dedicated committee to set the national minimum wage. Still, each discussion of its adjustment arouses dispute. In 1981, the minimum wage for US labourers was USD3.35 per hour, which didn't change until 1990; in 1997–2007, the standard stayed at USD5.15 per hour; in 2010, minimum wage workers earned an annual income of USD14,500, much lower than the official poverty line of USD17,374. Deaton argues that the constantly depressed federal minimum wage reflected the declining political influence of low-income groups, which in his opinion was directly related to the fall of trade unions, especially those in the private sector [33]. Alberto Alesina, the Harvard economist, similarly proposes that the lack of redistributional institutions was directly related to a weak labour movement and the unpopularity of socialist thought in the United States [34].

In addition to political reasons, inequality in the labour market was another important force behind intensified income inequality. Along with economic structural adjustment, the US low-income population relied on low-skilled employment sectors that were increasingly transferred to other developing countries, making it difficult to create more jobs for a relatively immobile local labour force with limited skills. The adverse economic effects of outsourcing also help explain the rampant populism in the United States over recent years.

Deaton presented many ideas on addressing poverty and inequality in the United States. He said that if democratic politics shifted to a plutocracy, non-rich groups would be deprived of their rights. He quoted the US Justice Louis D. Brandeis in saying that the country couldn't make it both ways: democracy and concentrating wealth in the hands of a few [35]. The failure of the *Affordable Care Act* promoted by the Obama Administration already revealed problems with US political system. While Deaton did not directly criticise the political system in his book, he agreed with Daron Acemoglu and James A. Robinson that institutions tailored to the elite are inimical to economic growth and poverty reduction [36]. Historically speaking, the United States offers a strong example of growth and poverty reduction, but put under a comparative lens, the United States is not necessarily a role model for reducing inequality. In this sense, Albert Alesina's book *Fighting poverty in the United States and Europe: A World of Difference* offers a sharp analysis of poverty in the United States.

Does Poverty in China End After 2020?

> 'Poverty' has long been defined by income thresholds. This is in itself tricky, but is also no longer adequate for China's changing circumstances: poverty remains, but its concept changes.

In 2011, China's central government set the goal of lifting poor populations out of poverty according to its new standard, and of helping all poor countries to escape the poverty list. Unprecedented financial and administrative resources have been invested by central and local government in a targeted poverty alleviation strategy.

Due to rapid economic development and rising living costs, in 2011 China raised its absolute poverty line to an annual per capita income of RMB2,300. This is significantly higher than the poverty line used in 2010. After economic growth, the new standard better represents the annual income that rural populations need to meet basic living needs, such as food and housing.

In early 2021, China announced its victory on the battle against extreme poverty and issued a white paper to summarise its experience in and contribution to poverty alleviation. Does this mean China witnesses the end of poverty? My answer is a no: lifting populations out of the current standard of poverty by no means brings the end to rural poverty.

First, even if populations have be lifted above the current poverty line of RMB2,300, various risks leave them still susceptible to falling back below the line: rural populations are extremely vulnerable, and people's basic living standards are not guaranteed. Consequently, even though statistically there was no rural population living in absolute poverty in 2020, there would still be a small group of people living near or under the poverty line of RMB2,300 of annual income.

Secondly, ongoing increases to living standards and costs means that it is not feasible to continue using 2011's calculated poverty line of RMB2,300 after 2020. At some point the poverty line will have to be adjusted; and when it is, absolute poverty will officially return. According to the calculated poverty line in 2010, an estimated 26.88 million people were living in poverty. The revision of the poverty line in 2011 elevated the number of people deemed poor to 122 million, raising public concerns. The same pattern will inevitably be seen with the next potential revision of the central government's definition of poverty.

To sum up dynamic changes within poor populations and possible revisions to the poverty line will lead to the continued existence of a certain number of impoverished people. Therefore, although China announced the completion of its rural poverty alleviation goal in 2020, it is important to also examine the situation of rural poverty after 2020, and to ensure that the poor are not written out of official figures in the ongoing 'numbers game'.

Although absolute poverty will continue to demand some attention after 2020, major progress in reducing rural absolute poverty has been achieved by the government's poverty alleviation strategy. Long a challenge in China's rural areas, absolute poverty thus basically came to an official end in 2020, and rural poverty has since entered a new stage that can be characterised as transitional poverty. This new stage is not necessarily calculated by absolute income but by income inequality, unequal access to social public services, and multidimensional poverty.

First, there remains a huge income gap between urban and rural residents. In 2020, the ratio of per capita disposable income for urban residents to that of rural residents was calculated at 2.56.[32] In 2019, the Gini coefficient in rural areas stood at 0.46 [33], demonstrating that income inequality has become a major problem in rural poverty.

[32] We updated the original version's 2014 data to 2020 data according to China's National Bureau of Statistics. Note by the translator.

Second, income is no longer the deciding factor in poverty. Many groups with an annual income of more than RMB2,300 are still unable to resiliently cope with risks due to a lack of property and social security. They have neither enough income to cover expenses incurred by diseases, natural disasters or the cost of education, nor a social safety net able to cover their deficit. An illness or a natural disaster risks dragging them into poverty and debt. All these risks contribute to transitional poverty.

In fact, income is no longer an objective measure able to reflect the real situation of rural poverty. We need new assessment indicators to evaluate new stages and types of poverty. When carrying out targeted efforts to alleviate poverty, some local governments have applied indicators other than income to identify the poor. For example, factors like housing, food consumption and education for children are also considered. These indicators relate to multidimensional poverty. Forming a new, objective system for evaluating rural poverty will be a major part of understanding and reducing rural poverty in the future.

New patterns of rural poverty mean that eliminating 'poverty' (in the traditional, threshold-determined sense) is no longer the target of poverty alleviation work after 2020. Groups in the 'transitional poverty' category and those susceptible to falling into poverty will become the new targets of poverty alleviation projects. These two groups of poor people experience a poverty characterised by multidimensionality. This requires speedy changes to transitional poverty alleviation policies and measures.

It is not the case that multidimensional poverty has thus far been ignored: China has already carried out multidimensional poverty alleviation programmes in rural areas. Particularly since the implementation of the targeted poverty alleviation policies, the central government has demanded that rural poor have access to food, clothing, compulsory education, basic medical services and safe housing, and that basic public services in poor rural areas meet the national average standards of quantity and quality. Central and local governments believe that the equalisation of public services in urban and rural areas is an important measure to reduce poverty. However, eliminating the urban–rural gap takes time, and current poverty alleviation efforts mainly focus on increasing incomes.

In recent years, the reduction of absolute income poverty in rural areas and the seriousness of transitional poverty demonstrate that China must adjust its poverty alleviation measures to this new stage of poverty. On the one hand, shares of agricultural income continue to decrease and rural residents are increasingly reliant on wage income. At the same time, wages contribute more to increasing inequality than increasing income. Although we can't say that the strategy of reducing rural poverty by raising incomes has come to an end, we can at least say that adjustments to income distribution in rural areas are becoming a major measure for addressing the problem of rural poverty.

On the other hand, the imbalance of social public services in urban and rural areas is a major cause of transitional poverty. Commonly, rural residents sink into poverty because of natural disasters, illness and school costs. There are many reasons for this. First, although there is a social security network for poorer populations, the subsistence allowances[33] provided for rural areas are often insufficient to counter the risks faced, and the widely covered New Rural Cooperative Medical Care System often do not provide sufficient support to guard against risks brought by a serious disease or critical illness. Secondly, the social security system is fragmented, undermining its effectiveness in ensuring basic living standards for impoverished populations with limited financial resources. Thirdly, although China has strengthened its support for rural education and health services, the price of these services is based on living costs in urban areas, which is still relatively high for low-income rural households. Some costs are covered by social security, but the high price of education and medical services absorbs an inordinately large proportion of rural residents' limited cash income. Finally, the current social security system in rural areas is essentially supplementary; frequently, it cannot cover necessary expenses. In China, college tuition and healthcare cost the same in rural and urban areas: urban residents have higher cash incomes and can usually afford these expenses, but rural residents, suffering from an urban–rural wealth inequality, struggle with the fees required. For rural populations, illness and the cost of educating offspring threaten to tip households into poverty.

[33] '低保', di bao (Rural Minimum Living Allowance or Subsistence Allowance). China's Dibao guarantee programme is one of the world's largest social safety net programmes. In 2011, eight percent of all rural inhabitants in China benefited from it. The Dibao programme provides cash transfers to households with earnings below a minimum level. Because the system is decentralised, however, it does not bring recipients above the poverty line. Studies also suggest that local authorities struggle to target the very poorest, leaving many of those who would most benefit unable to access the supplementary funding. Note by the translator.

It is clear that as new patterns of rural poverty emerge, efforts should be made to resolve the urban–rural divide and adjust development-driven projects to alleviate multidimensional poverty. China needs to unify poverty alleviation systems in urban and rural areas, prioritising the equalisation in the quality of services offered by the public sector. In particular, differences in the quality of social services, such as nutrition for children, primary and secondary education, and medical health services, will gradually become a major cause of new poverty. The rural poverty alleviation strategy needs to consider two integrations: integrated development between urban and rural areas, and integration between development-oriented income increasing approaches and public services equalisation approaches.

New patterns of poverty need new strategies; a new poverty alleviation strategy requires a new institution capable of responding to new conditions of poverty. Until the end of the 1990s, rural poverty reduction basically consisted of promoting rural and agricultural development. Since the 2000s, with the development of protection-oriented poverty alleviation projects (social public services, such as subsistence allowance, education and healthcare), rural poverty reduction has moved beyond an institutional focus on agricultural development and attracted the participation of multiple, closely intertwined departments.

China's recent attempts in connecting its poverty reduction system and subsistence allowance system, and integrating their relative resources revealed its institutional weakness in poverty alleviation. The fragmentation of poverty reduction portfolios in various bureaucratic departments has long contradicted the holistic requirement of advancing poverty reduction process. This contradiction will increasingly influence the effectiveness of measures needed to tackle the new patterns of poverty.

First, as rural poverty is increasingly characterised by secondariness and multidimensionality, it would be increasingly difficult for sector-based government departments to coordinate their actions. Unless the central government coherently mobilises resources through political and administrative means like in the targeted poverty alleviation movement, the current system cannot effectively integrate resources across the multiple sectors implicated. This is especially the case when professional management and resource management are based on different sectors, and when government departments have divided interests. Although political mobilisations can be very effective, they often lack sustainability.

Secondly, departments for poverty alleviation only run projects in rural areas, despite the fact that poverty exists in a state of mobility between urban and rural areas. With urbanisation, populations move from rural to urban areas, carrying their poverty with them. The urban–rural divide, and its fluidity due to movement, leaves rural-specific programmes unable to cope with new changes in poverty.

Finally, although China's poverty alleviation agency played a role in macro-regulation and coordination, as poverty reduction continues to cover more sectors and departments, a coordinated, coherent governance structure must be developed, at least to increase the efficiency of resource use and policy coordination. New patterns of poverty require a comprehensive governance system for poverty alleviation, which will be key to poverty reduction work in the post 2020 period.

References

1. Bowles, S. et al. (2006). *Poverty Traps* (p. 1). Princeton University Press and Russell Sage Foundation.
2. Guy, L. (2023). Gift Giving, Reciprocity and Community Survival among Central Alaskan Indigenous Peoples. *Humans, 3*, 47–59.
3. Douglas, M., & Forward: no free gifts. In Mauss, M. (1990). *Gift: The Form and Reason of Exchange in Archaic Societies* (pp. X, XIII). Routledge.
4. Aristotle. (1965). *Politics* (Rackham, H. Trans). Harvard University Press.
5. Weber, M. (2002). *The Protestant Ethic and the'Spirit' of Capitalism* (P. Baehr & G. C. Wells, Trans). (pp. 19, 368). Penguine Classics.
6. Samuelsson, K. (1993). *Religion and Economic Action: The Protestant Ethic, the Rise of Capitalism and the Abuses of Scholarship* (G. E. French, Trans). (pp. V–VIII). University of Toronto Press.
7. Tawney, R. H. (ED.). (1998). *Religion and the Rise of Capitalism* (pp. vii–xiii). Routledge.
8. Braudel, F. (1992). *Civilisation and Capitalism, 15th–18th Century* (pp. 484–509). University of California Press.
9. Acemoglu, D., & Robinson, J. (2012). *Why Nations Fail: The Origins of Power Prosperity and Poverty* (pp. 68–75). Profile Books.
10. Zinsmeister, K. (2019). *Less God, Less Giving? Religion and Generosity Feed Each Other in Fascinating Ways*. https://www.philanthropyroundtable.org/magazine/less-god-less-giving/
11. McKitrick, M. A. et al. (2013, September). *Connected to Give: Faith Communities*. https://rcfdenver.org/wp-content/uploads/2017/09/ConnectedToGive3_FaithCommunities_Jumpstart2013_v1.0.pdf

12. Weber, M. (1951). *The Religion of China: Confucianism and Taoism* (pp. 84–86). MacMillan Publishing Company.
13. Rousseau, J. J. (1755). *A Discourse upon the Origin and the Foundation of the Inequality among Mankind.* (pp. 23–26). Bottom of the Hill Publishing.
14. Rousseau, J. J. (1968). *The Social Contract* (M. Cranston Trans). (pp. 1–3). Penguin Classics.
15. Rousseau, J. J. (1968). *The Social Contract* (M. Cranston Trans). (p. 22). Penguin Classics.
16. Rousseau, J. J. (1755/2002). *The Social Contract and The First and Second Discourses* (S. Dunn Ed.). Yale University Press.
17. Flannery, K., & Marcus, J. (2012). *The Creation of Inequality* (p. 14). Harvard University Press.
18. Payne, K. (2017). *The Broken Ladder: How Inequality Affects the Way We Think, Live, and Die* (pp. 29–33). Viking Press.
19. Keith Payne, K. (2017). *The Broken Ladder: How Inequality Affects the Way We Think, Live, and Die* (p. 34). Viking Press.
20. Pogge, T. (2007). *John Rawls: His Life and Theory of Justice*(M. Kosch Trans). (pp. 3–27). Oxford University Press.
21. Rawls, J. (1971). *A Theory of Justice (Revised Edition)* (pp. 118–123). Harvard University Press.
22. Alesina, A., & Glaese, E. L. (2004). *Fighting Poverty in the U.S and Europe: A World of Difference* (p. 9). Oxford University Press.
23. Ravallion, M. (2005, June 25). *Inequality Is Bad for the Poor.* https://elibrary.worldbank.org/doi/abs/10.1596/1813-9450-3677
24. Lewis, O. (1966). The Culture of Poverty. *Scientific American, 215*(4), 19–25.
25. Banfield, C. E. (1967). *The Moral Basis of A Backward Society* (pp. 17–19). Free Press.
26. Ravallion, S. M., & Chen, S. H. China's (uneven) Progress Against Poverty. *Journal of Development Economics. 82*(1), 1–42.
27. Banerjee, A. V., & Duflo, D. (2011). *Poor Economics: A Radical Rethinking of the Way to Fight Against Global Poverty* (pp. 24–25). Public Affairs.
28. Sen, A. (1981). The Ingredients of Famine Analysis: Availability and Entitlements. *Quarterly Journal of Economics., 96*(3), 433–464.
29. Banerjee, A. V., & Duflo, D. (2011). *Poor Economics: A Radical Rethinking of the Way to Fight Against Global Poverty* (p. 26). Public Affairs.
30. Deaton, A. (2013). *The Great Escape: Health, Wealth and the Origins of Inequality* (pp. 178–179). Princeton University Press.
31. Pew Research Center. (2014, January 23). *Most See Inequality Growing, but Partisans Differ over Solutions.* https://www.pewresearch.org/politics/2014/01/23/most-see-inequality-growing-but-partisans-differ-over-solutions/

32. Deaton, A. (2013). *The Great Escape: Health, Wealth and the Origins of Inequality* (pp. 192–194). Princeton University Press.
33. Alesina, A., Glaeser, E., & L. (2004). *Fighting Poverty in the US & Europe* (pp. 122–123). Oxford University Press.
34. Deaton, A. (2013). *The Great Escape: Health, Wealth and the Origins of Inequality* (pp. 206–207). Princeton University Press.
35. Acemoglu, D., & Robinson, J. A. (2012). *Why Nations Fail: Origins of Power, Prosperity and Poverty* (pp. 91–92). Profile Books.
36. Tai, D., & Cai, R. (2023). Liangshi zhuchanqu zhengce yu nonghu shouru bupingdeng [The Policy of Major Grain Producing Areas and Farmers' Income Inequality]. *Journal of South China Agricultural University, 22*(2), 26–37.

CHAPTER 2

The Need to Help the Poor

Over two decades ago, when I started my work on poverty alleviation, I visited a poverty-stricken village up in the mountains with my colleagues and two non-Chinese friends. There we were struck by the tattered clothes of two little girls, sisters aged seven and six. The elder girl, staring at us with big eyes, made a deep impression on me. I later asked local officials about their family background and was told that their parents were sick and burdened with debts. We visited their bare, stone-piled house and found them a family in severe financial disadvantage. The elder girl was about to drop out of school and the younger one could not afford to go to school. At the time, the policy of waiving tuition and miscellaneous fees, supplying free textbooks and granting living allowances or other support was not available. When my colleagues and I suggested that we assist them, nobody objected, and my two international friends expressed willingness to contribute without hesitation. What impact might our intervention have had?

Poverty is both absolute and relative. When one faces people in absolute poverty, struggling below subsistence levels and unable to secure their basic needs in food, clothing or housing, anti-poverty efforts do not spark dispute. The girls' family may not be categorised as 'absolutely' impoverished, but still, no one objected to giving them support. When there is a wide gap in social welfare and wealth distribution in our society, assisting those at the bottom is for most people not controversial. Poverty alleviation is ethically legitimate. It is also, from a utilitarian perspective, socially legitimate: it satisfies both self-interested and altruistic incentives. Sympathy, pity

X. Li, *The End of Poverty and the Taming of Inequality*,
https://doi.org/10.1007/978-981-96-0684-9_2

and care spur us to help those in need, while social rationality suggests that we institutionally narrow the rich-poor gap to avoid damage to society and to reassure ourselves of a safety net should we find ourselves in a worse position.

Then why do some question the necessity of poverty alleviation? Here we should perhaps distinguish between two types of alleviation, which to an extent follow the two types of poverty. In some contexts, alleviation efforts are essentially humanitarian assistance for those in urgent need of extraction from absolute poverty. Those in the greatest poverty may face imminent threat to life, due to the inability to obtain medication, food, or adequate shelter. In other contexts, entrenched relative poverty may require more than the 'simple' provision of basic necessities. In these cases, efforts to help start to take the form of structural reform.

When support for those in need graduates to a more complex political, social and economic process, anti-poverty practise becomes complicated or even alienated. Controversies about the necessity of poverty alleviation are often about avoiding any negative externalities from this pursuit of social equality and preventing disorder and damage to society. A prudent and responsible poverty alleviation campaign is an important force for social harmony, while a politically irresponsible campaign may abuse the sympathy of the public and lose its ability to persuade. In modern society, poverty reduction is a highly complex political, social and economic process, so it is difficult to implement a responsible anti-poverty campaign. China has pressed ahead with targeted poverty alleviation from 2012 to 2000, devoting enormous economic and social resources to overcome absolute rural poverty. Despite the government's commitment, many problems arose in practise. The Chinese government thus determined to neither lower nor raise the standard in the hope of regulating its anti-poverty actions and avoiding adverse social effects.

Should We Respect the Choices of the Poor?

The dignity of the poor can sometimes best be protected by shaping their choices beyond what they think they want.

'Respecting the choices of the poor' is an almost indisputable principle of poverty reduction. However, if poverty becomes an accepted circumstance, and if the poor refuse to make changes, how can efforts to reduce poverty and help the poor keep their legitimacy?

Keith Payne is a psychology professor at the University of North Carolina, Chapel Hill, in the United States. His book *The Broken Ladder* is a must-read for students of poverty and inequality. From the perspective of experimental psychology, Payne's research offers a collection of illuminating cases of decision-making by the poor.

Payne's uncle Sterman lived in an abandoned barn at a landfill site. On winter nights, when temperatures were close to freezing, he slept by a coal stove in a corner of the barn. After much persuasion Payne and his father succeeded in convincing him to move in with them. However, Sterman refused to live inside the house and insisted on staying in an adjoining warehouse that used to be a pigsty. Later he returned to the barn at the landfill, where he died of lung cancer at the age of fifty-nine [1].

In Payne's book, Sterman's story is a tragic case of poverty. Undoubtedly, his fate resulted from his own choices. He declined help from Payne's father, ignored the doctor's advice, and when diagnosed with lung cancer chose whisky over painkillers. Payne's uncle is a typical case of poor people determining their own lifestyle. There are many people like Uncle Sterman in the world. Such choices perfectly accord with the argument 'the poor have the right to choose their own way of life', yet for those who work relentlessly to help the poor, such stories can be deeply discouraging.

I encountered many similar cases while carrying out an experiment on poverty reduction in a Chinese village. One farmer actively participated in collective activities but was reluctant to receive support to build a guest room in his house to gain extra income. I said to my colleagues, 'This is his choice, we cannot force him'. The construction of his guesthouse at the village entrance was only partially completed, and he used the house-building loans for other business enterprises. These failed and he lost money. By contrast, his three brothers built new guest rooms and established a catering service that generated tens of thousands of yuan a year. When I said to him, 'Look, you didn't make money!' he replied, 'I will make money next year'. He didn't realise that his three brothers would probably earn more than RMB100,000 the next year. How could he hope to earn that much in one year? On another occasion, I said to a farmer, 'Every day, you ride a motorcycle out of the village to earn a maximum of RMB100. You don't have much profit left if you deduct the cost of gasoline and the wear and tear to your motorcycle. You can make more money by staying at home and receive the guests, just clean up your guest room, and improve the courtyard of your house'. He smiled and made some improvements to his guest room, but he still rode out of the village every day. These farmer's choices contradict the economists' assumption that people will make rational decisions. They did not choose the obvious route to earn more money but instead, they made irrational decisions.

So, is poverty really a choice? In fact, both those who advocate for interventions to reduce poverty, and those who 'respect the choices of the poor', agree that the stories of Uncle Payne and those like him are tragedies. But why are there different views on whether, or how, to prevent these tragedies? If everyone lived a life like that of Payne's uncle, no one would think that Uncle Payne's story is particularly tragic; everyone would have had the same experiences. The problem surfaces as a matter of inequality: while most families spend their winters in comfortable houses, Payne's uncle was struggling. When most village families live in good wooden buildings that produce a considerable income, and others don't own such housing, the problem of 'the poor' arises. The issue of poverty is directly related to our values concerning inequality.

Any debate unfolds within a political space, within which the views of the political left, the right and moderates may vary. When it comes to inequality, however, the different wings of the political spectrum largely agree on its problems. Inequality does not only hurt the poor: it also harms the rich by causing serious social problems like crime. More devastatingly, it divides society and may cause permanent harm to everyone. The proportion of people who irrationally retaliate against society is much larger among lower wealth percentiles than at the top. Even though people that lived under disadvantaged conditions in their childhood may not engage in illegal or destructive activities in adulthood, a psychological shadow and sense of inferiority may accompany them throughout their whole lives.

Moreover, in many cases, an underprivileged childhood can produce incentive reversal—causing people to become more indifferent, selfish and unscrupulous. Corruption is often more prevalent in countries with higher levels of inequality. We often hear corrupt government officials explaining that they were born into poverty and that, while the people nourished them, their backgrounds finally kept them from living up to the expectations of the people. Most of these corrupt officials have proved unscrupulous and greedy when in power and have done great harm to society. The Chinese have a saying, 'The poor need to nurture morality and the rich need to nurture ambition', indicating that the poor often lack 'morality' and that the rich can easily lose 'ambition'. This proverb is not a discriminatory, moral judgment on the rich and the poor; rather, it suggests how people's behaviour is motivated and shaped through inequality. A person short of money may pick up a RMB100 bill found on the roadside, rather than leaving it for its owner to find it again or handing it in to the police. This person might thus open themselves up to societal condemnation for 'immorality'. A multimillionaire in the same situation, however, would not have bothered to look at the RMB100 bill. Although the psychological and moral impacts of wealth or poverty are very complex and the gap between rich and poor may not necessarily cause such specific social consequences, it is almost inevitable that inequality will eventually cause social harm to everyone.

'Respecting the choices of the poor' is not wrong in principle. However, real respect does not simply consist of asking the poor what they want to do, but of understanding the circumstances that lead to specific choices. In other words, what drags the poor into vicious cycles of self-destruction? Payne's study found that people in countries with high inequality, such as the United States, make wrong choices much more often than those in countries with low inequality, such as Canada. The proportion of people like Payne's uncle in Kentucky, where there is high inequality, is higher than in Iowa, where there is lower inequality. Inequality affects a person's choices: poverty and its limitations are not the result of a personal decision, but the product of a monopoly of opportunities by people of wealth and power within a system that permits this. When the poor have limited opportunities, 'respecting the choices of the poor' would become either an embrace of naivety or an evasion of morality. People who work on poverty reduction should not stop making efforts to help the poor at the moral barrier of 'respecting the poor'.

In fact, once a person falls into a vicious cycle, it is difficult to pull her/him out.

This however is far from being a reason to stop trying to alleviate poverty. No one poor is poor as a result of choice. Once a person has lagged behind for a long time, he or she will form a lifestyle that reinforces 'degeneration', the so-called destructive cycle of welfare. Poverty reduction should involve a sincere effort to break this vicious cycle. All human beings are born free and equal and should be treated in the same way. However, when there is inequality of rights and opportunities, one should not let the poor repeat their life tragedies, merely through the justifying slogan of 'respecting choices'. Instead, programmes should make a difference in the poor's lives and livelihoods. These programmes may seem 'immoral' since they do not result from the poor's choices and they are, to some extent, 'imposed' on the poor. However, if we do not provide the poor with alternative opportunities, ideas and programmes, what choices do they really have?

Payne shares a personal anecdote relating to this dilemma. His young daughter created a game that scared her parents, climbing to the edge of a bed or sofa and letting herself fall. She knew someone would be there to catch her, because she had never actually fallen to the ground. While Payne knew that catching her every time would only encourage her to continue this trick, he thought that instead of the hard lesson of not catching her, it was better to let her believe that someone would be there for her when she was at risk. Payne hoped to push her habits in the right direction through positive help [2]. It is difficult for us to extrapolate a general model out of this example in educating children. Nevertheless, helping people to make correct decisions rather than leaving them to 'learn from their mistakes' may be a better solution for changing the world, a point that also defends the legitimacy of interventionist measures for poverty reduction.

In the village where I conducted the poverty reduction programme, the farmer I mentioned earlier often sat half-naked in his big unfinished house. I didn't know what he might be thinking when he saw guests check into his neighbours' guesthouses. Once, he said to me, 'Professor Li, I'll build my house after I earn money from the sugarcane this year!' It suddenly occurred to me that my incompetence had indirectly contributed to his poverty. I had asked my colleagues to 'respect his choices' and avoid pushing him to complete the renovations to his guesthouse. In fact, this tactic did not respect his choices and rights in a real sense, because the farmer did not know how to solve his difficulties: his ability to make good choices was impeded by his lack of knowledge. He was seriously ill and wanted to pay off his mounting debts before building the new house with the income-generating guest room. The credit union urged him to pay off his debts every day. It wasn't that he didn't want to build the house. If we had tried harder to persuade and support him in its construction, he would have had a considerable increase in income like his three brothers and his life would not have been as difficult as it was now.

The biggest problem in the lives of the poor is constant daily difficulties and crises. Their behaviour is mainly driven by the urgency of the problem, not by its objective importance. They respond to crises with a short-term vision and use limited means that is available to hand. Anyone would choose a safe and familiar way to avoid risks, rather than launching on new ventures. This is path-dependence. 'Respecting the choices of the poor' sounds like considerate, reasonable and moral rhetoric, yet it overlooks an important pre-condition: there are very few choices or opportunities for the poor, and they often know very little about these choices or opportunities.

As I recall, when I first discussed the construction of new houses with the villagers, they all said that they would prefer a brick-and-mortar house like the buildings in the cities. In reality, they had no experience of living in brick or concrete houses. The local climate was hot in the daytime, cold at night and very humid during the rainy season and, since concrete houses are not well ventilated, staying in such houses would prove uncomfortable. In the end, my colleagues and I 'forced' the villagers to build wooden rather than concrete houses. Now, the villagers all agree that high-quality wooden houses are more comfortable for living and also profitable as guesthouses. People in other villages who built brick and concrete houses envied the wooden houses in this village. As they earn money from their wooden houses, again and again, the villagers appreciate the value of this 'forced' decision.

Thus we see that it is not immoral to provide more choices for the poor and to, sometimes, even persuade them to change their original life paths. On the contrary, 'respecting the choices of the poor' and leaving them to tackle their difficulties alone can constitute an evasion of one's moral responsibility to help the poor. Poverty alleviation is neither about imposing one's formulas on others nor simply facilitating the poor's choices, which can be, to some extent, a covering up of one's incompetence and indifference. Instead, as Sen has put it, it is about expanding the real freedoms that the poor can enjoy [3].

Why Are Some People 'Poor'?

Why the 'poor' are poor is a difficult question. We tend to blame poverty on the poor's laziness, lack of initiative, non-compliance to rules or non-collaborativeness with others. This is in itself a lazy assumption.

In my many years of work on poverty alleviation, I have regularly spent time with 'the poor'. Over the past decade, in particular, I have spent a lot of time with them discussing paths out of poverty. Despite having an academic and practical knowledge of their situations, and despite making efforts to mentally stand in their shoes, I sometimes found it still hard to understand them. In many cases, I was entrenched against my will in discriminatory thought patterns, continuing to assume that they were 'poor' because of their way of thinking.

Let me give you a few examples. At one point, we planned on building a small square on the way into Hebian Village and needed to slightly adjust the position of two houses. One household rejected the proposal, and we had to give up on the square that would have improved the village and the lives of that household. We also designed new houses for the village: they had their bathrooms behind them, to let in sunshine and look more attractive. Despite our efforts, one household still built its bathroom in front of the house. On another occasion we provided building materials for the households to renovate their own houses and asked households to contribute their labour to improve the muddy roads that got in the way of transporting the materials into the village. This was an obvious need, but only a few volunteers showed up. One of my colleagues got very disappointed: 'No wonder they are poor!'.

Why the 'poor' are poor is a difficult question. We tend to blame poverty on laziness, lack of initiative, non-compliance to rules or non-collaborativeness with others. This is in itself a lazy assumption. When one spends time with the poor, one recognises that these reasons are insufficient to answer the question. For instance, if we asked rich communities to contribute labour to repair their backyard pavements like we asked the 'poor', would the rich respond actively? If we asked urban residents to take responsibility for their section of public facilities, would they agree? I don't think they would! Take for example our request that the two households agree to slightly move their houses in order for the square to be built. Would this be acceptable to richer people? We only have to look to the 'nimby' phenomenon to get our answer. We often asked farmers to support our poverty alleviation programmes at their own cost and received negative responses, which we blamed on their ignorance. But if we placed urban residents in the same situation, would they be willing to offer support at their own cost? Not necessarily. Some people may disagree with the comparison and believe that, since urban residents pay taxes, the government should take responsibility for improving the urban environment. But farmers pay taxes too and have paid even more taxes than their urban counterparts in the past.[1] Why are public road and health services unavailable in rural areas when they are available in cities? Isn't it unfair to ask people who have also performed their civic duties to the best of their capacity to also contribute their labour and then accuse them of laziness when they do not? I don't approve of populist propositions or hope to become a populist advocate, but it doesn't prevent me from thinking about 'substantive fairness' for the 'poor'.

Apart from personal inadequacy argument, we tend to attribute poverty to two reasons. The first hypothesis is that of so-called deprivation in wealth creation and especially capitalist exploitation, resulting in the absolute and universal impoverishment of the proletariat. But why has poverty been significantly alleviated in many developed capitalist countries? Is it because the exploitative bourgeoisie has been ironed out? Obviously not. The second hypothesis is that of the so-called culture of poverty. In many circumstances, even if poverty is not widespread in a society, many people are still in poverty. Their poverty does not result from wealth deprivation, leading to the 'culture of poverty' theory. When discussing the 'poor' in China, we are unconsciously influenced by these theoretical paradigms.

Under the impact of classical Marxist theory, Chinese scholars regard poverty in China as the result of unfair wealth distribution and take income distribution as a main indicator of poverty. Thus, income becomes an indicator for identifying the 'poor' and deciding where to target poverty alleviation efforts. The problem here is that people in different areas with similarly low incomes may not all be 'poor'. For instance, I was in Germany once and met some young people who made a monthly salary of only EUR1,000, far lower than the country's average income. I said you must have been counted as poor in Germany. They said no because they had a job. Since they had a job with income, social security, a monthly benefit of EUR500–800 in the case of unemployment, and medical insurance, they were not considered 'poor' despite their slim income. However, suppose a farmer in China earns tens of thousands of RMB a year but has no access to medical security. In that case, they may immediately become 'poor' if a serious disease strikes.

[1] In 2006 China abolished its thousand years-long agricultural taxes levied on farmers or rural households. Note by the translator.

Low incomes do not necessarily cause poverty, and social security in modern societies may be an important factor in determining poverty and the risk of poverty. Poverty is not only affected by individual security but also by public facilities. If public facilities like those provided in cities—for instance, subsidised public transport, adequate education and healthcare systems—were available in rural areas, poverty in the true sense would be unlikely even if individual income was low. Incomes should not be the main measure of poverty; instead, we should consider people's access to welfare security programmes. Wealth deprivation and the 'culture of poverty' cannot sufficiently explain why some people are 'poor'. While these factors may prevent one from getting rich, they do not necessarily reduce one into a state of poverty. A national failure to provide inclusive and equitable access to public services is the underlying cause of why some people are poor in modern society.

The Tragedy of Ms Yang[2]

Rural poverty alleviation programmes can save lives, but are difficult to implement. Delegated resources, and knowledge of the local political context, are vital.

In 2016, China was shocked by a tragedy in a small rural village. A peasant woman in a northwestern province first made national news and then was discussed in the international media, her name even appearing in The New York Times. Ms. Gailan Yang, twenty-eight years old, first killed her four little children and then committed suicide. She had lived all her life in Agu Shan village, an impoverished village without gas or water supply in Kangle County in Gansu Province. She had lived in the village all her life and spent her days undertaking backbreaking agricultural labour. She was reported to be relatively isolated within the community. Her husband had travelled as a migrant worker to a nearby city, but had struggled to find work. Ms. Yang struggled to support her family on the money he sent back and the produce she could cultivate, which was reduced by an unusually cold winter followed by an unusually dry summer. Her family

[2] This article was first published on Guangmingwang (12 September 2016) at http://www.xinhuanet.come//politics/2016-09/12/c_129277774.htm.

had been stripped of welfare benefits two years previously after the village decided that their income surpassed the standard of being 'poor'.

In the aftermath of this tragedy the press blamed the murder-suicide on the government's implementation of the subsistence allowance system (Dibao). Government spokespersons bristled in response, causing negative interactions between the public and the government. I am not sure that it would be reasonable to attribute this event to the improper execution of the subsistence allowance system. At the same time, we have to recognise that failures in the implementation of social welfare programmes and other anti-poverty interventions do cause real social problems that need our close attention.

First, the way in which the subsistence allowance policy is implemented is inconsistent with the reality of life in rural areas. Dibao is a means-tested programme. The local government categorised households based on a locally assessed poverty line: this meant that across China there were, in 2017, over five hundred local poverty lines, with large disparities nationwide. The local government then calculated the number of households requiring a subsistence allowance and then notified the central government of their assistance needs. However, in areas with a high incidence of poverty (especially in poverty-stricken villages), living conditions often only varied slightly between villagers. Both types of households—those who are qualified as Dibao households or poor households—received a free-of-charge state transfer. These transfers inevitably introduced power struggles to the local context, as village officials and relatively affluent groups rushed to take for themselves the largest share of the free transferred resources. Even where this problem was not present, the fact that households had almost equally poor living conditions forced local governments to allocate the transfers equally. Where there was not enough to go round, households would rotate yearly to receive a subsistence allowance. This is especially common in poor villages. The introduction of the subsistence allowance had a great impact on the complex rural socio-political context. The allowances turned into something rare and coveted, and their ability to contribute to the fight against poverty was reduced.

Second, the implementation of the subsistence allowance required setting thresholds for benefiting. This could be challenging. Identifying poor groups for targeting poverty alleviation policies requires reliable statistics, using an authentic and valid system that villagers widely recognise. Without this, any form of household identification and criteria for eligibility for the subsistence allowance would be highly controversial. Though a household's qualification for the allowance was decided through village discussion, the process and criteria for identifying the rural households eligible to receive the subsistence allowance could remain vague. The households in extreme poverty, with urgent special needs, could be relatively easily identified in the countryside. But generally speaking the quota for eligible households was above the number of households in extreme poverty—requiring urgent assistance—but below the number of rural households needing subsistence allowance and poverty relief. This would inevitably lead to the exclusion of some poor groups. Despite villagers' practise of open review and the transparent appraisal of eligible households, the fact that there wasn't enough poverty relief to go round made this practise more of a consensus-building exercise rather than a real process for allocating transfers. This explained why, after the village appraisal process, some villagers still disputed the list of households considered to be in poverty and thus eligible for the subsistence allowance. It would often be the case that some impoverished farmers, in urgent need of the subsistence allowance, were not covered after the community appraisal. Excluded farmers tended to feel angry and frustrated, wondering why they had been overlooked when peers—whom they knew to be in similar situations—had received help. This even led to some extreme behaviour including revenge actions. A campaign intended to help the poor was alienated from its original purpose, revealing the incompatibility of social security programmes with rural realities.

Third, the recent populist trend has increased social and governmental attention towards vulnerable demographics. To quell populist voices, the government has been forced to keep increasing the number of covered groups. With limited financial resources, the number of qualified households outgrew the available support. As prices continued to rise, effective support was undermined, and, in some villages, the subsistence allowance even turned into average welfare where everybody got a little bit support but nobody got sufficient support. In a sense, rural subsistence allowance policies should focus on improving the quality of available support rather than on expanding coverage. Greater attention should be paid to cultivating reasonable identification and exit mechanisms.

Lastly, implementing rural poverty alleviation measures requires delegating power to lower levels. Rural poverty alleviation is a complex social undertaking for which local governments lacked sufficient professional resources. The challenge of identifying households eligible for the subsistence allowance requires resources. All the rural poverty reduction policies were ultimately implemented at the township level, which, without sufficient human capacity, failed to implement the policies thoroughly or correctly. Since there are hundreds of thousands of civil organisations in China, the government could alternatively try to purchase anti-poverty services from social groups to solve this problem. Poverty alleviation by social organisations can rapidly make up for the insufficient governmental organisational resources and ease the political and social tensions, significantly mitigating the risk of potential conflicts between the government and the public.

Why Couldn't Mr Yong Get Rich?

> Escaping poverty is not merely a matter of individual capacities. Systemic barriers to opportunity are what really determine outcomes: if someone is born in the wrong place, they face low incomes and slow advancement.

Almost everyone who had been to Hebian Village knew Mr Yong. He was called (elder) Brother Yong, though he was young, the same age as my daughter. Living in the village, I sought his help a lot. I lived at the highest point in the village, surrounded by rainforests, big trees on all sides. I am used to life in a city. Especially in the rainy season, the chirping of crickets disturbed my sleep; every day, Mr Yong would come over to look for crickets with a flashlight. He could find them in mounds, crevices and the wild grass. Once he had cleaned them out, my village home was quiet. Mr Yong's wit often surprised my colleagues and students. He led the village in building the courtyards and paths I had sketched; he and his team built all the brick courtyards, micro landscapes and stairs in Hebian. As versatile as he was, Mr Yong was good at carpentry and the first young man in the village to learn to build wooden buildings.

Mr Yong was sturdy and agile and climbed trees easily. I liked to chat with him. He knew the plants and animals in the rainforests very well and was familiar with the uses of many tropical plants. He was sincere, kind and honest, but to my surprise he was still single. I had told him I would get him a particular type of minivan, a Wuling Sunshine, as a wedding gift if he got a girlfriend and married, but it had been years, and he remained single. He used to make a living from sugarcane but earned more in recent years with the income from guestrooms and a subsidy as a cooperative employee. I often wondered why Mr Yong, who was much smarter than many rich urban residents, was stuck in poverty. He was like many young people in Hebian Village: hardworking, clever, but poor.

My impression of the people I met in Hebian Village was at odds with the public messaging from the government. In the battle against poverty, slogans such as 'the lazy cannot be lifted out of poverty' can be seen everywhere in the Chinese countryside. During my frequent visits to farmers' homes in poor villages, almost all the officials would condescendingly lecture the poor, stating that one should be self-motivated and industrious with the government's support. This lecture was given without much thought, repeating widespread cliches. The idea that poverty results from laziness has been embedded in our social ideology. I was often asked if the people in the village I worked in were lazy, and I would say no. Then I would be asked: 'If they are not lazy, why are they still poor?'.

Where indeed does that question come from? It certainly isn't new. Turning again to the United States, the mainstream opinion on poverty in the eighteenth century is reflected in Poor Richard's Almanack, by Benjamin Franklin. The almanacks reflected, but also profoundly influenced, discussions of poverty in America. For Franklin, poverty is an individual failure. He, and others of his time and since, attributed poverty to laziness, lack of initiative, and weak abilities. This has been the offhand consensus of most modern societies, China included.

Even in the United States, empirical science does not support Benjamin Franklin's theory that poverty stems from individual failure. Researchers compared the poor's attitudes to life, work and initiative with their wealthier counterparts and found almost no difference [4, 5]. It is not a mere matter of research and policy, however, that poverty is not attributable to individual laziness. More importantly, this narrative is an ethical and moral issue. It provides the rich with a natural excuse to evade their social responsibilities and a political justification to maintain their economic position and privilege. It also undermines our efforts to establish a fair and just value system across society. Additionally, it conceals defects in our systems and policies and prevents us from building a fair society through systematic reforms. Since society criticises the poor for laziness—and sometimes worse—the poor are socially excluded, and their exclusion is chalked up to individual defects rather than systematic injustices. In this way, the political roots of poverty remain conveniently behind a curtain.

My colleagues and students fully agreed that Mr Yong and the villagers were poor but never lazy. Far from being harmful to society, they were sincere, hardworking and smart. They were only poor because they were not employed in a high-income, high-welfare industry. But why was this? If he had been employed by any urban landscape gardening company, Mr Yong would greatly contribute to the company, and his income and welfare would be considerably improved. In the wider world, he might well have met a girlfriend and eventually found the right Mrs Yong. However, he did not have access to a decent education and could not compete with graduates from the School of Architecture at Tsinghua University or even junior college graduates who majored in gardening. After living in Hebian Village for over five years, I became familiar with many young people in Hebian Village. Hebian Village was isolated from opportunity. To be born in Hebian Village was to start at a disadvantage. This is exactly why I have repeatedly mentioned the 'poverty trap': when people are cut off from places and networks where there is the chance of wealth, they and their families and peers are far more likely to be trapped in cycles of low income and slow advancement.

The American sociologist Mark Rank had powerfully criticised the popular American conceptualisation of poverty that poverty resulted from inadequacies of the poor. Instead, he argued from his studies in the US, poverty stems from structural failings, prime among them lack of access to employment and education and ineffectiveness of social safety net. He showed that the most important reason for poverty was the US economic structure's failure to provide decent jobs for all its inhabitants. Millions of US families are struggling on or below the poverty line—a poverty line higher than China's, but still one that reflects a difficult standard of living. He also soberly pointed out the problem of social mobility, believing that social classes are typically self-reproductive. The children of working-class or low-income parents tend to remain in or around the same social strata, while the rich inherit an affluent life. [6] Opportunity begets opportunity. The Chinese saying that 'wealth never survives three generations' may have some truth—even those with opportunities may not know how to take them—but it is easier to slip from the top stratum than it is to climb up from the bottom.

In recent years, I was often invited to explain the importance of the battle against poverty. Many people were convinced of the significance of this battle, and I would emphasise the importance of eliminating absolute poverty. However, today's key problem is that many are in a poverty trap caused not by laziness or a lack of hard work but by systemic constraints. Take Mr Yong again, or his peers among the young in Hebian Village. Even if they could travel to a city with better economic opportunities, employers would be reluctant to hire them because they do not have a proper record of formal schooling, and few speak good Mandarin. Even if they took the initiative to attempt the opportunity of a better labour market, their outcomes could match that of the ill-fated husband of Ms Yang in the previous section. There are many 'poor' people, just like Mr Yong, in China. They are poor because economic and social systems exclude them. This exclusion is not intentional but naturally results from economic and social transformation. As modern economic and social systems cannot prevent poverty, government intervention becomes necessary.

Removing structural barriers is not easy. If a government wishes to claim to be just, however, it must attempt it. The translation of political commitment to effective action in poverty reduction thus becomes vital in realising fair and just governance. I believe it should be the number of poor citizens, not the number of rich citizens, that should be used to measure the success of governance. As China has found in implementing its poverty alleviation ambitions, especially in rural villages, eliminating poverty is an extremely difficult process.

Why Hasn't Mr You's House Been Put up?

Unexpected results in a state programme supporting house-building offer insights into the challenges of poverty alleviation. It is lack of opportunity, not lack of knowledge, that keeps people in poverty.

Those who have visited Hebian Village will have been impressed by the tall house at the village entrance, a stark rise that everyone entering the village must pass. I say house, but in truth it remains something of a construction site. It's been four years, but the house hasn't been entirely put up yet. During every visit, I would seek out the owner of the house, Mr You, and his wife for a chat. They used to live on the hillside where the cooperative office now sits. Their house then was a wooden shed, often with shabby clothes hanging outside to dry for everyone to see.

Their household was later relocated to its current position during the period of homestead adjustment. It was one of my greatest challenges when running the poverty alleviation experiment in Hebian.

At the start of our work, government funds for relocation and other purposes were secured. This was very good. As a registered household in poverty, Mr You's family was entitled to an RMB40,000 subsidy for house-building (which the government would grant after the house was built and evaluated) and RMB60,000 interest-free loans for 20 years. After decades of practising anti-poverty fund administration a far more complete set of administrative measures has been developed in China, but they are not problem-free. Such funds used to be extended directly to farmers, but, in many cases, farmers would use the funds to pay old debts or buy food. This is an understandable decision. If I was constantly pressured to pay back an overdue debt or had no food or clothing for my children, the first thing I would do upon receiving a sum of money would be to repay the debt and buy food and clothes; other things, such as housing renovations, would follow on later if all went well. Indeed, the fact that the poor typically know far better what they need than policy-makers do is a key reason for the growth of cash transfers in development. From the perspective of a policymaker distributing anti-poverty funds for specific purposes, however, the unintended uses of money allocated for housing, education, or any other purpose can be frustrating.

Seeking a way around this problem, Chinese policymakers gradually introduced a range of fund administration measures. One of them is the requirement of a financial contribution for support. Many large-scale poverty alleviation programmes requested that farming households contribute funds of their own to support state poverty alleviation funds, which would then be fully allocated after the project was completed. In essence, this is a fund matching scheme intended to make sure that more money is channelled towards useful activities. Even though this seems like a reasonable measure, it had unintended effects for poverty alleviation. First, in many cases those who benefitted the most from these programmes were not the poorest—as Professor Sangui Wang, a poverty expert, found after systematically evaluating implementation of China's anti-poverty policies at the village level [7]. Second—and relatedly—the fact that funds were allocated after a project is completed does not align with the reality of poverty in rural areas. From the perspective of state bureaucrats, such an approach at first glance makes sense. As we have noted, beneficiaries of state support often don't use the money in the intended ways; allowing access to the money after the intended activity uses the funds as a carrot, incentivising the 'correct' action. Beyond its paternalism, however, the approach ignores the fact that impoverished households have no financial means to begin projects. When Hebian Village started to build houses, we mobilised villagers to first get loans from credit cooperatives, to be paid back after the poverty alleviation funds were granted. But the loans came with an interest rate, and the farmers, who meticulously worked out their accounts, were unwilling to request them. In 2015, Mr You refused to apply for a loan, even declining the RMB60,000 interest-free loan from the government.

On one visit to Mr You's, going to him for my regular conversation about construction, I found a collection of people who looked like local government officials had arrived before me. They stared at me, smoking, and I looked back at them. I knew all the officials in the township, but I had never met these people before. Later on I asked around, and other villagers told me that the credit cooperative had sent representatives to Mr You's to demand repayment. Chronically sick, Mr You carried a heavy debt for medical therapy, and the credit cooperative's patience was wearing thin. I started to understand his reluctance to take out government loans. In order to secure the RMB60,000 interest-free government loan for house-building he first had to request a loan from the credit cooperative, but he was unlikely to get a reasonable interest rate with his poor credit record.

After studying his case with government officials and taking into consideration his medical troubles and his children's educational expenses, we decided that as long as he put up the main structure of the house, the work would be considered done and he could receive the fund. Later, Mr You prepared timber on his own, borrowed some money from relatives and finally did put up the basic structure of the house. Mr You received nearly RMB110,000 of financial support, and the 20-year interest-free government loans were later exempted for payback. Nonetheless the construction of his house was never completed, even after the structure had been built and the state support had been provided.

I tried to find him in the village several times, only to find he was not home. I had to learn from other villagers that he had spent the money contracting a sugarcane field, not on building the house. Everyone is an economist in their own livelihoods. Though we could blame Mr You for misappropriating poverty reduction funds and had to withhold further support, it didn't change the fact that he was responsible for his own fate. When I finally met him some time later, I asked him if he had used the money on sugarcane fields, and he replied, 'Yes, I did. The sugarcane field will earn me RMB200,000 this year. Please be assured that I will build the house once I have made money'. His words left me feeling bitter: he deemed the house-building as something requested from me—an outsider, instead of a means that would generate additional funds to improve his livelihood as he saw in sugarcane growing. He and I, the supported and the supporter, lived in two different worlds. This was the meta-question of poverty and the underlying reason behind the failure of our poverty reduction programme.

After that I stopped pressuring Mr You to build the house and instead waited for him to make the expected money. In 2019, I was told by other villagers that elephants had damaged his sugarcane field at a heavy loss. When I met him, he said, 'I suffered a loss, but I can still make money'. The outbreak of COVID-19 kept me from further visiting the village. I tried to glean information from photographs to see whether Mr You had put up the house. Though I noticed a few new planks, it seemed he hadn't. Many people in the village didn't believe in what Mr You said, but I did. I believed that he would build the house when he earned money, and that his inaction only indicated that money was scarce, not that he had no intention of following the plan he had shared. If his sugarcane hadn't been eaten by elephants or flooded by storms, I trusted he would make more than RMB200,000 because he was the best poor economist and had placed his investment where he could expect the greatest possible return. The guestroom that I had advised him to build at the cost of RMB100,000 would make at most RMB10,000 annually. Although many villagers did not make much of this sum, I told them a steady RMB10,000 annual income would lift them out of poverty. By contrast, Mr You said to me that his RMB100,000 investment to contract sugarcane fields would secure an RMB200,000 return; the technological and market risks were minor because he was familiar with growing sugarcane. He only encountered setbacks because of storms and elephants. In any case, he was an economist in life, and the greatest expert on his own circumstances, abilities and needs. Mr You was not stuck in poverty because he was lazy, but for institutional reasons. Elephants destroyed the crop he badly needed, but the state did not provide him with adequate compensation. This is not a unique story. If insurance or guidance for the poor's investments were available, or if farmers' compensation for wildlife damage was increased, I believe Mr You and others like him could not only overcome poverty but become affluent.

Once, my family asked me how someone they knew, an executive director of some company, made money. She didn't work but merely travelled and took photographs. I answered that she put her money together with others' and invested it for returns. The poor also know about making money with money, in their own ways, but never have the opportunity to try. Wealth accumulation requires certain conditions. The uneven distribution of opportunity consolidates into entrenched social inequality. In the context of social inequality, the poor remain poor because they are stuck in a poverty trap that is difficult to address.

I hope to meet Mr You soon to discuss new paths. In the past few years, his hard work relied on the initial RMB100,000 loan, and, fortunately, RMB60,000 of this sum did not need to be repaid. When organising economic activities to support the poor, should we ask them to follow our advice, or put our support in their hands, allowing them to make decisions? It's a complex question. I am generally not critical and tend to be optimistic and romantic, which is why I can't become a good scholar. I wonder if institutions can offer startup insurance, investment guidance and even investment banking for the poor to turn their assets into capital—would this be more effective than industrial poverty alleviation programmes?

Why Don't the Poor Save Money?

> The choices made by poor people reflect both the constraints of their situations, and the real mental effects of poverty upon decision-making processes: it is hard to plan for the long term if ambitious goals seem unattainable. In the face of this, community support networks and help in creating new opportunities are crucial.

My colleagues and students all liked to hang out with Mr Yong because he was simple and smart. The students helped him draw up a savings schedule for some of his guestroom income and supervised his spending. We had no means to conduct randomised controlled trials in the village, and so were conducting some simple interventional studies. In 2018 I walked past Yong's yard and saw in it a brand-new Yamaha motorcycle. These are quite expensive. It belonged to Yong's elder brother. Yong's brother had made a fair bit of money by building houses for the villagers and running his guestroom. I knew that his old motorcycle worked just fine and asked him why he didn't save the money. I received no reply but a smile. (He was a man of few words. While he didn't speak much, others spoke of him—he often ran around outside, causing village gossip.) Later, I heard he made more money with his savings but did not inquire further.

I often asked villagers why they did not choose to save their money. They almost always gave the same answer: they had no money to save. I had no idea how much they had made before I arrived, but I could see the figures after the local cooperative was founded, which kept books on each household's income from guestrooms. I knew how much each household earned, and it was clear that many young singles earned at least a small income, more than enough to live on in an impoverished village. Knowing this I often asked them if they had savings; I believed they should save money for future investments or events, like getting married. But the farmers seemed to live life differently from how I imagined. Our communications were not always verbal. I asked Yong if he had used up his earnings every time we met, and he always smiled a positive answer; then, I asked where he had spent the money, but only received another smile.

I didn't get more clarity into the financial situation of Yong's brother with the Yamaha, but I did gradually learn about the economic sociology of poverty-stricken villages. Yong's second elder brother had no money for the weekly educational and boarding expenses of his two children, and Yong had to give him a hand. Even where villagers seemed only distantly related, they were really nonetheless part of a large and surprisingly close-knit family. If you could trace the lines of family interconnections, you would probably also be tracing the lines through which lending and borrowing took place. Borrowing was an integral part of economic life in Hebian Village, and the circulation of limited funds throughout the village helped maintain their livelihoods. Hebian used to rely on the income from sugarcanes before the Yao Guestroom project started to provide them with an alternative, but the income from sugarcanes was only available at the beginning and end of the year. Besides sugarcane farming, villagers collected Fructus amomi, a traditional Chinese medicinal material, and could obtain a considerable income in good harvests. Taking odd jobs outside the village was another source of income. Since incomes were mainly concentrated at the beginning and end of the year, the villagers spent much of the year without access to cash and could not buy cigarettes, alcohol and daily necessities. Almost every household had a motorcycle, and so also needed fuel. The village economy was therefore characterised by a constant need for cash. Villagers with a slight level of affluence could try to save money to meet daily needs, while those unable to make money had to borrow. As far as I know villagers generally only borrowed small sums on which there was no interest; large debts, for those who incurred them, would require interest.

We tend to observe the poor's economic and social issues from the perspective of the formal economy and normative institutions. Often, we attribute poverty to a lack of savings. Abhijit Banerjee and Esther Duflo, after examining the poor's approach to savings and the logic behind poverty and self-control, argued that the temptation to spend was the same for the poor and the rich, but that the consequences of unproductive spending were more serious for the poor. A small spend on a minor indulgence is a tiny percentage of a rich person's income; for someone scraping by on the poverty line, it is a larger proportion of their earnings [8].

This is not at all to say that they cannot save; the fact that even the very poor can nonetheless hold fairly large weddings confirms that when something is important, they can save if they have the chance. However, the ambitious, long-term goals for which development thinkers might want them to save are often, from their perspectives, simply unrealistic. Given a choice between self-deprivation during a difficult time in order to pursue a goal that seems distant to the point of impossibility, and something pleasant without perceptibly increasing the distance to the goal, it is easy to choose the small indulgence. Urban residents have money; for them it is easier to save for an apartment or a car, which they know they can with some effort achieve in a certain time. In Hebian, such ambitions are very remote. Even just a driver's licence costs thousands of yuan. It is not that the poor are poor because they are unambitious. On the contrary, they are unambitious because they are poor. The rich save to invest and increase the value of their net assets in the future. The poor have limited resources and pitifully little capital and are unlikely to save for future resources. In the modern market economy, the poor have no privilege at all. The affluent are not bothered by the cost of daily consumption, and urban wage-earners save monthly wage surpluses in banks or invest in the market to increase their assets and make more money. By contrast to the rich, the poor villagers of Hebian were—to my observation—often baffled by the expenses of daily life. Mr Zhou in Hebian Village told me that his two sisters would have trouble going to school without income from the guestroom. In this sense, savings were not an economic issue for the people in Hebian Village.

We often claim that it is the lack of access to financial systems that leads to the 'backwardness' of the poor's economic activities. In fact, they do engage with financial systems, but not ones that are immediately visible to us. The community serves as a bank for the poor. In Hebian, this bank was free from formal rules about savings and lending and management costs. Instead, it is run informally through a system of mutual knowledge and trust. Villagers are accountable to each other. With the entire village acting as a large capital pool, each household was likely to support their peers so long as they had money in hand. For instance, house-building in Hebian relied largely on mutual support amongst the villagers. The poor didn't save, not because they were ignorant of the benefits of savings, but because savings for them have low liquidity. They depended on cash daily; savings would make everyday expenditure inconvenient. If the villagers were to deposit money in the bank, they would have to make a motorcycle trip to withdraw it. In the beginning, few villagers had bank accounts. Many opened one only because the poverty alleviation programme's funds for house-building and income from the cooperative were transferred via banks. The increase in village bank accounts made it possible for my students to supervise Yong's savings.

Another reason why the poor do not save enough is that they spend money where they 'shouldn't'. In a recent survey, we found that higher incomes in Hebian corresponded with a surge in expenditure on cigarettes and alcohol. My colleagues always tried to dissuade the villagers from smoking or drinking to save money. Mr Deng, a key opinion leader here, never had a break from cigarettes and alcohol and claimed his spirits would be too low if he worked without smoking. The affluent may spend little on cigarettes and alcohol because they pay closer attention to their health. The villagers know less about the health consequences of drinking and smoking, and their income was only enough to support a little smoking and drinking, but not much. Perhaps, again, this is because when ambitions seem less attainable, something pleasant is needed—even if it is only small—for support.

Consumption beyond subsistence is an important part of life for both the rich and the poor. A few years ago, when I was having a meal in Germany with the head of a local Christian charity, he told me he was busy mobilising donations and calling upon Germans to drink less beer and donate the money to poverty reduction programmes. I replied that this was easy since beer does not cost much. He responded that beer was very important to Germans; it was not easy to ask them for a bit of sacrifice, which was why he had to remind them that it was God's will. If affluent Germans need a religious reason to sacrifice a beer, this shows that the significance of consumption beyond subsistence cannot be considered simply economically. The poor's consumption of cigarettes and alcohol was just a part of life, like travel and dining with friends is for the rich. If it took God to persuade the rich to drink less beer, how should we demand the poor to smoke less?

People working on poverty alleviation tend to think from the position of the haves and feel that the have-nots' attitudes are inconsistent with the actions needed to gain wealth. Still, the poor would be in a more miserable situation if they did not have the freedom to live in their way. A seemingly poor village was, in fact, run by the rules of 'economics of the poor' and 'sociology of the poor'. It's difficult for us to see these rules. Nevertheless, each day of living in Hebian Village helped me to better understand the economics and sociology of the poor. Money flowed between villagers, invisibly supporting them to buy daily necessities and pay for their children's education. In recent times some things have changed: they now save money in banks. It is safer than keeping money at home, and moreover the challenges related to distance have been erased by WeChat—a social media based multi-functional application that can be installed on mobilephones. They still don't see savings accounts as a form of investment, but prefer to keep money in the bank for safety. The ease of WeChat, conveniently accessible on their mobile phone, allows them to transfer money to friends and family, continuing to weave the tapestry of small transactions that constitute Hebian's relationships of support. A village like Hebian is like an invisible bank, reliant on the trust of the community.

The Cycle of Poverty

Poverty can perpetuate itself, trapping individuals in short-term struggles at the expense of long-term preparations, and dripping down to trap subsequent generations. Outside assistance, access to opportunities, and education can help to break these treadmills.

One day, I received a WeChat message asking to borrow some money. I didn't recognise the sender's name, but he addressed me as 'teacher' and I wondered if this might be one of the students who had attended my classes before. Upon inquiry he said his name was Gang, and I guessed he must be a villager from Hebian. I asked how much money he needed, and what he wanted it for. He needed RMB3,000 for his wife to give birth in hospital. I transferred the sum via WeChat, and he promised he would pay me back. I asked other villagers about him and was told he was the son of the 'mad woman' in Hebian. Although I was acquainted with this woman and her young children, I couldn't recall this young man who seemed to have got married and become a father. I also had no idea how he connected to me via Wechat.

When I returned to the village, I asked about Gang and learnt that he was under 18 and had married his pregnant girlfriend, herself a teenager. Most Hebian villagers got married and had children at an early age. The villagers I spoke with said that he wouldn't be able to repay me, and that I shouldn't have lent him money. In fact I had not expected him to pay me back, but I wanted to help the unfortunate newborn. Later on I saw a girl holding a baby in the village and wondered whether this was the child I had helped, but Lu himself never came to pay me back or even to express thanks. A while later, Lu again texted me to ask to borrow more money. He was leaving to find money as a migrant worker, and his family needed a home by any means possible. He promised to pay back all his debts once he had made money, and I lent him another RMB500. Later on he contacted me again to ask to borrow still more money, but this time I declined.

As some psychologists suggest that while the affluent tend to make long-term plans, poverty encourages people to become shortsighted and oblivious to the future, striving to acquire what they need in the short term without giving enough thought to the longer span of their needs [9]. This inevitably leads to future uncertainty and stress—as Gang, stumbling from one crisis to another, had found. Perhaps this affected his young wife. Jay Belsky, a developmental psychologist, has found that girls raised in stressful or disorderly environments are more likely to experience early pregnancies. [10] These mothers, especially when in poverty, are also likely to give birth early. Such trends could be both a reflection of poverty, and also a contributing cause. This is why poverty alleviation workers often viewed many features of poverty as being themselves part of the origin of poverty, and hoped to change such behaviours of the poor through education or persuading which however often rendered futile.

Young people in the village were generally poorly educated. Many dropped out by junior middle school, and only a few made it through to high school. Mr Deng told me they learnt little of worth at school, and that therefore the costs were not justifiable; the children would still be farmers after graduation. It was better to drop out early to make money by tapping rubber trees or cutting sugarcane. His words partially revealed the truth of poverty: the cyclicity of low opportunity. I wondered if Hebian youth would still return to the village after graduation to become farmers if they had the chance to attend the top kindergartens, primary, and middle schools in Beijing? Of course, the analogy was unfair.

I once visited the primary and middle schools in the township. There I was told that the school dormitories and facilities had significantly improved with the support of new educational development programmes. The school meals, in particular, had been important. Village children were willing to go to school because the food offered there was better than at home. This was somewhat encouraging. Nevertheless, the headmaster said the biggest problem was neither school meals nor dormitories (due to favourable policies and subsidies, farmers could afford their children's education): the most significant challenge was a lack of high-quality teachers. The school was struggling to find an English teacher who would like to work in such remote areas, and the quality of Chinese and math teachers needed to be improved.

This disclosed some clues regarding the cycle of poverty in the area. On the one hand, poverty was indeed a vicious cycle, where young people reduced to poverty were unlikely be able to plan for and invest in the future as children from affluent families did. Low-income youths prone to early pregnancies were stuck struggling to imagine a path to a successful future. The next generation, born to parents unable to easily look beyond the immediate, were of course influenced by the example they were given. We can compare this cycle to experiences in previous centuries, and to patterns elsewhere in the world. In harsh times, as Keith Payne notes, when the future was full of uncertainties and the chances of survival and reproduction was slim, it made sense to give birth to more children at an early age. This was the most efficient option. Payne calls this cycle 'live fast, die young' [11]. Of course, this is the basic logic behind the struggle for survival. Survival may not be so simple as the mere transmission of the lineage. As in many places—such as in Niger, where there is an average of nearly seven births per woman—children may be seen as an insurance option against an inadequate social safety net. As we discussed in previous chapters, the 'economics of the poor' are not always simple. Decisions that to outside observers seem irrational or short-termist might also be due to the mental constraints brought by poverty, or might in fact be coping mechanisms.

Even in impoverished villages like Hebian, early marriage and early childbirth were not necessarily driven by pragmatic concerns. Still, one thing was certain: in the struggle for survival, they would all make short-term decisions to meet immediate demands, and this could cause lifelong predicaments. Hebian villagers urgently needed money to pay medical bills and daily expenses and borrowing was part of their daily life. They often subsequently had to engage in nearsighted, risky endeavours to earn money to repay these debts. In such a cycle, they were susceptible to deception and exploitation and might even commit crimes. Their difficulty in extricating themselves from immediate pressures made it hard to plan for the future, causing them later to again have to borrow, and again to struggle to repay. We called this situation the individual cycle of poverty.

Meanwhile a family would often pass this livelihood pressure on to their children, through family education, an intergenerational transmission of poverty that may be called the intergenerational cycle of poverty. When many village families faced the same predicament, their means of coping with this immediate livelihood pressure affected other families in the neighbourhood, forming a culture of poverty. Many people attribute poverty to a culture of poverty, implying that the poor would be lifted out of poverty if this culture changed.

I myself have some sympathy with this culturalist perspective, but I couldn't avoid persuading the villagers to look further. My colleagues and I repeatedly discussed the future of Hebian's youth, and my colleagues even initiated many cultural activities such as films and sports. I meant to build a library, but villagers said that no one would be interested because many books were on politics and few taught them how to get rich; library books required care and would become mouldy in the area's high humidity.

The longer I stayed in the village, the more ignorant I felt. As a poverty scholar, living and working in a poverty-stricken village, I felt increasingly helpless in my perceptions of poverty. This book's discussion of the poverty trap and structural poverty stems from my experience in this village. It was Hebian village that taught me about poverty.

Poverty alleviation was intended to break the individual and intergenerational cycles of poverty. We could not seek solutions solely from the poor or resort to educating the poor in an condescending way. Yet, the poor are not necessarily the origin of either cycle of poverty. As in my example regarding educational institutions, if children in Hebian went to a fine school and attended junior college after high school like children in cities did, I believe their fate would be significantly different.

During my work in the village, I set up a small non-governmental organisation that hired a local girl, a member of the Hani ethnic group, who finished college and obtained a Master's degree at the Minzu University of China. She was the organisation's executive director and is currently a project manager with the China Charity Federation. She was a typical example of how education and access to new opportunities could alter an individual's fate, but she was an exception to the rule, given the many particular reasons for her success. In poverty alleviation, we must examine why exceptions succeed, but we must also study why such exceptional cases are not universal, in order to create approaches that reduce the barriers preventing everyone from enjoying the same successes. We are unlikely to persuade people to invest in education without proving that educated people generally have a more promising future than the uneducated. Sometimes, government officials would investigate school dropouts by door-to-door visits, offering support to families in difficulties to ensure their children could go to school or stay in school. However, once we secure funds to improve the quality of education in poor areas and closely associate local education with children's futures, there will be no need to encourage children to go to school.

Recently, three Hebian youths went to college. When returning to the village for vacations, they brought new hope to the village youths.

Life in a Malawian Village

A short diversion into life in Malawi shows a parallel example of short-term needs creating cycles of poverty.

My colleague Professor Tang Lixia once visited a village in Malawi to implement a Chinese foreign aid project. From the experience, she wrote a short article on the life of the poor in this African village. Africa is the continent most enmeshed in poverty, and people seldom question the necessity of poverty alleviation there. The village Professor Tang visited was in the south of Malawi, less than 20km from the town of Balaka and accessible via a bumpy car ride—Malawi had no highways, and villages were accessible by dirt roads off trunk roads. The majority of villages had no access to electricity. Water was provided by wells built through international aid programmes delivered by various UN agencies, NGOs, or country-specific aid organisations. Chinese initiatives have also built 600 wells in Malawi. These programmes were critical for local villagers who would otherwise have had to travel far to get water. This village had no access to electricity, though it was only a few kilometres from urban residential areas. Almost no public facilities were available, and the village consisted of small houses—of no more than 20 square metres—scattered in an unorganised fashion.

Most houses were built with bricks and roofed with thatch, while households with a better financial status had asbestos roof. Two thatch-roofed grocery stores sold cooking oil and snacks. The cooking oil was sold in bags at 50 Kwachas (RMB0.48 or USD0.07) for a full bag and 30 Kwachas (RMB0.29 or USD0.04) for a half bag. Prices were adapted to the cash shortage, as local farms had neither deposits nor money to store food. They ate whatever they could afford and did whatever they could to earn money.

In the 2014 sowing season most planted seedlings were washed away by floods, and it was too late to resow. Then in 2015 a severe drought significantly reduced corn production. Whereas the villagers commonly harvested 50 sacks (at 50 kg per sack) per acre which were sufficient to feed one family, the 2015 harvest only yielded one or a half-sack of maize per acre. The market price of maize doubled from 4,000 Kwachas (RMB38.4 or USD5.5) per sack in 2014 to 8,000 Kwachas (RMB76.8 or USD10.9) per sack in 2015. Though the harvest season in June and July was just over, the farmers had no more maize at home and only ate one meal a day. Those in this situation considered themselves poor. When villagers were asked whom they considered rich within their population, they replied that 10 out of the 80 households were rich. Wealth was judged against a threshold of two meals a day: houses able to eat more than once were considered wealthy.

Next year's harvest season was still far away, and Professor Tang asked how the villagers would get by. Luckily, Balaka was one of the major towns in Malawi and home to a few cotton companies and farms. With the decrease in maize yields, income from cotton farming became especially important for the villagers. Many owed debts to contracted cotton companies with whom they had previously done business. If they sold cotton to these companies, their debts would be deducted from the price of the cotton. In these cases, farmers would receive limited cash and might as a result starve in desperate times. Consequently, most farmers chose to sell cotton to non-contracted companies which would not deduct debts. The contracted cotton companies, for their part, could no longer recover their loans: the farmers to whom they had lent were destitute, and there was no money to be collected. This avoidance of repayment was a weapon of the weak and desperate, and it had severe consequences for farmers' production in the next years. However, they were unlikely to concern themselves with next year's worries at this stage. They had to get money for food today.

Some villagers would go for odd jobs to the companies and farms, earning 500 Kwachas (RMB4.8 or USD0.7) a day, and some would mow lawns for 1,000 Kwachas (RMB9.6 or USD1.4) a day. They used the 500 Kwachas earned to buy five piles of cassava to feed their families for one day. Then, they would do other odd jobs to earn food for another day. They could buy 4kg of maize with 500 Kwachas but chose cassava because they had to travel far to buy maize, and it cost money to process maize into flour and required other vegetables if eaten as a side dish. It was much easier to eat cassava, which was convenient to buy. The poor carefully use their wisdom to survive from one day to the next. In the long term, however, more stability is needed, and this must come from other actors. The resilience of the poor can never be a justification for inaction. Cassava provides calories to allow survival, but provides little else: it contains very few nutrients. No one can thrive on cassava alone.

When Tang requested to take photos of them, they said: 'We are starved now and will not look good in the photos'.

Are Women More Likely to be Poor?

Feminisation of poverty, as a concept may help us better understand poverty as embedded in social relationships, yet to tackle feminisation of poverty in the real world can be extremely complicated.

In 1978 Diana Pearce, then an assistant sociology professor at the University of Illinois, published an important paper [12] which studied gender inequality in labour and incomes on the basis of employment statistics for the United States between 1950 and 1970s. She raised a strong argument that although the employment rate of American women had improved, two-thirds of the country's poor population over 16 were women. Her study was mainly based on wage income data as one of the most important indicators of women's poverty. Pearce illustrated the proportion of women in impoverished demographics and the proportion of female-headed households amongst poor households. Pearce coined the concept of the 'feminisation of poverty' and profoundly influenced subsequent methodological studies on women, poverty and gender inequality with highly persuasive income data. Notably, she used poor individuals and households as a total sample to estimate the proportion of women in poverty and the proportion of female-headed households. She did not use individuals and households than included the poor and non-poor as the total sample. To better estimate the incidence, intensity and depth of poverty later studies mostly adopted the method of measuring the proportion of the poor in a total sample including poor and higher-income groups, which has become the mainstream method in current studies of income indicators in the feminisation of poverty. Still, her paper had a big impact on the field, and on my own thinking and work.

In the early 1990s, when I was studying in the Netherlands, I took a course on gender and development. Essays on Pearce's study were included in the reading materials. Despite the fact that a decade and a half had elapsed between the publication of her paper and my studies in the Netherlands, the impoverishment of women was still a new and stylish topic at the time. I barely digested it before trying to systematically introduce the concept to thinking in China. After I returned to China, my colleagues and I conducted surveys on gender and development in rural areas in Hebei. At the time, I was unlikely and also unable to criticise western development theories. In 2019, I published a paper [13] based on my poverty alleviation practise in Hebian Village. For a long time, I agreed with the theory of lifting women out of poverty through economic empowerment. Pearce's work probably had a big influence on my thinking.

In my poverty alleviation practise in Hebian village, the Yao Guestroom was the project's core. We intended it to develop an avenue for the economic empowerment of women. Once women had access to a relatively independent economic space, we thought, their economic contribution to the family would become explicit, and they would be empowered. They would run the guestrooms; their male family members would see what effect this was having on the household's finances; and, as the managers of this revenue stream, the women's agency would increase. However, practise indicated otherwise. My students used to meticulously calculate the division of labour between men and women in running Yao Guestrooms and found, at every step of the work, that women devoted far more time and labour to these tasks than men. In one conversation I had with a woman who cleaned guestrooms and received visitors, I asked if the income from the guestrooms was counted as hers. She replied that it was not her income, but her family's. In some households the guestroom income was transferred to the women's bank accounts. But no matter whose income the money was counted to, women's income from what we had envisaged as a relatively independent revenue stream was eventually transformed into welfare expenditure for the whole family, including the husband. As the guestroom income rose, we found that family expenses on cigarettes and alcohol—both mostly consumed by men—surged, while spending on women increased only mildly. I named this phenomenon the 'alienation of empowerment'. Tweaks to a system might give the appearance of greater agency, but if the fundamental culture and distribution of power does not change, the results may be only skin deep.

In her 1978 study Pearce focused on American, black, working-class, single-parent households living on wage income. She found two things. First, the livelihoods of single-parent households were more vulnerable than two-parent ones, and this was the case for male-headed single-parent households as well as female-headed. Second, working-class households living on wage income were more prone to poverty due to low income and childcare costs. These are very interesting findings, but they are closely related to the differentiated income between different classes in the US. Pearce's study on the feminisation of poverty, I realised after leaving the Netherlands, might not point to a global phenomenon.

In developing countries, many households do not live on fixed incomes. Especially in rural areas, households are self-sufficient and do not depend on cash incomes. Thus, it is difficult to use the economic income to indicate the relationship between poverty and women. Meanwhile, the conclusion that poverty is feminised based on female-headed single-parent households does not consider the situation of two-parent households. In a poor two-parent household, both men and women might have low incomes, and men might even have a lower income than women. Instead of pointing to the feminisation of poverty, it might be more reasonable to define poverty as structural. This reminds me of Karl Marx's theories, which argued that class exploitation was a primary cause of poverty while women face another exploitation through their unpaid reproductive labour.

It should be pointed out that gender issues reflected in the economic measurement of poverty do not necessarily indicate that poverty itself is differentiated between men and women. But gender differences will always remain, even if class perishes. A further question is whether gender differences are themselves the cause of the feminisation of poverty, or whether poverty in fact intensifies gender inequality. Before answering this question, we should clarify the meaning of poverty. Poverty is the absence of welfare measured both spiritually and materially, and on such a basis, gender-based inequalities will lead to a differentiation between poverty for men and women. For instance, if one measures a household's income living on wage income, a wife usually attends to the children and the elderly. She cannot undertake a higher-income job that requires time and energy. Thus, income difference is shaped. Since housework is traditionally performed by women and is excluded from the social value system of labour, poverty comes about to the disadvantage of women. Many people object to the connection between gender differences in income and poverty, believing it is unreasonable to conclude that women are in poverty because of gender differences in labour and income. Even with this difference, many women do not consider themselves in poverty, a perception mainly rooted in gender awareness. The absence of welfare for women has been the norm in many societies, indicating that society is still under patriarchal influence. If we use welfare in the material and spiritual dimensions as indicators to study the state of men and women, the result tends to be more objective. For example, if measured in multiple dimensions such as time spent on leisure, entertainment and control of household resources, the feminisation of poverty objectively exists.

In our own work and observations, we also found that poverty carried different implications in different conditions, various dimensions and even within different discourses. Preparing anti-poverty interventions to tackle the feminisation of poverty can be extremely complicated. One illustration of this stands out from my own experience. Towards the end of the 1990s, I was closely engaged in approaches aimed at reducing women's poverty in China. International development projects at the time mainly concentrated on poverty and gender, and we found that this required us to change some of our conventional practises. The Canadian International Development Agency—as it was then—initiated a programme aiming to increase incomes among Uygur women in Hetian, Xinjiang. We arranged for these women to join training meetings and study tours, but many complained about their heavy workloads and objections from their husbands. We attempted to apply a gender framework to the Chinese context, but social and cultural norms, made things hard for us. The stark objectivity of poverty legitimised aid and intervention. Often, however, the differences in living standards between men and women were not that great. The relativity of poverty, especially when it comes to the feminised poverty, made interventions even more difficult.

In the development community, many tend to have the preconceived idea that women are more vulnerable to poverty, and poverty reduction projects naturally regard women as primary targets for aid. Having a gender-sensitive concept in mind is good for understanding 'poverty as the outcome of a system of social relations' [14] on the ground, but classificatory interventions may also bring unintended risks. First, without conditions of social empowerment, programmes aimed at supporting women's economic development would dramatically intensify the burden for women and could not be sustainable. Second, social relations between men and women are the primary relations of human society, whereas an over-emphasis on the dichotomy of gender relations while neglecting the inter-dependency of these relations may cause a fracture in social relations in the real world.

Why Is It Hard to Identify?

To study poverty and work to alleviate it, we must identify 'the poor'. This is not a homogenous group, and even villagers will disagree about who among them are poor. Our benchmarks for help will often be clumsy, but they are still necessary.

I started my work on poverty reduction in the mid-1990s. I was mainly engaged in technical work for international organisations' development assistance projects in China, designing, implementing and evaluating projects. For every project, the first question that needed to be answered was 'how is this benefiting the poor'. This of course required that we first identify the poor. At the time I didn't understand why almost all projects mounted by international organisations had to be oriented towards the poor. (It was not that I disagreed with the focus.) Now, I realise that Western countries offering development assistance began to examine aid's effectiveness in the mid-1990s. At the development and cooperation ministerial meeting of developed countries held in Paris in 1996, the ministers passed a proposal by the OECD's Development Assistance Committee to put poverty reduction high on the agenda of international development assistance. The elimination of poverty became, in fact, the primary goal of development. Since then, all assistance from developed countries must consider its contribution to poverty reduction, and all the Chinese projects I have been engaged in targeted poverty alleviation.

In one of my early involvements, colleagues and I worked on a community development project for two villages in Yanqing County, just beyond the northernmost fringe of Beijing. We met with village representatives to identify who was poor, discussing households and ranking them in order of wealth. This was a participatory approach, intended to gather information that local government officials might not have. It was mostly used when the resources of a programme was limited and a specific number of villagers had to be identified as targets of the programme. The measures were introduced in some of my books [15–18]. I was most confused when a villager came all the way from Yanqing to the university in Beijing where I worked, complaining that he was impoverished but not included in the list. I replied that the list was based on ranking by his own peers, and that was a decent method, exclusion of the list meant that a person was not poor. Twenty years later, I used the same method to identify poverty-stricken households in Hebian Village by sitting village officials and representatives down in my shabby temporary office in the village, of which I still keep a picture. My student Xu Jin drew votes of assent on a record board, but a few villagers said it was unfair when the result was presented. They had witnessed the whole process and not complained until this point, so I asked which part was unfair. One replied that the whole village was poor, and no one was much wealthier than anyone else. As far as these few were concerned, it seemed, the whole exercise was almost meaningless. Everyone in the village needed help. It has been 20 years since the question raised by the Yanqing villager, but scholars like me have advanced little on our understandings of this important issue.

In the recent rhetorical escalation of the battle against poverty in China, 'households in poverty' became a significant political, economic and social symbol. In the eyes of farmers, being officially poor was certainly no badge of honour but also no longer really a source of shame: it was instead regarded as an important identity to gain benefits. For local officials, the existence of poor households in their jurisdiction meant the availability of external resources. Also, anti-poverty responsibilities were given more weight than previously, and reducing poverty offered opportunities for promotion. It was now in everyone's interest to identify the poor, but this was technically complicated. Poverty elimination had recognisably evolved into a political, social and economic matter.

In 2012, the Chinese government identified an annual disposable income of RMB2,300 per capita (2011 constant price) as the rural absolute poverty line. In theory, farmers earning less than this figure were defined as poor. The poverty line chosen made sense when viewed from an office in Beijing, but seemed painfully arbitrary to a villager informed that because they earned a smidge more than their neighbour, she would receive support but they would not. How should we identify the poor in reality? In rural areas, farmers often are not dependent solely on crop yields; they often sensibly make income from diversified sources, such as migrant work, the sale of their products, and land rental. From the outside, understanding a farmer household's revenues could be difficult. The challenge was even greater if we tried to break households down into individual members: the households themselves typically did not keep books and had no means of distinguishing individual members' income. Even if they did have the details of every income stream, would they report them truthfully when they knew that they stood to gain a lot if they were considered to be below the poverty line? The challenge grew again if we tried to look beyond a simple income-based set of eligibility criteria. Suppose poverty was defined as a general absence of welfare rather than a low income. In that case, farmers might not be categorised as poor if their land production and living conditions were adequate despite a low cash income. In some cases this would penalise ingenuity; farmers making good choices to adapt to their circumstances would lose support, while farmers making poor choices would retain it. Such a system would risk incentivising undesirable behaviour.

Conversely, farmers without residences might still be poor even if their disposable income was above RMB2,300. Chinese farmers were not living on formal wages, and their diverse income sources made it difficult to identify the poor through the criterion of annual disposable income. To this end, the battle against poverty adopted the goal of 'freeing farmers from worries over food and clothing and giving them access to compulsory education, basic medical services and safe housing' to make it easier to provide the poor in rural China with opportunities, even if they could not be easily identified at a granular level.

Neither an income nor non-income standard was sufficient to address the objective difficulty of identifying the poor. Logically speaking, everyone in a village was perfectly aware of who among them were relatively rich and poor, but when viewed from outside the local context it was clear that poverty was in fact universal in many villages. Given the minor wealth differences between farmer households, poverty alleviation officials were faced with the decision to only target exceptional destitute cases such as elderly adults with no families, the disabled, the sick and those without homes or the ability to work. However, 'poor' households outnumbered these destitute persons, and identifying the poor became a complex social issue.

In theory, 'the poor' is a group deprived of general welfare, such as food safety, nutrition, education, health or work (for reasons such as physical disability and market systems). In society, those at the bottom of the income ladder were considered poor and shared the following characteristics. Socially speaking, they showed the lowest mobility and typical intergenerational features of social class. Politically speaking, they did not actively participate in the political process and were underrepresented. Economically speaking, their income was not only low but also unstable. Culturally speaking, they were regarded as representative of the culture of poverty and marginalised by the mainstream society.

In modern developed and underdeveloped societies, the poor share similar features, and there are similar reasons behind poverty. Among many causes of poverty, institution or structural failure is believed to be one important origin of poverty. The United States highlighted social equity, but ironically, it is one of the most unequal societies worldwide. Comparative political studies tend to take fairness and justice as integral to comparing states' political systems. The size of the poor population and the degree of inequality are most likely to reflect a state's fairness and justice. Relations between different political systems and fairness, justice and poverty, are extremely complicated, and we must not draw hasty conclusions. In A Discourse upon the Origin and the Foundation of the Inequality among Mankind, Jean-Jacques Rousseau discussed the relationship between political systems and poverty. Plenty of modern studies have also analysed this topic.

I wrote in the previous paragraph that 'the poor' share certain characteristics. This is true, but it is wise to add a caveat. I have often used this phrase, 'the poor', and it offers a useful but imperfect shorthand. We cannot analyse poverty or create poverty alleviation programmes without using it, but we must also look beyond it to recognise that this group is not the homogeneous unit that it may appear at a glance. 'The poor' are in reality a fragmented bloc. Poverty is intersectional and multidimensional. In an affluent household, a wife could be poor. Her poverty may not be directly reflected by food or clothing, but she may be deprived of her rights, even the right to decide her own life. There are plenty of such cases globally, and we need to take gender into account when discussing poverty. Similarly, age has different implications for poverty. Certain ethnic or religious minority groups are also disproportionately prone to poverty. In China, ethnic minority groups are located in mountainous, remote areas and experience a high incidence of poverty. Poverty is also not unique to rural areas, but can also occur in cities. In short, those who lack opportunities are more likely to be poor. A lack of opportunities is often experienced in rural areas cut off from activity, but it can also be experienced by members of groups whom society cuts off, such as women, the elderly, or minority groups.

Our work to aid this demographic—'the poor'—thus needed dynamic, portable and reliable benchmarks for identifying those most in need, and for looking beyond high-level definitions. We often used a 'participatory' approach, as I sketched above, in which we would identify beneficiaries through conversations with their peers. This was not our sole method, however: as long as we knew which groups and people were prone to poverty, we could work to seek them out and ensure that they had access to help.

How Do the Poor Support Each Other?

The poor rely on mutual support networks and community-based institutions. These were important traditionally and remain important now, but are often overlooked by the public and by policymakers.

It is natural to assume that the poor are primarily supported by the rich. The poor are poor: from the outside, one might imagine that they have little to go round and will prefer to keep what resources they do have for themselves. From such a starting, the question, 'How do the poor support the poor?' might sound strange. Yet poor societies indeed have their own poverty alleviation strategies. In reality, this should come as no surprise. Western societies are individualised and have traditional means of poverty alleviation, such as religious charities and civic organisations. Traditional Chinese rural society also resorted to redistributional charities to keep rural order.

Rural societies, short of modern tools for production, used to depend on individuals' physical strength. Kinship and local community networks were used to share the labour force for mutual help to maximise the outcome of material production. Mutual help in labour was the basic logic behind rural collective survival and inevitably led to food sharing. Food sharing mechanisms were spontaneous and resulted from rural systematic arrangements. Traditionally, public fields and granaries were built in the countryside by the village community as a collective response to poverty and assisted people with extreme difficulties. This welfare practise was very common in Chinese rural society, which could be seen as an indigenous form of poverty reduction. Unfortunately, we seldom tap into the treasure of traditional practise to inform today's anti-poverty efforts.

While rural society used to be more organised according to more collective principles, the existence of the rich was not forbidden. Here, traditional ethics and morality were gradually transformed into what can now be viewed as particularly 'Chinese' beliefs regarding destiny, good fortune and retribution, which was a traditional ethical mechanism for adjusting wealth between the poor and the rich. The legitimacy of wealth was established by believing that it was either the result of destiny—if the person was lazy—or of good fortune, if hardworking. If this legitimacy were to be undermined, the rural order would be disrupted. That is not to say that rural society approved of unrestrained wealth acquisition. The value system of wealth included the belief that the rich must share their resources to avoid retribution. This was why the rich in a rural society always gave to the poor. They couldn't survive in rural areas without almsgiving, which was another important mechanism for maintaining rural stability and can be counted to some extent as a form of poverty alleviation. Rural societies depended on collective mechanisms and mutual help to survive difficulties, and almsgiving served to check inequalities.

This represents the basic concepts of contemporary poverty reduction. Regretfully, state anti-poverty actions always took individual welfare for the modern society as the criterion and thus often runs into dilemmas in rural areas.

References

1. Payne, K. (2018). *The Broken Ladder: How Inequality Affects the Way We Think, Live, and Die* (pp. 139–141). Penguin Books.
2. Payne, K. (2018). *The Broken Ladder: How Inequality Affects the Way We Think, Live, and Die* (pp. 141–142). Penguin Books.
3. Sen, A. (1999). *Development as Freedom* (p. 18). Anchor Books.
4. Lichter, D. T., & Crowley, M. L. (2002). Poverty in America: Beyond Welfare Reform. *Population Bulletin, 57*, 1–36.
5. Rank, M. R. (1994). *Living on the Edge: The Realities of Welfare in America* (pp. 174–175). Columbia University Press.
6. Rank, M. B. (2004). *One Nation Underprivileged: Why American Poverty Affects Us All* (pp. 49–51, 69–73). Oxford University Press.
7. Wang, S., et al. (2014). 2007. Zhongguo xinshiqi nongcun fupin yu cunji pinkun miaozhun [Poverty Alleviation and Poverty Targeting in Rural China in the New Era]. *Journal of Management World, 01*, 56–64.
8. Banerjee, A. V., & Duflo, E. (2007). The Economic Lives of the Poor. *Journal of Economic Perspectives, 21*(1), 141–168.
9. Shah, A. K., et al. (2012). Some Consequences of Having Too Little. *Science, 338*, 682–685.
10. Belsky, J., Steinberg, L., & Draper, P. (1991). Childhood Experience, Interpersonal Development, and Reproductive Strategy: An Evolutionary Theory of Socialisation. *Child Development, 62*, 647–670.
11. Payne, K. (2018). *The Broken Ladder: How Inequality Affects the Way We Think, Live, and Die* (pp. 48–50). Penguin Books.
12. Pearce, D. M. (1978). The Feminisation of Poverty: Women, Work, and Welfare. *Urban and Social Change Review*, 11, 1–2, 28–36, 78.
13. Li, X., et al. (2019). 'Funv pinkun" lujing de jianpin yichu yu fuquan yihua: Yige shaoshu minzu funv fupin shijian de fazhanxue guancha [Alienation of Empowerment and Spill over of Poverty Reduction Based on Women's Poverty Approach: The Observation on a Women's Poverty Reduction Project in a Minority Village in Southwestern China]. *The Journal of Chinese Women's Studies, 02*, 5–16.
14. Green, M. (2009). The Social Distribution of Sanctioned Harm: Thinking through Chronic Poverty, Durable Poverty, and Destitution. In T. Addison, D. Hulme, & R. Kanbur (Eds.), *Poverty Dynamics: Interdisciplinary Perspectives* (pp. 309–327). Oxford University Press.

15. Wang, G., & Li, X. (Eds.). (2003). *Canyushi fupin peixun jiaocheng[Participatory Poverty Alleviation Training Manual]* (pp. 19–21). China Financial & Economic Publishing House.
16. Zou, T., Li, X., & Qi, G. (Eds.). (2003). *Jishu fazhan yu nongmin canyu [Technological Development and Farmer Participation]* (pp. 14–23). China Agricultural Press.
17. Li, X. (Ed.). (2002). *Canyushi fazhan gailun[Introduction to Participatory Development]* (pp. 26–28). China Agricultural University Press.
18. Li, X. (Ed.). (1999). *Shui shi nongcun fazhan de zhuti[Who are the Main Actors in Rural Development?]* (pp. 59–61). China Agricultural Press.

CHAPTER 3

What Needs to Be Done?

The work of fighting poverty never truly ends. Perhaps we will one day reach utopia, but until then, there will always be work to carry out. This is because—to continue from the conclusions of the previous chapter—ending poverty must address both the absolute and the relative dimensions of poverty. Even absolute poverty, we should remind ourselves, is in a way 'relative', exemplified by the fact that the absolute poverty line can shift over time to reflect changes to living standards and purchasing power. Across different social stages, people at the bottom of society live in absolute poverty. People in relative poverty include the population categorised as living in absolute poverty, but mainly refers to those living some distance below the average income of the entire society. In any population, the indicators of poverty are relative. For instance, wealthier people in a developing country may be impoverished compared to 'poor' people in a developed country because average living standards vary across nations—but these groups may have very different perceptions of their own relative wealth or poverty. On the other hand, absolute poverty measured by basic human needs such as food, clothing, and housing is comparable across different countries, despite differences in their respective standards. The World Bank's international absolute poverty line is a common measurement tool based on purchasing power parity (PPP).

Where does this leave us? In China, I have long found that the absolute and relative dimensions of poverty make poverty alleviation work extremely

X. Li, *The End of Poverty and the Taming of Inequality*,
https://doi.org/10.1007/978-981-96-0684-9_3

complex, and very difficult. First, poor populations must be identified, determining who will be targeted by assistance efforts. On the face of things, it is easy for projects to target poor demographics through indicators of absolute poverty, especially if these indicators are simple and easy to assess. As a shortcut, objective characteristics such as disabilities, a lack of access to housing or previous recognition by government programmes, can help. Receipt of the state's 'five guarantees'—food, clothing, medical care, housing, and funeral expenses—is for example a convenient and often uncontroversial way of identifying the poor and cutting out those who do not need assistance. And yet, as explored in the previous chapter, even an 'objective' set of criteria can stir anger and leave professionals doubtful. Resources are limited and a line must be drawn somewhere, but the difference between those on one side of the line and those scarcely on the other side can be very small. Definitions of poverty are often unavoidably arbitrary, and there will always be undercoverage or leakage problems. The more indicators used, the harder it can be to identify the poor, even those in absolute poverty; they can squeeze in or elbow out certain people from the category of poverty.

Second, poverty reduction is a constant effort to eliminate absolute poverty and alleviate relative poverty. The recent battle against poverty is to eliminate absolute poverty by setting up the goal of 'two worry-frees and three guarantees'—freedom from worries over food and clothing and guarantees for access to compulsory education, basic medical services and safe housing. Eliminating or alleviating poverty is not as simple as changing indicator values. It involves complicated political, social and economic processes, and it is challenging to change political and social structures, which are often deeply entrenched. Poverty is not so much about individuals but about structural and institutional issues related to economic and social transformation and an institutionally uneven distribution of opportunity.

Third, poverty reduction plays out differently in different contexts, both within a single country such as China, and in contrasting political systems such as Europe or the US. This means that we must be adaptive: our anti-poverty strategies, policies and measures must respond to the realities of poor populations. Going into this work with the assumption that we know better than the poor, and that their ongoing poverty is the result of defective thinking or an inability to seize the opportunities in front of them, is quite misguided.

Why Does the Fight against Poverty Differ in the United States and Europe?[1]

In China we tend to regard Europe and the United States as a monolith, and they do share similarities. However, when it comes to real issues, we find wide gaps between them, and sometimes even disputes.

Our approaches to poverty in China do not fully align with those in Western nations. Not long ago, I was invited to a China-United States dialogue on poverty at the China Institute in America.[2] The introduction, given by Professor Irwin Garfinkel of the University of Columbia, revealed that US policies are entirely different from our expectations. The conversation really centred on American views and policies regarding impoverished populations. It left me reflecting on the differences between China and America, but also upon the differences between the United States and Europe.

The US and continental European countries are western, democratic, developed, and prosperous states with similar cultural and religious foundations. Chinese people tend to refer to both continents as 'the West', assuming that their politics, society, and culture are similar and that policies on poverty are consistent. However, as we explored in a previous chapter, we find vast differences when we closely compare their political and social perceptions of the poor.

European and American attitudes and policies on the poor mirror their differences in public redistribution policies. Furthermore, progressive tax rates in continental European countries are much higher than in the US, and Europe regulates the labour market through laws and trade unions that protect low-income populations more closely than the US. People at the bottom of the income ladder in Europe generally have greater support than in the US. In general, US redistribution policies lag far behind Europe. The share of government expenditure in GDP is around

[1] Published at The Economic Observer (2018-12-24) at http://www.eeo.com.cn/2018/1224/344061.shtml.

[2] Founded in New York City in 1926 by American educators John Dewey, Paul Monroe, and Chinese scholars Hu Shi and Kuo Ping-Wen, China Institute in America is an internationally-renowned U.S. nonprofit organisation dedicated to deepening the world's understanding of China through programmes in art, business, cuisine, culture, and education. Note by the translator.

30% in the US, 45% in continental Europe and over 50% in the Nordic countries. Discrepancies between welfare expenditures account for two-thirds of the difference. Why is there a large difference between Europe and the US, which share cultural traditions and religious foundations?

A large part of the reason comes from differing attitudes to inequality and distribution, and the effects that this has upon policy related to poverty and indeed the prevalence of poverty itself. The United States is in several ways 'exceptional', as Seymour Lipset [1] remarked in the 1990s: it embraced a market economy some time before Europe, and it has never had strong political parties founded on labour movements. Individual striving, and by extension an acceptance of the inequality that varying levels of individual success will create, has long been important. This inequality will inevitably impact a country's political situation, even if it is accepted. One would expect the majority of the poor to vote in favour of taxing those richer than them and redistributing money across society.

According to the 'median voter' theory, a loose tipping point is reached when the median voter has less income than the mean voter. At this point, the median voter—and thus a majority—will have a personal interest in supporting greater distribution. Studies of European voting patterns appear to match the theory's prediction, and patterns elsewhere also support it (with caveats)—but in the United States other forces seem stronger. The pre-tax income gap in the United States is far wider than in Europe, but its tax rates are much lower. There is a common belief—in the United States and outside it—that American social mobility is high while Europe's is low: in the United States a rich person might become poor tomorrow and vice versa, whereas Europe is set in strata. This narrative places the onus for escaping poverty on the American individual, and suggests that government support is less necessary. According to the World Values Survey, 71% of Americans believed one can overcome poverty through hard work. Only 40% of Europeans agreed, by contrast. The American dream lives on in the American imaginary.

But is it borne out in reality? In 2013 the Harvard economists Alberto Alesina and Edward Glaeser published a brilliant comparative study, *Fighting Poverty in the United States and Europe*. It set out to examine the differences in distributive policy, exploring why Americans were less willing to reallocate money from rich to poor. Its findings explode the American mythos: the poor in America and Europe invest a similar amount of time and effort in work and thus should according to the 'American dream' have the same chance of upward mobility—but poor Americans were in fact less upwardly mobile [2]. Why is this? Clearly America's raw belief in accessible social mobility is not borne out. Perhaps, though, it could affect major policy areas such that mobility is harder to achieve? A number of economists have proposed that, in particular, tax policy may play a key role. Some people hold that taxation efficiency in Europe is higher than in the US. I find this hard to believe: tax avoidance in Italy and Greece is far higher than it is in the US. But the amount taxed is very different, and European states all place a far greater emphasis upon national social protection provision than the United States does. This fits with our recognition of the role of the emphasis upon individual striving to escape poverty. If one believes that this is possible, less can be expected of the state, so less taxation is justifiable; and if one believes that gains are made by individuals through their own merit, it is less fair to redistribute their earnings. A belief in the power of the individual to escape poverty and obtain riches may thus counter-intuitively make actually escaping poverty far harder, if it is internalised in redistribution policy.

Constraints in the wider political systems also make a difference to the poverty approaches in Europe and the US. Both have democratic systems, but they differ considerably in their institutional arrangements. Most European countries practise proportional representation in their election systems (but not all; the UK, for example, does not). This works to the advantage of left-wing parties supporting more welfare distribution and establishment of welfare states. Conversely, because the US two-party system only requires a simple majority to win elections, new and marginal parties are prevented from succeeding in mainstream political life. More radical voices proposing greater redistribution may have significant fringe support, but unlike in Europe they are unable to gain any traction in the mainstream. Both main parties are wary of being branded 'socialist'. The separation of powers under the US Constitution is mainly intended to prevent the government from making radical changes in overall policy direction, and the expansion of welfare is one of the sensitive issues on which the executive struggles to make headway. The Constitution was drafted in the 18th Century, when centralised welfare states were both ideologically unfeasible and logistically impossible; it does not make any provision for the expansion of welfare, and the US Supreme Court has repeatedly rejected proposals (as has the Senate, for political reasons). The Obama Administration's setbacks when trying to initiate health care reform stand as a case in point. In a sense, the difference between European proportional representation and US simple majority is an underlying cause for their discrepancy in welfare distribution.

Differences in European and American electoral systems were gradually shaped over different historical courses. Before the First World War some European countries (Belgium, Finland, Sweden, the Netherlands, and Switzerland) were swept by workers' movements; with low enforcement capacities, these movements could not be suppressed. After the War these workers' movements flourished, and socialists and communists actively promoted constitutional reforms in the interests of the working-class. The development of proportional representation in elections was a particularly significant shift. In the US, by contrast, socialists and communists failed to drive constitutional reform. The simple majority required to win an election, together with multi-layered institutional arrangements, made it impossible for any marginal party to fundamentally change the constitution. The US Constitution was primarily drafted by rich white Americans in 1787 and intended to protect the private property rights of a few [3]. It has subsequently been amended several times, but it remains of its era, and cannot easily be updated to safeguard social fairness as we understand it today. The core reason the US Constitution has not significantly changed is the absence of socialist and communist movements in the country.

Many factors affected socialist and communist movements in the US. First, because of the US' broad geographical scope and the capital city's distance from industrial cities, workers' movements were unlikely to sweep the entire country as in Europe or pose a direct threat to state power in the capital. Large-scale workers' movements such as the Chicago workers' strike could therefore develop and gain local victories, but struggled to spread to other areas. Second, unlike Europe, American people were highly mobile, and workers subject to exploitation might easily move to other places. As Lipset remarks, one of the reasons America is 'exceptional' is that it was for many decades a frontier society. People whose lives were unsatisfying in one place could easily try their fortunes in wide open expanses [4]. Many people did get prosperous in this way, a reason for the American belief in individual effort. Third, in the US, an immigrant country, race preceded class and discrimination obstructed cross-race solidarity in the working-class. Karl Marx and Friedrich Engels noticed this phenomenon in their early study of workers' movements. Fourth, the powerful military force in the United States contributed significantly to its political stability and successfully repressed multiple workers' strikes. For instance, the Pullman Strike that broke out in Chicago in 1894 was suppressed by the US federal army. Fifth, unlike Europe, the United States never experienced major post-war turmoil, where people lived on the edge of starvation. Although The Depression led to a kind of moderate 'Europeanisation' of American politics, and class factors became more important in differentiating party support, the pattern, gradually inverted after the second world war as a result of long-term prosperity [5]. Its post-war prosperity provided little soil for socialism or communism to grow.

In addition to the aforementioned electoral and political systems, differences between Europe and the United States in religion also partly explained their discrepancies in poverty perceptions. Their religions shared the same origin but were not identical. Calvinist and Protestant ethics in American culture drove many American people to regard economic success as the result of individual effort. Many immigrants from continental Europe to the United States believed that personal hard work could change their fates and did not count on social protection for risk prevention. Research shows that defence against risks and demand for social security are highly correlated; low risks lead to insufficient demand for social security and redistribution. Historically speaking, the Catholic tradition in continental Europe adhered to the belief in generosity for the poor. The religious tradition, together with socialist ideas, fostered social redistribution policies in Europe.

In China we tend to regard Europe and the United States as a monolith, and they do share similarities. However, when it comes to real issues, we find wide gaps between them, and sometimes even disputes, such as differing opinions on the War in Iraq. At the current critical juncture of globalisation, the two diverged again. Europe experienced the impact of globalisation and related problems of domestic and international inequality. Still, it has not turned against globalisation like the United States has (even though it was more closely impacted by the refugee crisis). Their differences cannot be sufficiently explained from a merely geopolitical perspective. Historical, political, social and cultural differences are important factors that shaped their respective policies and approaches, not only in tackling poverty, but also in handling international matters.

Who Should Be Helped?

At a first glance, poverty alleviation seems to be about helping the poor, but if given a deeper thought, it's those who are more wealthy and powerful that needs 'help' to change their thinking.

Poverty alleviation,[3] as it literally implies in the Chinese language, means helping the poor. After nearly two decades of engagement in this work, I have, however, increased doubts about some of its basic, widely-accepted values. I do not question the objectives of eliminating poverty or the basic motivation to support the poor. Still, I am uncertain about many concepts and approaches adopted in the anti-poverty campaigns.

I used to visit a Yi village in Chuxiong, Yunnan which had graduated from poverty. As I saw its beautiful residential houses with Yi characteristics and rolling hills planted with mango trees, I imagined its impoverished past. When chatting with a village official, I asked why the changes here were so dramatic. Three times, he excitedly attributed all this change to the government. Many might find his words propagandist, but he was telling what he thought of.

He didn't take the credit for his improved life by saying it resulted from his hard work. Of course, his advantages would not come without his own hard work. Nevertheless, in the villagers' plain perceptions, such a life was not something they could realise on their own. While an enhanced lifestyle and environmental improvements should not be construed as the government's gift—since serving the people is the basic value of government—the villagers' words simply imply another question: who should be supported in poverty alleviation.

The purpose of poverty alleviation is to help the poor shake off poverty. However, when it comes to specific work, we find the target of poverty alleviation is not necessarily the poor but the structural nature of poverty. We cannot rule out poverty caused by individual failure, but social, economic and political structures impact even these situations in the final analysis. In general, I endorse a structural understanding of poverty. When I discussed with government officials anti-poverty policies, we did not deliberate on how to change the awareness of each

[3] '扶贫', fu pin, in the Chinese language, fu means to support or to help, pin means the poor. Note by the translator.

impoverished individual but how to change policies and systems. In the Hebian village's case, we explained to the local government that government funds for rural areas were administered in a decentralised way, controlled by different departments and failed to be integrated for anti-poverty purposes, the local government responded positively by making fund integration policies accordingly. Such government policies enabled Hebian villagers to have a comprehensive poverty reduction plan which included housing renovation, road hardening and village greening. The villages could thus construct quality wooden buildings with guest rooms that generated additional income, instead of building a new metal roof housing that could not serve as a source of additional income.[4] Therefore, even though many believed I played a critical role in advancing Hebian Village's poverty reduction, the villagers and I would not hesitate in saying that the changes should be attributed to the government. It may be me who pushed for the change, but it is the government who made the change happen.

The great achievements in China's poverty alleviation were often made in periods when policies were extensively formulated. For instance, institutional reforms including introduction of the rural household responsibility system had drastically incentivised rural households to increase agricultural productivity thus increasing their incomes in the beginning of China's reform era, the early 1980s, while rolling out of educational and other subsidies in 2000s had greatly eased the burdens of the poor. Researchers and decision-makers may not have realised it, but discussions on each policy change was in the first place helping oneself. Correcting old policies and piloting on the new ones is actually a process of self-criticism and self-improvement. We used to say agricultural development relied on policies, input and technologies, but not mentioning

[4] Poverty reduction funds in China is mostly sector-based, i.e. the department of housing administers house-related poverty reduction projects and funds, the department of transport administers road-building poverty reduction projects, the department of health administers health-related poverty reduction programmes, each has respective project application, using and management policies that do not necessarily align to others. The poverty office, at different government levels, administers itself a specific poverty reduction budget which is mostly oriented to village industrial development. Though this budget increased rapidly in the recent battle against absolute poverty, it was still small compared to other rural poverty reduction related funds from line departments. Although the poverty office is tasked with coordinating poverty reduction policies across different departments, it encounters enormous difficulties when doing so on the ground. Note by the translator.

the farmers. Without a doubt, farmers were the main players in agricultural development, but the main constraints were in policies, input and technologies. The same applies to poverty reduction.

The causes of poverty are varied. In many circumstances, institutions were an important cause, such as China's urban–rural dual system. Under this system, migrant workers could not settle down in cities due to lack of an official urban registration record, and their children were either left in villages or went to migrant schools in cities which usually suffered from lower quality education compared to their urban counterparts. The urban–rural gap in public services disadvantaged the rural population in education, medical services and other areas, which were all institutional reasons for poverty. Poverty alleviation is to gradually eliminate such institutional factors.

When I started to work on poverty alleviation in the mid-1990s, I intended to 'transform' the poor. Even when I arrived at Hebian Village, I still believed poverty alleviation was about changing the poor's thinking and improving their capabilities. As mentioned in this book, the meta-questions of poverty involve conventionality and modernity. These issues seem overambitious in a landscape analysis of poverty because it is neither specific nor practical and induces the impression that the poor are poor because they are backward. As I reflect on poverty alleviation, I don't mean to co-opt the poor's standpoints because I may easily get caught in the populist maelstrom of self-criticism. Instead, I hope to discuss why the poor have been left far behind the locomotive of development.

Institutions and policies are personified because policies are made by people, and institutions are maintained by people. People's concepts, values and standpoints influence policy-making. If institutions and policies are important factors behind poverty, isn't poverty alleviation about changing the perspectives of the policymakers, those wealthier and more powerful? When we interact with the poor, our poverty-alleviation policies can be improved by learning to change our thoughts.

As I mentioned earlier, the measure of social civilisation is not the size of the rich population but the size of the poor population. Of course, poverty is a relative concept and wealth inequality will always exist. If all impoverished villages could develop as Hebian Village did, villagers, though still comparatively poor, would not be the same poor people they used to be. This is the goal of the battle against poverty. The goal of eliminating extreme poverty in society is attainable. Many people have been to western or northern Europe, where many were poor, but extreme poverty was absent.

I always wonder, if kindergartens in poor villages were as good as those in cities, children in poverty would have the advantages of urban children. If the quality of teachers in primary and middle schools in impoverished areas were the same as in Shanghai and Beijing, the probability of inequality and poverty for Chinese youth would be significantly lower. While it is difficult to realise parity in public social services, we can narrow the gap. Many measures were initiated to attain this goal but were simply too difficult to execute. Consequently, poverty alleviation seemed to be about helping the poor. Many slogans can be seen in poor villages, calling upon the poor to not wait for assistance but be self-reliant, as if poverty was solely the result of ways of thinking and laziness. In fact, the underlying problems of poverty do not have to do with the poor themselves.

The statement that the origin of poverty does not lie with the poor can be controversial. Many cases show that, under almost identical conditions, some people become prosperous, but others remain poor. In Hebian Village, brothers from the same family had different fortunes: some were better off, while others became poorer. However, in a systematic review of poverty, it's unreasonable to use individual success or failure as proof for concluding whether poverty should be attributed to individual or structural reasons.

Will Poverty Reduction Lead to Prosperity?[5]

> Successful poverty reduction must be sustainable. Interventions from outside can't deliver the change needed except on a temporary basis: to be successful, interventions must be locally owned and durable.

For over three years,[6] I have been engaged in poverty reduction in Hebian Village, Yunnan. One of our major initiatives is Yao Guestroom, helping farmers to build guestrooms for accommodating tourists to boost

[5] Published at WeChat official account 'xiaoyunzhupin' (2018-05-18) at https://mp.weixin.qq.com/s/O1jtMKL9kFl0ET5PeVqxaQ.

[6] This article was written in 2018, three years after the author Li Xiaoyun started his poverty experiment in Hebian Village which went on after 2018. Note by the translator.

their income, but I have recently pondered what else we can do to help the village. I chatted with a local farmer and said, 'You made some money from the guestroom in your home, didn't you?' I knew that he earned around RMB8,000 from our Yao Guestroom initiative in 2017. He replied: 'No, actually, it's nothing'. I was surprised by his answer. Farmers could make RMB100–150 a day as agricultural workers in nearby villages, and it would take over 60 days in the work to earn an equivalent income of RMB8,000 (very few villagers could engage in this work for such a length of time in one year). They also earned income by planting sugarcane and selling fructus amomi. We had developed the Yao Guestroom initiative as a low-effort means for villagers, especially women, to make an equivalent income by renting and cleaning the rooms. I explained this fact to the farmer: the money he had made from his guestroom represented quite a success. Rather than acknowledging this, he said: 'Professor Li, we are waiting for you to lead us to prosperity'.

Can I lead Hebian Village to prosperity? The villager's question got me thinking. We have quite a few billionaires in the country, but can they lead people across the country to prosperity? Probably not. Is the farmer's statement therefore unreasonable or even ridiculous? Surely not—it's only natural for farmers to hope for prosperity. I of course have the same hopes for myself. For instance, I regret not purchasing more apartments when housing prices were low. After this conversation, I started to reflect on poverty alleviation and prosperity. Government officials and people like me told farmers they would get rich as long as they worked hard to fight poverty. What an ambitious and irresponsible promise! We carelessly raised people's expectations, although we were probably incapable of realising their hopes. Poverty alleviation had been confused with prosperity. I was left wondering whether this was the fault of the language we had used in our conversations and communications, or whether we ourselves had conflated the two concepts in our minds.

Let us be clear: poverty alleviation and prosperity are related—but they are not synonymous. Poverty alleviation seeks to give people access to basic welfare, and to help them to escape serious deprivations. In other words, it seeks to put people on the path to prosperity. But prosperity itself is—unless one comes from a fairly ascetic strand of philosophy—more than the mere absence of poverty. Our experiment in Hebian Village has thus far helped some, but not all, villagers to escape from poverty. But for most of those villagers, it has not yet brought them to prosperity.

Just as definitions of poverty shift as overall living standards change, so too one's understanding of what it means to be prosperous rises ever upwards as one becomes wealthier. When I started poverty alleviation experiment in Hebian Village, I discussed the construction of new houses with the local villagers. I presented my architectural designs with colourful, beautiful pictures that contrasted the dark and shabby office where we sat. They couldn't believe they would live in such nice houses one day. Today, they live in houses even nicer than the design sketch, and their former homes seem uninhabitable now. Their standard of living has risen dramatically—but as in the case of the villager that told me he was still waiting for prosperity, they are not yet fully satisfied. That is quite natural. As we will discuss, they have escaped absolute poverty, but are still in relative poverty when one compares their lives to those of the wealthier households of Beijing or even the smaller cities.

With the government's anti-poverty resource portfolios supporting our poverty alleviation experiment, Hebian Village has been transformed from a poverty-stricken village in three years, and I am proud of our success. I designed a series of comprehensive poverty reduction experiments, centring around developing a tourism-oriented new industry that was based on creation of the Yao Guestroom, village conference room, restaurants, bars and convenience stores. This new industry would gave farmers access to additional income sources besides sugarcane and fructus amomi. The Yao Guestrooms have developed into a village industry. In 2017, many households made over RMB30,000 from guestrooms and catering, and those without a catering service still earned more than RMB10,000. From the perspective of welfare, poverty has been eliminated in Hebian Village, but many villagers still persisted: 'Professor Li, please help us make money!'.

After 2018, many Hebian villagers sought driver's licences, which cost around RMB10,000. I was concerned that they were incurring high costs before investing in income sources. A young villager told me: 'Professor Li, watching you drive a car gave me the itch to drive too'. This desire was only natural. The changes of Hebian that only took three years to happen was a good showcase of China's targeted poverty alleviation actions. However, this conversation did not merely demonstrate local farmers' desire to get rich but also underlying problems with our poverty experiment in Hebian.

I seldom convened plenary meetings in the village, only twice in three years' time, but I held one recently to explain that the real difficulties in Hebian's development had just begun. Over the past year, my colleagues, students and I were preoccupied with promoting the Yao Guestroom industry, enhancing publicity, contacting client resources, signing contracts and issuing invoices. My colleagues and students almost all became receptionists on site. The villagers, however, had barely participated in this process—not because we didn't want them to, but because they were unfamiliar and untrained for the jobs we needed to do. In fact they were to a large extent cut out from all planning and operations. The only thing they knew was how many visitors would stay in the guestroom per day. In the meeting I explained that I was worried that when my colleagues, students and I left, the farmers would be unable to keep up the initiative and earn the guestroom income. At this, many farmers called out: 'Professor Li, you can't leave!'.

The Hebian experiment was confronting a real challenge, and one that such initiatives must always face. Would the project become sustainable by itself, or would it only work while my colleagues, students, and I stayed in the village to manage it? I suddenly felt guilty for raising their expectations, developing an industry incompatible with their skills and culture, and then asking them to run everything after we leave. Poverty alleviation projects that only work with ongoing outside support are of very dubious use. Of course, we had already started to cultivate the farmers' independent management capacities by setting up a village cooperative and appointing villager assistants. Nevertheless, I was aware there was a long way to go before they could master the skills to run the Guestroom Project.

The predicament of the Hebian experiment testified to the universal difficulty of bringing those stuck in the poverty trap onto the track of development. If some enterprises specialise in serving villages as we do now, there is still hope for sustainable poverty reduction in Hebian. The question is, where are these enterprises or civil organisations? With philanthropic resources declining in recent years, I even registered a small civil organisation, 'Action Against Poverty', in Mengla County. However, grassroots philanthropic efforts have limited social influence and, more importantly, are often short-staffed, lacking high-quality human resources. None of my students showed interest in engaging in similar work after graduation.

Assisting people isolated from the modern market economy to realise prosperity is feasible in theory but demanding in practise. If a group of skilled people in the village can set up a culture and tourism company on their own, Hebian will genuinely thrive. However, in a poor community based on kinship and egalitarian values, it is challenging to ask a few farmers to advance their personal interests without attending to the others'. It's also hard to establish contract-based social relations in this traditional community. Any slight inequality in client distribution will instantly break contractual relations. My colleagues and I once discussed hiring a management team for the cooperative, supported by resources from the philanthropic community in the beginning phase, and then gradually paid by the village cooperative as the village's tourism and leisure business developed. When I shared the plan with local farmers, they seemed to agree. But we didn't really start this initiative due to insufficient start up resources.

In our anti-poverty practise in Hebian Village, my colleagues, students and I realised the difficulty of ensuring that a poverty reduction effort is truly sustainable. This reminded me of problems with support for aboriginals in Canada, the US, Australia and New Zealand. Though the comparison may not be strong, the reality before us is that when we measure poverty with modern welfare standards and assume that the poor can follow 'our' path to prosperity, we have already put ourselves in a predicament. I'm not biased with any cultural discrimination or developmental conditions. Still, we must realise that the path to overcoming poverty and reaching prosperity is often based on modern ethics that are always conflicting those of the poor's. My hands are tied before the predicament.

My experiments in Hebian Village have generated positive results, and some called it a big success. However, many colleagues and friends feel ambivalent about the project. On the one hand, we may praise each other for the sake of social etiquette and personal ties, and, on the other hand, we genuinely feel that our three years' hard work has been worth it. But I know that my colleagues and I haven't yet found the clue to a sustainable path to poverty elimination in Hebian Village.

Poverty and Social Exclusion

Poverty and exclusion reinforces each other: exclusion begets poverty, and poverty makes the poor further excluded. It is for this reason that poverty interventions, mounted by outside actors, are important: they can break the cycle.

The connections between poverty and the structural failure of society; cultural relationships; and personal failure can all be drawn and can all be useful, but they neither fully account for poverty's persistence or illustrate its social consequences. In particular, they overlook the exclusion of the poor, which is both a consequence of poverty and a reason for its continuation.

Consider how the poor are represented in popular culture, a subject that we have already discussed with regard to Benjamin Franklin and others. We only feel sympathy and pity for impoverished people that we believe abide by the law and have no 'pernicious habits'. But generally, there is a scepticism of the poor: just by virtue of their economic standing, they are considered less able, the cause of their own misfortune, and even their honesty can be interpreted as ignorance. This is surely unfair. Many social 'virtues' are defined by the behaviours and norms of the rich: education; refinement and love of culture; and so on. The poor will often be excluded from access to such traits and behaviours, which is both a cause and result of their poverty.

In many circumstances, once relatively poor people come to have some money, they are inclined to spend at least some of it the way the rich do, to show off or to enjoy themselves—even if this is something that is not really in their interests. This is a longstanding observation, in economics referred to as 'conspicuous consumption' [6], a phrase first coined by Thorstein Veblen in 1899. We can learn more of why this happens in revisiting the more recent work of Keith Payne, which found that social comparison impacted people's choice and beliefs [7]. Since basic social value systems are subject to the influence of the rich's cultural values and their control over social rights, the poor, though large in number, often feel inferior and helpless. The rich frequently assert, often implicitly, that the poor deserve their conditions and ascribe poverty to personal failure. Some of the poor are even reduced to socially condemned behaviours such as theft and drug trafficking, which establishes a connection between poverty and crime, leading to social exclusion. For instance, the apartheid in South Africa and the systemic discrimination against black and other ethnic minorities in the United States claimed in part to derive their legitimacy from the association between race, poverty and crime. Methods of systemic discrimination were supposedly adopted to uphold social order. Once living in close proximity to the poor, the rich feel insecure. In many countries, the rich build high walls around their residential areas in the name of protecting their safety, only to build one hedge after another of social differentiation.

Social exclusion derives from and intensifies inequality, shaping a vicious cycle. The poor's conditions are not improved, and the rich's safety cannot be guaranteed, which is the social cost of poverty and inequality and our primary motivation to fight poverty. In this sense, poverty alleviation seeks to fulfil two dimensions, advancing idealism and utilitarianism, seeking both social justice and individual interests. Thus, we cannot take social exclusion for granted.

In Hebian Village there is a woman whom I often heard shouting and cursing in the morning. She also prevented any construction around her yard. Local villagers believed that she was insane, and even tried to hospitalise her. Her shouting was always in Yao, which I did not understand, and other villagers told me she was calling others malicious names. We tried to understand what drove her to furiously confront the entire village. Once, she said to me she could barely support her children at school and her husband, a man of few words, physically too weak to do farm work. She wept and told us that other villagers had taken advantage of them and took their land many years ago, but that she was determined to take the land back. Other villagers dismissed her accusations about the land issue quite lightly.

My students and I talked with her several times, and we never received the impression that she was not in full possession of her senses. When we visited her shabby place, she was polite and would offer small stools for us to sit on. Local villagers considered her very competent, finishing all the farm work on her own. However, while others had put up new houses and produced income from their guestrooms, all she had was an empty frame overgrown with weeds. The increasing gap between her living standards and other villagers' living standards intensified her rebellious state of mind. Others blamed her for her aggressiveness and viewed her as the 'public enemy' of the entire village.

I believe this was an extreme example of a vicious cycle of poverty caused by exclusion. The woman was originally from another village and her husband was an honest man, but far from being competent on either economical or social terms. It was first by accident that one villager burned some of the family's land but didn't provide 'sufficient' compensation, and afterwards some others had land disputes with her which was deemed as taking her land according to her. The woman was angry about the 'loss' of the land but could do nothing about it except shouting at other villagers. She therefore found herself increasingly excluded, which exacerbated mental ill health or some form of severe distress resulting from her situation. This mental and relational difficulty led to further isolation, which increased the difficulty of escaping poverty. Individual and societal factors combined to harm this unfortunate family. In fact, she was not wholly excluded. Town leadership tried to offer care and support to help her overcome poverty. The village held multiple meetings and decided to help her put up a new house by contributing voluntary labour and money on two conditions: that she would stop scolding others, and that she would support the planned construction around her house. She did not reject this offer, but she added her own condition: that the occupied land be given back to her. Though many argued that the plot of land was not necessarily hers and was used by others, she nonetheless persisted, arguing that since she had cultivated the plot, the land was hers. From my own perspective her claim seemed reasonable; village land used to be mountain land and belonged to whoever used it, and since her family had cultivated the plot, she could be fairly described as the owner and whoever occupied it should give it back. It appeared however that more influential, powerful people in the village had seized her land. She exercised her only capability to revolt against the infringement of her rights. However, she didn't win other villagers' support and was gradually alienated from the whole village.

In poor villages like Hebian, livelihoods depend on social networks. According to the villagers, a well-maintained connection with relatives and neighbours would win support and help. The 'insane woman' had many relatives in the village, but her household was socially isolated; she never engaged with other households, and her children seldom played with children of other families. Holding her daughter's hand, she would walk through the village scolding others, passing her anger on to her children and causing a negative psychological impact. In a previous chapter,

I have told of her eldest son, who asked me to lend him money because he had a child at a young age, becoming another burden on the family.

If we don't analyse the case from the perspectives of inequality and exclusion, we will naturally view the household's poverty as individual and household failure. However, exclusion is not always reflected in grand political narratives, such as discrimination against black communities. It also exists in small social scopes and groups, caused by non-equivalence in rights or possession of opportunity or wealth. In this case, we noticed a connection between the protection of basic rights and poverty. I was not sure whether the daily yelling of the 'insane woman' was always about the plot of land, but it was certainly a topic about which she was vocal. Over the years, the village and external authorities had offered her help, but she regarded the help as 'charity', an additional string to pull her to compromise. She was not yelling and scolding anyone in particular, but she wanted to express her frustrations, or even to uphold her rights. The villagers believed she was blackmailing the government and the village to pursue greater interests. They considered that help only spoiled her and tried to tame her since she was getting more disruptive.

Let us temporarily put aside the origin of her poverty and consider the troubles she caused to the village. She was not an adverse case of extreme poverty connected to crime, but the social consequences of her poverty severely undermined the village's harmonious social environment. Her ear-splitting scolding disturbed guests staying in the village every morning.

What can we learn from this example? What does it tell us about the relationship between poverty and social exclusion? Firstly, the two interact in both directions. The woman lost her land and became embittered; she was therefore isolated from her neighbours, which made it harder still for her and her household to recover. Secondly, both poverty and social exclusion are embedded in—are the product of—social and political processes. The woman's land was taken by people who are influential in local political life; she did not have the influence to recover her loss. If we imagine the web of village relationships as a network, we can only picture the influential landgrabbers as a larger and better-connected node than the poor woman and her household: those who are already isolated are at greater risk of being exploited. Thirdly, exclusion can happen without a genuine motivation. It is easy to assume that those excluded are marginalised because 'society', or key actors in society, have chosen to keep them down: this is not always the case. In this example from Hebian, more influential actors made an opportunistic choice to seize someone else's land, and as a result that person was excluded. But in fact she was not wholly excluded even after this: the villagers made efforts to try to build bridges for her, although without going so far as to challenge the status quo on her behalf. Fourthly, and perhaps most importantly, patterns of exclusion, dispossession and exploitation can become entrenched quite quickly, leaving some groups unable to recover. In this case, a single household has been 'down and out' for some time. Where local law enforcement is lacking knowledge or capacities, or where it has been corrupted by social relationships, those who are excluded can find it very challenging to regain opportunities. Exclusion can persist, sometimes almost invisibly, for generations.

Assisting the marginalised is often controversial and challenging. In Hebian, other villagers accused the woman and her household of trying to obtain more than they should. But this is why the work of poverty alleviation is so important. Without outside intervention, the situation in that village and for that woman would be very unlikely to change. But with help targeted towards the poorest and most vulnerable, there is the possibility that she—or perhaps her grandchildren—can have a better life. I don't know whether the Yao Guestroom project will deliver that for this family; but if we don't, I hope another programme might.

Turning Poverty Reduction Resources into Foundations for Development[7]

> Poverty reduction resources from government are not one-time subsidies, if well used, they can form solid basis for long-term development.

In 2019, China's Number One Document[8] proposed to focus on targeted poverty alleviation by adhering to prevailing standards without

[7] Published at The Beijing News (2019-02-20) at http://www.bjnews.com.cn/feature/2019/02/20/548777.html, and included into this book with revision.

[8] Number One Document,'yihaowenjian', the first policy document issued every year by the central government of China, usually at the beginning of a year. The first No.1 document was released in 1949 when the People's Republic of China was founded. Between 1982 to 1986, China's No. 1 Documents all focused on its agriculture, rural community and farmer issues, the so-called three-rural or 'san nong' issues. Since 2004 (up to 2024), China has issued consecutively twenty-one No.1 documents which all focused

elevating them blindly. In my understanding, it advocates distinguishing between fighting poverty and achieving prosperity. Achieving prosperity requires long-term individual effort and policy support, whereas poverty overcoming poverty is about solving subsistence problems as per prevailing standards. The current prevailing standard for eliminating poverty is to achieve an annual income of RMB2,300 per capita and eliminate worries over basic food and clothing, guarantee access to compulsory education, basic medical services and safe housing, in short, two worry-frees and three guarantees. Overcoming poverty is the foundation of achieving prosperity, but the two should not be equated.

To prevent the 'blind elevation' of standards (without lowing standards either) is to prevent the 'pan-impoverishment'. Many officials are eager to ask for government money and do whatever is necessary to qualify their areas or villages as impoverished. Poverty alleviation, as a political task and part of basic social security efforts, is intended to reflect social justice, not to be used by non-impoverished areas as an excuse for getting more resources which could generate severe poverty leakage problems.

Yet how does the government identify where to focus the battle against poverty? The 2019 Number One Document clarified that the focus should be given to areas trapped in deep poverty. Anti-poverty forces and resources must be concentrated in such areas and not used for development elsewhere.

Regarding targets and measures for poverty alleviation, the document emphasised long-term mechanisms such as industrial poverty alleviation as the foundation of sustainable development. Poverty alleviation is not a one-time task but concerns helping local areas establish sustainable development. Industries must be healthy because they will not reduce poverty if products have no market once an investment is introduced and enterprises are set up.

Besides, the document proposed to consolidate the achievements of poverty alleviation in two dimensions. First, no one should return to poverty. Poverty alleviation will be meaningless if a village is lifted out of poverty one year and then falls back the next year. In addition to proposing long-term mechanisms for preventing a return to poverty, the document also put forward multiple security measures. Second, the incidence of new poverty should be avoided.

on three-rural issues. The No.1 document has become an synonymous for most important rural-related policy document. Note by the translator.

The Chinese government planned to win the battle against poverty by 2020, but areas lifted out of poverty will remain the priority of rural revitalisation policy after this date. The document highlighted the importance of integrating poverty alleviation with rural revitalisation. In my opinion, areas that have recently risen out of poverty remain a challenge and will need government assistance to realise revitalisation.

After eliminating poverty, attention should turn to prevention of new poverty. Long-term mechanisms are needed to accommodate development beyond 2020. Poverty alleviation and prevention of the return to poverty is insufficient still, new poverty should be prevented strategically.

My poverty reduction experiment in Hebian Village reveals that anti-poverty resources are not one-time subsidies but the basis of development. The battle against poverty is about using governmental poverty reduction resources thoroughly as per policies; only by doing so can we establish long-term mechanisms.

I believe we should reduce poverty by developing industries in local areas, and new business forms should be fostered at the very beginning.

In Hebian, we used poverty alleviation resources to renovate villagers' houses and improve public facilities. Investment turned into development resources. For instance, improved public facilities in the village paved the path for tourism; a guestroom was designed in each villager's house to generate income from local tourism. In 2018, the guestrooms produced over RMB800,000 income for the village and lifted it out of poverty. This benefit was delivered because poverty alleviation resources were used to further development.

While developing new business forms, we found many young people were not interested in traditional agricultural production. People might deem rural areas unenlightened, but the young are attracted to modernity, especially in the Internet era. Since they are not interested in agricultural production, we have to attract them to more appealing vocations.

We did not introduce external enterprises to Hebian Village but let the villagers run and manage all the industries. It's important to identify the interests of the young, such as tourism, culture, and digital industries, and develop appropriate job opportunities. We must also equip the young to manage new businesses by training them in knowledge and skills.

The Evolution of China's Poverty Reduction

China's poverty reduction priorities have developed with the country. As transitional poverty generally eases with its economic development, chronic poverty remains the most difficult challenge.

The development of China's economy and society has gone through many historical stages. After the founding of the People's Republic of China, land reform and the initial industrialisation process laid a solid material foundation for the country's future economic and social development. During this period, the Chinese government accumulated valuable experience of development. It is probable, even, that without the positive and negative lessons learned from its experience in the period of more than thirty years after the founding of the People's Republic of China, the reform and opening-up policy would not have been adopted. Since the reform and opening-up policy, China's social and economic development has gone through three stages. I will briefly outline the evolution of China's economic policy and its relations to poverty policies, without going into great depth.

The first stage ran from 1978 to 2000. During this period the Chinese government made economic development its central task; social justice and protection of the environment were considered important, but secondary. At this stage, boosting economic growth was the primary focus of development. In the first 20 years after the adoption of the reform and opening-up policy, China prioritised development in all concerns, following the doctrine of 'development is the absolute principle[9]'. During this period, due to the long-term capital shortage and the massive funding demand for economic development, the country could not provide sufficient funds for social security and environmental protection. Wide coverage of social security and poverty reduction programmes was thus not affordable at the time. With rapid economic growth, the urban–rural and rich-poor gaps gradually widened. Poverty in rural areas ceased to be a widespread problem. Instead, poverty became gradually concentrated in certain areas and groups of people.

[9] The quote is from Deng Xiaoping, who served as the paramount leader of the People's Republic of China from 1978 to 1989 after chairman Mao Zedong. Deng led China through a series of far-reaching market-economy reforms earning him the reputation as the 'Architect of China's Reform and Opening-up'. Note by the translator.

The second stage ran from 2001 to 2013. At this stage, China began to transition from development centred on economic growth to a form of development with a greater emphasis on sustainability and inclusivity. In the first decade of the twenty-first century, the Three Rural Issues,[10] environmental problems and corruption rose to prominence. Numerous parts of government and society responded strongly to an increased focus on the reduction of social inequality and of the urban–rural development gap. This followed the Chinese government's shift from a prioritisation of economic growth to a more inclusive vision of development. The main reason for this change was that the country had accumulated considerable wealth in the previous economic growth stage, especially following China's accession to the World Trade Organisation (WTO) in 2001. After accession, China's foreign trade increased sharply, and rapid urbanisation led to a massive shift of labourers to the non-agricultural sector. The contribution of agriculture to the country's GDP dropped abruptly. As part of this inclusiveness shift of focus, the Chinese government launched a rural tax reform programme (which abolished all forms of agricultural taxes levied on farmers), rolled out a series of rural social security policies, and increased attention to environmental issues.

The third stage ran from 2013 to 2020. During this stage China has deepened its pursuit of sustainable and inclusive development and has attempted to combat multiple new challenges emerging due to changing circumstances. The country's demographic structure, industrial structure and social structure have undergone fundamental changes. The management of welfare distribution, environmental issues and corruption have become significant difficulties.

These shifts made it inevitable that sustainable and inclusive development, rather than mere economic progress, should become a key part of China's national agenda. The CPC committed itself to this more holistic developmental vision at the Fifth Plenary Session of the Eighteenth CPC Central Committee in 2016. The resulting document—*The Suggestions of the Central Committee of the Communist Party of China for the Thirteenth Five-Year Plan for National Economic and Social Development*, hereafter referred to as *The Suggestions*—signalled China's entry into a development stage during which the CPC is committed to advancing

[10] The three rural issues, 'san nong wen ti', mean issues related to the development of agriculture, rural community and farmers. The three issues are usually put high on China's development agenda. Note by the translator.

economic, political, cultural and environmental dimensions of development in addition to party building. According to *The Suggestions*, all the rural poor under the current standard should by 2020 have been pulled out of poverty and all counties identified as poverty-stricken should no longer merit that description. Rural poverty had hindered China's coordinated economic and social development, and it was hoped that regional development discrepancies would be alleviated within a relatively short time-frame. Indeed, after more than 30 years of economic development, development-oriented poverty alleviation efforts and rural social security work, all rural residents had basic food security in the early 2010s, which formed the material base and conditions for further actions to overcoming poverty.

At the general level, rural poverty reduction efforts currently focus on absolute and relative poverty caused by unequal distribution of income and welfare. A little more specifically, two types of poverty are particularly prevalent in rural areas.

One type is that of transitional poverty, which is also known as 'short-term poverty'. This type of poverty is mainly caused by rapid industrialisation, urbanisation, and unforeseen disasters, which lead to a decline in economic income and affect residents' wellbeing. The absence or inadequacy of a social security mechanism intended to support poor people also contributes significantly to transitional poverty's prevalence. As factors that cause income loss disappear, and as favourable conditions for economic development emerge, many people in transitional poverty are able to extricate themselves. Not all can, however; due to various reasons, some fall into chronic poverty.

Chronic poverty is the other prevalent type in rural areas. People in chronic poverty cannot benefit from economic activities, holding their income at a very low level over an extended period of time; this, coupled with the lack of social security, gradually drags them to the bottom of the income and wellbeing ladder. Those in chronic poverty constitute the majority of the poor population base, while the group that moves from transitional poverty to chronic poverty every year constitutes the incremental part of the poor population. Among these groups, some are completely incapable, due for example to disability, and need the support of the social security system; some are capable but cannot escape poverty by themselves due to structural factors. Among those in transitional poverty, some live in absolute poverty. Some of these people can escape poverty through economic development with the support of the government; some will be dragged into chronic poverty. Others are transitionally poor, but in a form of relative poverty. Some of their situations will degrade further, into transitional absolute poverty; some will be dragged further still, into chronic absolute poverty.

It should be pointed out that, as observed in the first section, relative poverty will exist for a long time, and that if the country cannot achieve full social security coverage, absolute poverty will also remain with us. From the perspective of welfare, it is only when everyone's right to an adequate standard of living, including food, clothing, housing, education, and medical care, is protected and the standard is adjusted annually in accordance with the welfare level of the whole society that absolute poverty can be eliminated. Therefore, in a sense, the distinction between absolute poverty and relative poverty is not very meaningful.

However, the definitions of transitional poverty and chronic poverty that are used will have significant policy implications. As of the end of 2014 there were still 70.17 million poor people living under the poverty line in China, but it is unclear how many people were in transitional poverty and how many were in chronic poverty. Through my observations and estimations, this consisted of mostly chronic poor, if we define chronic absolute poverty as five consecutive years of poverty in terms of housing, education, medical care and income. Although the population in chronic absolute poverty is distributed in rural areas across the country, due to the difference in social security measures in different regions, the population in absolute poverty in developed areas is much smaller. Most of the population in chronic absolute poverty is distributed in remote mountainous and economically underdeveloped areas. In these areas there is a tendency for intergenerational transmission of poverty, which constitutes one of the most difficult challenges faced by China's poverty departments.

References

1. Lipset, S. M. (1996). *American Exceptionalism: A Double-edged Sword* (pp. 31–52). W. W. Norton & Company.
2. Alesina, A., & Glaeser, E. (2006). *Fighting Poverty in the US and Europe: A World of Difference* (p. 16). Oxford University Press.
3. Ovetz, R. (2022). *We the Elites: Why the US Constitution Serves the Few*. Pluto Press.
4. Hadley, T. (1848). The Constitutional Position of Property in America. *The*

Independent, 834, 837–838.
5. Purdy, J. S. (2018). Beyond the Bosses' Constitution: The First Amendment and Class Entrenchment. *Columbia Law Review, 118*(7), 2061–2186.
6. Lipset, S. M. (1996). *American Exceptionalism: A Double-edged Sword* (pp. 80–81). W. W. Norton & Company.
7. Lipset, S. M. (1996). *American Exceptionalism: A Double-edged Sword* (pp. 37–38). W. W. Norton & Company.
8. Veblen, T. (1899). *The Theory of the Leisure Class: An Economic Study of Institutions* (pp. 3–47). Macmillan.
9. Payne, K. (2018). *The Broken Ladder: How Inequality Affects the Way We Think, Live, and Die* (pp. 28–29). Penguin Books.

CHAPTER 4

Why Is It So Difficult to Eradicate Poverty?

China began working on rural poverty alleviation in 1982. This sudden new focus was allegedly because senior leadership was shocked by the poverty they saw when visiting the Sanxi Areas.[1] At the time many farmers in those areas lived in cave-houses. In some families, an entire household shared a single pair of pants. The level of poverty will sound hard to believe for some Western readers. Though China was generally underdeveloped when the Reform and Opening Up period began, the Chinese government still decided to focus poverty alleviation efforts (then called 'agricultural development') in the Sanxi Areas. It was believed that poverty could be overcome by improving agricultural production and increasing food production. Back then, poverty alleviation was focused mainly on reducing hunger. I was born in the Sanxi Areas, and have the most vivid memories of this kind of extreme poverty.

Since then a lot has changed. There has been a quite remarkable transition. In August 2020, my colleagues and I surveyed Dingbian County, Shaanxi Province, where I was born, and Yanchi County, Ningxia Region.

[1] '三西地区', san xi di qu, literally three western areas in China, includes Hexi and Dingxi areas in Gansu Province and the Xihaigu area in Ningxia Hui Autonomous Region. Note by the translator.

X. Li, *The End of Poverty and the Taming of Inequality*,
https://doi.org/10.1007/978-981-96-0684-9_4

As I recalled, in the 1980s, many people lived in cave-houses in these counties. We visited the village and cave-house to which my grandparents fled from the Gansu famine in the 1960s. They lived in this cave-house until my parents helped them move out in the 1980s. We took group photos with the villagers and local officials in front of the cave-house. I was sent to this village for summer vacation as a child, and the elderly residents still remembered my name. Today, the village had been lifted out of poverty, and the earlier look of impoverishment was nowhere to be seen. This is a story of success and relief. By contrast, many poverty alleviation campaigns—in some parts of Africa, for example: I worked in Tanzania and many other African countries in 1990s—have generated results that are almost imperceptible.

Engaged in development studies and poverty reduction work, I have often wondered why overcoming poverty can seem easy but nonetheless turn out to be very difficult. The work is indeed very hard. Otherwise, why would China found itself needing to pursue a 'battle' against poverty to realise the goal of eradicating absolute rural poverty by 2020? Of course, I am far from the only person to have this view. The entire state structure for poverty alleviation in China works on the assumption that nothing will happen overnight or without difficulty. I remember when Liu Yongfu, the then Director of the Leading Group Office of Poverty Alleviation and Development of the State Council, visited Hebian Village: one of his comments was that my work in this remote village was not easy. I responded that the most difficult part was not at the very local level but at national decision-making and policy-setting level. He agreed that no achievement in poverty alleviation could be made without leadership's close attention. Many people may take this as merely a necessary political discourse, but it genuinely inspired me, who had been engaged in anti-poverty practise for years both at home and abroad. In China and elsewhere, the most valuable resource for poverty alleviation is real political commitment. To execute the commitment involves the most precious government resources: not only money, but time, political capital, the willingness to take risks and to become unpopular with some groups. The greatest determinant of the success of poverty alleviation is a country's political courage [1], expressed in its willingness to take actions to break structural constraints and fundamentally change the distribution patterns between the rich and the poor. I'm not saying that China is the best in this regard, but it has been trying.

'Poverty Trap' in Use

Academic debates about the 'poverty trap' continue to rumble, but its use is proven in practise.

Why are some countries poor and others rich even when they share a similar geographical environment? Why are nations internally divided between rich and poor? Why do some countries succeed, and others fail after practising the same market reform? Why do certain hardworking and capable groups remain in poverty? To answer these questions, economists have developed the concept of the 'poverty trap', a term that describes a situation in which individuals require significant investment, basic funds and supportive human capital to fundamentally change their livelihoods and escape poverty. Without these resources, they cannot acquire the resources to escape a self-reinforcing cycle of poverty.

Jeffrey D. Sachs has been a supporter of the theory of the poverty trap. One of the most active scholars in international poverty studies over the past 20 years, he used to be an economics professor at Harvard University and later continued his international development studies at Columbia University. As a panel member for the former Soviet Union's 'Shock Therapy' in the 1990s, he was criticised for his liberalist propositions. Most prominently, he helped the United Nations develop the 'Millennium Development Goals' (MDGs) and served as a special international advisor on MDGs to the UN Secretary-General. He also frequented the China Development Research Foundation, attending the China Development Forum almost every year. For two years, he and I met at a sub-session to discuss aid, and I developed the impression that his belief in aid was not as firm as his books suggested. He published *The End of Poverty* years ago, which was a reference for postgraduate students of development. Consistent with his general belief in eliminating poverty through aid, this book proposes that we can shake off global poverty through the big push model. Sachs held that, due to geographical and other reasons, some countries were trapped in a vicious cycle of poverty, despite their potential for development. In his opinion, only aid could push them towards the trajectory of development; otherwise, they would stay trapped in poverty [2].

William Easterly is a renowned development economist with a sizeable list of publications, such as *The White Man's Burden*, *The Elusive Quest for*

Growth and *The Tyranny of Experts*, that has had an immense influence on development studies. He is also a former senior economist with the World Bank. Nobel economics laureate Angus Deaton, who used to chair an independent evaluation of the World Bank's policy research, wrote that Easterly's research exerted the biggest influence on the World Bank at the time. Easterly questioned the significance of assistance in development, holding almost opposite views to those of Jeffrey Sachs'. In his opinion, the fact that many previously poor countries have become prosperous while some formerly rich ones have become poor indicated that a poverty trap is a cruel pseudo-concept that deceives the poor [3].

Conceptual disputes among scholars are common, and regardless of Sach's views in favour of the poverty trap or Easterly's arguments against the concept, it is undeniable that poverty is often chronic; you could also call it 'deep' poverty. I am not going to defend the theory of the poverty trap here, but merely hope to demonstrate through my own experience in poverty reduction projects that poverty traps do exist.

In 2015, when I visited Hebian Village, not a single decent dwelling could be seen. Hebian is an ethnic Yao village and its customs were new to me. Since Han people would generally build houses as soon as they were financially able, I asked the local villagers if they would also build houses when they had earned enough money. They all responded positively. So, I started to calculate the cost of building a habitable house. After repeated discussions with the villagers, I concluded that the construction of a habitable wooden house would cost RMB100,000–150,000. In 2015, local villagers' annual disposal income was approximately RMB10,000–15,000, but most local households' cash expenditure exceeded RMB10,000. I later learned that the debt ratio of local villagers was quite high and, even if a villager could secure RMB10,000 in balance annually, it would still take ten years before they could actually move into the new house. Local villagers would have to spend all of their savings on building a new house, with no spare money for investment and production. Moreover, it was unlikely that they could secure RMB10,000 in balance each year and, per the income levels of 2015, they would not be able to move into a safe dwelling place until 20 years later. This is a vivid and practical case of a poverty trap that I have encountered on many occasions, in which existing poverty prevents escape from ongoing poverty.

When travelling to remote areas, ethnic minority areas, and mountainous villages, we may wonder why these villages are poor. It is highly likely that, similar to Hebian Village, many such villages are caught in poverty traps. These traps can be caused by a variety of reasons. One is that these groups' livelihoods are alienated from mainstream society's economic activities. For instance, after the outbreak of COVID-19 wreaked havoc on the new, tourist-based forms of business in Hebian Village, reducing guestroom incomes to nearly zero, villagers were forced to migrate to Jiangsu and Zhejiang for work. According to my colleagues, most of them returned soon after setting off for the simple reason that, illiterate and unable to speak Mandarin, they were not capable of working in electronics factories in developed areas. These factories were in urgent need of a labour force, but these villagers were not eligible as workers. The phenomenon was not new to the pandemic but had also occurred over ten years ago when most migrant workers ended up returning to the village.

The concept of a poverty trap does not convincingly explain all phenomena related to poverty. As I will go on to discuss, when an economically under-developed country remains in universal poverty, if this situation must be called a poverty trap, it's an institutional poverty trap that entraps the whole country. This may share some characteristics with a local-level poverty trap, but it is of course a different one.

The concept of the poverty trap underpins many poverty reduction projects, and I carried out my experiment in Hebian Village according to this hypothesis. I sought government funding for relocation and renovations so that each local household had nearly RMB100,000 for house construction. Originally, our idea was that if the government's anti-poverty funds were used to help villagers construct houses, these funds would be converted into fixed assets; the houses could at least be mortgaged to secure funds. Afterwards, amid discussions, the villagers and I came up with a plan to simultaneously build houses with guestrooms so that the Yao village could host visitors and gain income. The guestrooms were supported by external assistance. From 2017, guestrooms and meeting facilities began to generate income for the villagers. By the end of 2019, this income significantly increased, with the average household income rising by more than 30% compared to 2018. The case of Hebian Village explicitly manifested the usefulness of the poverty trap theory to alleviating poverty: a capital injection allowed a vicious cycle to be halted, and a virtuous cycle of revenue growth to be begun.

However, the success of poverty alleviation practises based on the poverty trap theory doesn't necessarily guarantee sustainable success. Many friends have asked me whether the Hebian Village experiment was sustainable; I reply that it is very difficult to know. First, an important concept in the poverty trap theory is that human capital is a fundamental requirement of rising above the poverty threshold. Hebian Village could only shake off poverty with high-input support. The new businesses of homestays and tourism depended on external help, because local villagers were not yet capable of managing these operations. Moreover, I couldn't anticipate when the villagers would learn enough to effectively respond to market demands without outside assistance. We thus see more evidence of the existence of the poverty trap: a cycle of disadvantage often requires external intervention if it is to be reversed. When a group is left far behind the train of modernisation, they will find it difficult to catch up with the speeding train on their own. This is why many impoverished villages like Hebian remain backward. Second, poor households that have barely escaped the poverty trap are not resilient to risks and any major market fluctuation will affect their investments. The tourist-based economy of Hebian Village produced zero income in the first quarter of 2020. Although we had already started to develop composite industries—like growing winter vegetables, traditional Chinese medicines, and bee-keeping—to diversify the village's sources of income and offset risks, the pandemic hit the new businesses hard and also wreaked havoc on agricultural commerce. After two years of prosperity, Hebian villagers were reduced to the same dilemma by COVID-19. However, their state of wellbeing was completely different. The entire village infrastructure and living environment have fundamentally changed and, despite the pandemic's impacts on incomes, multi-dimensional poverty has been profoundly eased.

Is It Difficult Because of Culture?

> Overcoming poverty is difficult largely because poor villages are enmeshed in the 'culture of poverty'. This is not to discriminate against the poor but to indicate that the poor population has developed particular social relations and material production systems that offer low-level material gains.

When speaking of eradicating poverty, many people think of working to increase farmers' incomes, offering impoverished households basic educational and medical assistance, or granting a subsistence allowance to people unable to generate income. These measures are very necessary, and we continuously implement them in our poverty alleviation practise. But despite their necessity, they are not always free of controversy. Outside of the professional poverty reduction community we hear dissenting voices, in China as elsewhere. The primary doubts concern whether this assistance is the only way to reduce poverty and whether anti-poverty efforts might actually counter-productively support the idle. These doubts can sound somewhat heartless, but they are not always unreasonable.

Is straightforward assistance treating the symptom, rather than the cause? The purpose of poverty reduction has to be to help people to find a sustainable improvement in their living standards. Of course, this is easier said than done. When the question of how to fundamentally address poverty is raised, we still do not have ideas that are effective in every situation. Why is overcoming poverty difficult? Oscar Lewis' proposal that there is a culture of poverty tended to alarm people as discrimination against the poor, but it actually touched on the root of difficulties faced by many poverty reduction efforts.

Poor individuals are often marginalised, but they are not wholly isolated from society, and poverty is keenly influenced by the production and reproduction of social relations. Particular social, political and cultural relations intertwine to form the whole of society. Social relations and material production are necessarily connected; different social relations produce different modes of material production, which further developed corresponding values, identities, social norms and capacities. In a system, people develop routine habits and productive skills based on particular social relations.

In a poor community, everyone is used to daily productive activities. I came to know this well in Hebian Village. Many people would carry swill to feed the pigs each morning, tap rubber trees in the forests, transplant rice seedlings and help each other cut and harvest sugarcane. These farming habits lead to various village rituals, such as each household butchering a pig when it was time to transplant rice seedlings or to start cutting sugarcane. In a traditional impoverished village, kinship and geographical networks produce social and productive relations that enable mutual support, overcome problems of labour division, and maintain village order. Each villager would grow up, get married, bear children in this production network and live a harsh but—in the absence of major natural disasters—peaceful and predictable life. This is why, when I first arrived, Hebian villagers said it was hard to tell who was rich and who was poor in the village, every household was more or less the same. Although viewed by outsiders as poor, villagers themselves did not regard themselves as being poor. The barriers to social inclusion were not high, and the actual differences between rich and poor were not so great in the village.

To practise targeted interventions in such villages, it was important to identify which households were in poverty and which were qualified to receive subsistence allowance. The focus on this individual welfare gap is the paradigm of modern poverty reduction. Modern society, consisting of individuals and controlled by the market and bureaucratic and government organisations, inevitably contains welfare gaps between individuals. As a result, we tend to target anti-poverty efforts at individuals—or at individual households. However, poverty alleviation is highly difficult in villages where poverty is pervasive, and where welfare is often not individual but networked or relational.

Overcoming poverty is mainly difficult because poverty-stricken villages are enmeshed in the 'culture of poverty'. The point of this statement is not to discriminate against the poor but to indicate that the poor population has developed particular social relations and material production systems that offer low-level material gains. This is a vicious cycle of poverty, and the more dependent a village is on such relations and modes of material production, the poorer it becomes.

I mentioned Mr You in a previous section. In June 2020, I met him again in Hebian Village. In 2019, he had told me that he would make money by growing sugarcane. When I asked a year later if he had made money, he began to repeat the same old story: he had made some but was left with almost nothing after paying his debts. He was hardworking, but he dreamed of making a great fortune overnight, and wasn't satisfied by gradual progress. The way he wanted to realise his goal was still attached to rural values, networks of social relations and modes of production. Being an average farmer with a binding credit, skill and knowledge constraint, he can not become a successful 'entrepreneur' [4]. He had to borrow money for renting land and hiring labour. He was basically mortgaging output without money, hoping to earn a big return by expanding scale. I told Mr You that his plans for wealth were an illusion.

For villages where poverty is universal, poverty will continue to be produced and reproduced for as long as the whole of rural social relations remains unchanged. Eliminating poverty means replacing the social relations that produce and reproduce poverty. This touches on the ethics of development, and is a big contributor to the difficulty of real poverty alleviation.

What Is Standing between the Poor and a Better Life?

> Attitudes, and institutions, are important things that stand between the poor and a better life.

As I have explained, targeted poverty alleviation had become a national campaign in China in the period of 2013 to 2020. Many Chinese departments and organisations had at some point sent people to impoverished villages to contribute to long-term anti-poverty projects. This concerted effort had borne some fruit. Still, we had a great deal left to do. This had baffled some. Many of my colleagues, friends and students had frequently complained to me, 'Professor Li, poverty reduction is really hard!' Even a senior colleague of mine, who used to work with me on village poverty reduction, would often sigh now when remembering our work: 'It was such a challenge'. I agree with him. Why, exactly, is overcoming poverty so challenging? I am still not wholly sure.

A while ago, when my cousin visited my mother, I asked her upon her return about the valley where my aunt's cave-house stood. There used to be tens of households in the valley, and it was a very impoverished community. Water would gather in the houses' cellars, and the inhabitants would drink it. Now, most have relocated to the nearest town, a small example of the urbanisation that has taken place across the country. My youngest cousin now lives there alone, in a house built with government anti-poverty support, raising a dozen sheep. Like many, this small county in northwestern China has been changed beyond recognition, and my aunt's village has been lifted out of poverty. As urbanisation increases, the rural population finds employment in urban areas, and rural poverty is alleviated or eliminated. Is this, then, what poverty reduction is all about? It seems easy: allow the rural poor to move to live and work in urban areas, where they can earn more money. The persistence of poverty despite urbanisation, however, implies that it is perhaps not so easy.

In my view, the key factor in our failure to assist everyone in escaping poverty is our fundamental understanding of what poverty is. This is not to say that poverty is not the result of many factors: many aspects contribute—we all know this. Even though we know this, though, society still often regards poverty as a personal failure on the part of the poor. Of course, a person's success is related to their personal efforts, but disadvantage cannot be simply traced back to incapability. The belief that incapacity causes poverty has misguided our anti-poverty endeavours and covered the root causes: unequal social structures, systems and even policy arrangements. Convinced that personal success depends on individual efforts, we always emphasise self-reliance in poverty alleviation and take this as an internal motivation for overcoming poverty. But why should we work on poverty alleviation if overcoming poverty is an individual endeavour that depends on internal motivation and personal efforts? Undoubtedly, the poor are unlikely to escape poverty without effort, but why are so many people still trapped in poverty while trying so hard?

Personal factors are only part of what leads to poverty. Excessive emphasis on their importance will distract our attention from poverty's political, economic and social causes. In fact, almost all countries with a low incidence of inequality and poverty have pro-poor political, economic and social mechanisms. The most developed global power, the United States, suffers the most severe poverty and inequality in the developed world mainly because individualism is ingrained in its national ideology. Many Americans are convinced that economic success or failure is entirely determined by personal effort; this belief, expressed through electoral choices, causes the country's underdeveloped social security network.

China's work in poverty alleviation is admirable for both eliminating structural constraints and mobilising the initiative of the poor themselves. The idea that the poorest in society can escape poverty without support in education, health, social security or employment, is ludicrous. That, at root, is why poverty reduction is so difficult. Institutional reform is not easy, especially when deeply held attitudes must be changed first.

The Challenges for Targeted Poverty Reduction[2]

> We used our limited modern culture to communicate with the 'pre-modern' culture of the village, which was difficult.

One thing I have learned over the past two decades of work on poverty alleviation will surprise no philosophers: that people understand welfare and happiness differently, and that these perceptions will vary according to culture, place, age and moment. For instance, urban residents might think residential houses in remote areas that are wooden, shabby and windowless are uninhabitable. Yet local people get by just fine and would be surprised if you tell them there is something wrong with this mode of living.

'Modernity' did not arrive all at once in rural China, but when it did, it brought with it the creeping realisation of greater possibilities and new approaches. This was, in my view, not always a good thing. The arrival of 'modernity' left local residents with the depressing knowledge that their income was insufficient to support 'modern lifestyles'. This forced new choices upon them, with good and bad effects. Educational and medical expenses came to take up a large share of rural expenditure. This was a new departure, but a good one. On the other hand, some areas came to be swept with the new trend of consumerism, such as buying new mobile phones and cars and engaging in costly festivities or recreational activities.

It is not unreasonable for rural people to want these things. Development, and poverty reduction, has as its goal the ideal of giving people greater choice. The greatest challenge to this lies where whole areas and populations are in deep poverty. When a broad population has been connected to the wider economy, individuals that are 'left behind' and remaining in poverty are not very 'problematic'. Even when their poverty is caused by real laziness or by disease, it is still relatively easy to lift individuals out of poverty if the general population is affluent.

To address regional poverty, however, is more difficult. Lack of opportunity can beget lack of opportunity. In poor villages, the local labour force lacks skills and capacity to work outside the region, may face

[2] First shared at the salon 'How to Cope with the Era of "New Poverty"' jointly held by Narada Insights and Beijing Cultural Review, and then published at Narada Insights (2017-07-24) at http://www.naradafoundation.org/content/5397.

language and cultural challenges when working there, and therefore finds it hard to travel outside the region for work when there is little work available locally. Without resources introduced from outside the region, its villages are often stuck in a somewhat pre-modern state. Such areas are generally below our view of welfare standards in modern China.

In villages where there are few impoverished households, the local government can mobilise inhabitants without needing to bring in significant resources for support. (My mid-2010s surveys in poor areas in Sichuan have reinforced this viewpoint.) In such places economic development and transformation will gradually solve the local poverty. It may take time, but it will happen.

It will take longest for areas and populations in deep poverty. Their poverty is not caused by laziness or backward concepts and ideas but by the wide gap between their social culture and modern ethics, their inability to grasp basic market rules and possible external control of local resources.

In response, the priority is to interrupt the intergenerational transmission of poverty. Transmission involves children and parents, and children are most susceptible. If children receive proper preschool nutrition and education, and their concepts compatible with modern ethics (such as science and rational thought, individualism, etc.) are gradually nurtured, they will be able to gradually catch up with development.

Beyond work at the individual or household level, support for the construction of infrastructure in poor areas is also vital. Potable water, reliable and sufficient electricity and adequate roads are all necessary infrastructure that without them development will not get far. Once these are improved, time and energy of the poor can be reduced. In Hebian Village, government repaired an 8 km road that connected the village to the outside world, which made it more convenient to sell local sugarcane and decreased traffic accidents. The amplification effects of infrastructure can often be far greater than the cost of building the infrastructure itself: it may be a financial cost, but it is a socio-economic benefit.

At the regional and community levels, development practitioners should seek to use local advantages to increase residents' income. This can allow development to be sustainable: without this, a cycle of fiscal transfers (such as subsidies), or an extended social welfare net, may fail to meaningfully improve conditions. This underpinned our thinking in Hebian, where we developed guestrooms in villagers' houses for tourists. In my opinion, poverty alleviation in absolutely poor areas must focus on supporting the creation of sustainable local industries able to generate high enough incomes to stimulate local initiative.

This will inevitably have consequences for equality, which may require some distributional interventions. Forty years ago in China, the gap between rich and poor was limited, and the Gini coefficient was around 0.2. As the economy developed, the gap was gradually widened. Though economic growth produced admirable effects and reduced poverty, these opportunities were not universally distributed or seized. Some regions—such as more rural ones—had less access to new opportunities, or gambled on poorly chosen projects and came to lag behind.

The poor in these areas require support through social welfare, but only up to a point, and always with great care. For instance, the government could build houses for each household and give support to each poor labourer. While well-intentioned, however, social welfare can create moral hazards and social ills, exemplified by conspicuous consumption in some areas when people become wealthy.

Another way is to influence impoverished populations with relatively 'modern' culture, a cultural and ethical challenge I face myself. As a researcher on development, I often wonder how to connect poor populations with the modernised world and want to distil some common elements of them. Though cultures differ, some might see drinking and smoking as harmful while others regard it as part of the quality of life—some commonality should exist beyond cultural specificity. It is important to preserve a group's cultural characteristics while helping them catch up with the modern world. In Hebian Village I found some clues in the house. In our experiment, we encouraged villagers to build wooden houses on posts, a traditional style of houses widely seen in Yao, Dai communities and in the Southeast Asian region. But we also ask them to install wide instead of narrow windows in the house and segment the interior space to accommodate a modern life, including kitchen, bathroom, living room and bedroom, one or two of the bedrooms could serve as guest rooms for visitors. The new houses look both traditional and modern.

When I arrived at Hebian Village, there was no space for outsiders at all. All we could do was slowly introduce and embed new ideas, beginning with a simple guestroom with a bathroom, shower and hot water. Some villagers found problems with these ideas, and we occasionally found ourselves in mild conflict with them, but we were not changing the village entirely, only transforming a small space with faucets and hot water. We used limited modern culture to communicate with the 'pre-modern' culture of the village, which was difficult. For example, villagers didn't perceive the utility in installing a toilet in the bathroom, since they were more used to a squatting one. They also kept some habits of eating animal flesh raw. In this way, we carefully put into practise concepts like the poverty trap and modern transformation. I am a sociologist, I know I have to be culturally sensitive and I try my best to understand their cultures and feelings.

Hebian Village is increasingly running by market rules. It has encountered some problems along the way, such as which households should receive guests first, how to distribute customers, running businesses in a corporate or cooperative form, and whether businesses should be run by villagers or outsourced. Solving these problems requires modern ethics, thoughts and skills.

While it has been our NGO that has contributed to the development of these skills and to the wider poverty alleviation project, it is ultimately always the government that makes improvements possible. Without broad commitment to poverty alleviation, and support in accessing the economy, developing infrastructure, obtaining education and so on, our small efforts would have very little effect. The work of NGOs is ultimately only a supplement to the work of the government. China has 600,000 social organisations; they can support poor areas and populations and safeguard social justice, and each can contribute to poverty alleviation as professional players. Many of these other public interest institutions, moreover, have also supported Hebian. My practise in Hebian, working with both government representatives and peer organisations, has illustrated that the government, higher education institutions and civil society organisations could work together to achieve positive change. We have played a supportive role, and I was pushed to the front line to experiment in poverty alleviation. My experiment is a small but significant step. I'm now in my fifties—let's look back at the value of the experiment in ten years.

We have set up several initiatives to increase incomes in Hebian Village. Genuine eco-friendly and organic agricultural products are fairly rare in China, and their high retail value motivates farmers to produce these items. For instance, insecticide-free organic rice is very labour-intensive and does not grow as abundantly as non-organic rice; as a result, its price point must be many times higher than that of regular rice to motivate farmers to plant it. I also suggest that we fix agricultural production and procurement at a specified rate, which will discourage farmers from falsification. Ensuring that farmers do receive this higher price means that eco-friendly agricultural products must be marked to enable traceability and supervision, and there is still work to be done on this front.

More large-scale options are also available. Cooperatives can be set up for mutual supervision. For example, ten households can team up to plant a certain rice area, and only a certain pre-estimated amount of rice is purchased. This will make it easier for farmers to identify and supervise the products and allows labour to be shared.

Pro-poor tourism is a form of tourism intended to economically improve poor areas. It helps local farmer households to become autonomous players in the economic chain, bolstering their local income with money from other parts of the economy. If this is to be fully successful, I insist that the majority of economic benefits from pro-poor tourism should go to farmers rather than travel agencies. The key lies in pricing power, poor villagers should have controls over how to cooperate with others and how to distribute benefits between them such as a specified proportion of income for villagers from a guestroom. The Hebian Village project has developed successfully because a labour force was available to clean rooms and wash sheets. Guestrooms are not a suitable business idea for villages in deep poverty without a labour force to do this. In those cases there is still hope: the inhabitants can run modernised hotels, outsource asset management, and earn dividends. However, if the industry is contracted by external capital, farmers may be displaced as main players.

The Burden of Deep Poverty[3]

Deep poverty—persistent lack of opportunities and modernity ethics, and varied welfare deprivation—persists in pockets. Eliminating it is challenging, and relies on increased access to public goods.

Currently, China's rural poverty is mainly present in deep poverty and transitional poverty. Though the two are interconnected, reflecting imbalanced development, they are also different. Transitional poverty are very

[3] Published at www.gmw.cn (2017-04-24) at http://theory.gmw.cn/2017-04/24/content_24284434.htm?from=timeline&isappinstalled=0.

often manifested in pockets of poverty while the broad population of a given area have largely escaped poverty. Deep poverty results from the lasting accumulation of multi-dimensional poverty and are usually manifested in areas where poverty is pervasive. It is mainly reflected by an absence of welfare for groups of various sizes and is far more difficult to eliminate. It describes group poverty in entire villages or even larger scopes and is generally related to regional economic and social underdevelopment. Whether China's battle on extreme poverty could be won largely depends on how the deep poverty is being addressed. In this sense we need to reexamine the deep poverty in rural China.

What do I mean by 'deep poverty'? Areas of deep poverty suffer an absence of what I call 'modernity ethics'. In China, demographics in deep poverty are mostly distributed across remote mountain areas and areas inhabited by ethnic minority groups. These areas have long been granted support, but many outsiders feel that they are embedded in a 'culture of poverty'. Their inhabitants are characterised as 'lazy, unorganised and slow' or 'being constantly waiting for, relying on and asking for assistance'. It is worth noting that poverty alleviation in these areas overlooked the fact that local populations were culturally out of step with the ethics of modern prosperity. Simple preaching in modern ethics failed to substantially change this situation because they had developed their own subsistence equilibrium based on a relatively low material supply. Economically, socially and culturally, these areas lack 'modernity ethics'. Since mainstream anti-poverty concepts failed to culturally resonate with disadvantaged groups, anti-poverty support based on material supply caused a simple give-gain paradox. To transform material support into sustainable poverty-eliminating resources, the subsistence ethics of the poor must gradually align with modern prosperity ethics, but the task is highly challenging. In the long run, the intergenerational transmission of poverty can be prevented through education; in the short term, solutions that fit the cultural context of impoverished populations should be explored. However, inculcating modern ethics in this region may cause social disorder and loss of cultural diversity, as illustrated in the aboriginal poverty reduction cases in North America and Latin America.

Those in deep poverty can be considered to be in an 'economic poverty trap'. A major characteristic of deep poverty is that the poor's incomes can only support subsistence but cannot improve quality of life and educational, health or cultural needs. Constrained by a subsistence culture, those in deep poverty often cannot effectively transform their resources into income-increasing assets like people in more developed areas do, while external market forces seize a large part of their returns from resources. Moreover, many new or 'unnecessary' reasons for spending consume the poor's income. For instance, in a deeply impoverished village, a young villager has an annual disposable income of less than RMB5,000–6,000. Still, per capita spending on cell phones and cigarettes may reach RMB3,000–4,000 a year. Furthermore, poverty relief is insufficient to support them to escape the income poverty trap. For instance, many areas adopt the anti-poverty measure of giving each household ten ducks and five pigs. However, the livestock do not generate a high-income after the cost of their upkeep is deducted, and consequently, many farmers just sell them for cash. The key to breaking the income bottleneck for the poor population lies in exploring opportunities for high-intensity income growth and creating conditions for materialising these opportunities, which requires delicacy, innovation and a good understanding of the local context. The poverty relief currently available in poor areas is mostly provided through regular support as part of ubiquitous state programmes, but we seriously need targeted and innovative last-mile efforts. We should be aware that poverty cannot be solved solely by government officials and poverty alleviation institutions—but nonetheless, national policies need to be enacted as soon as possible to encourage research institutes, higher education institutions and social organisations to research innovative solutions that can be applied to individual contexts. My Hebian experiment may be a case for social organisation-led and state-driven last-mile innovation.

Furthermore, deep poverty is related to the unbalanced supply of public goods. That is not to say that public goods meant to rebalance opportunity access have not already been made available, but that they have not yet been closely targeted. Targeted poverty alleviation delivers a greater proportion of resources through a more fine-tuned approach than broader anti-poverty programmes. The central government has devoted unprecedented attention, fiscal support and administrative resources to poverty alleviation programmes. However, the supply of public goods in areas in deep poverty remains unbalanced.

Why is this, taking a brief detour? Firstly, the administration of the subsistence allowance in these areas is flawed. Compared with average areas, incomes strata in rural society in deep poverty are barely differentiated, and the welfare gap between groups is very limited: all are poor. The allowance quota granted to villages pro-rata is often controversial. Because the amounts provided to impoverished rural areas by state are inadequate, many local administrations are forced to distribute the subsistence allowance to households *on a rotational basis*. Under these circumstances, the subsistence allowance is often further segmented into different categories. This expands its coverage but causes leakage effects, spreading relief over more houses and undermining the security of the basic provision support for those in most urgent need. Secondly, in areas of deep poverty, non-competitive public goods are in severely short supply. On the one hand, this directly causes deep poverty; on the other hand, the high cost of goods can play a large role in consuming the slim income of the poorest, keeping them from making investments. As the most deeply impoverished villages are far from major towns, villagers have to pay more for shopping, the education of their children, and medical services. For example, villages with hundreds of inhabitants—even some over one thousand—can lack kindergartens, clinics, schools or basic business facilities, and may be wholly inaccessible on rainy and snowy days. This is in part due to the higher cost of providing these services in more isolated, rural areas, and due to an unfortunate governance loop: local services are supported in part by local revenue-raising, and where revenues are low, local government will struggle to provide services. This makes transfers from central to local government all the more important. Unlike villages in transitional poverty, those in deep poverty are low in mobility. Movement costs money, and poorer households cannot easily set aside money for travel to where labour markets are better. Location is an asset. Those in rural poverty do not have this asset, and cannot afford the investment necessary to obtain it—through migration to a city. Work in urban areas can be transformative for households remaining in rural areas, and the money sent back can (but does not always) allow investment and a change in living standards. This migration is often temporary, however, and many young people who have been educated ultimately return to rural areas due to cultural and other reasons. The supply of more non-competitive public goods in these rural areas would not waste public resources. Instead, it will create material conditions for local anti-poverty efforts and, over time, considerably reduce poverty. More importantly, the provision and maintenance of non-competitive public goods can promote alignment of traditional social cultures to development. Once immediate hazards are resolved, such as real hunger, deep poverty is best addressed by prioritising the provision of non-competitive public goods. This allows the growth of capacity, opportunity, and over time of prosperity. It is the difference between a blood transfusion—short-term transfers of public money through closely-managed, in-kind assistance—and 'blood-making', helping local economies to have the resources and opportunities needed to start growing sustainably. In short, poverty alleviation requires creating conditions for the poor populations to develop their capacities and have sustained access to opportunities. If these opportunities rely on continual access to transfers without changing the fundamental situation, the benefits risk ultimately remaining temporary.

A specific challenge faced by demographics in deep poverty is the leakage of poverty-reduction benefits under the 'market mechanism'. People in deep poverty are disadvantaged in terms of financial and economic literacy. Most anti-poverty measures aim to drive industrial development through external market actors, but the poor population is at a disadvantage in this unequal game. Since agriculture-based development is relatively unprofitable, contract models can increase farmers' incomes. However, the farmers only control a small share of the value chain, and market approaches such as corporate plus farmer households and cooperatives tend to benefit privileged groups. Areas and villages in deep poverty find it hard to find capable leaders, and a lack of representatives causes severe leakage of poverty-reducing benefits under the market mechanism. For instance, over the past decade, the development of the banana industry in southern Yunnan created many business owners, but few local farmers became rich as a result. Most of the profits were taken by intermediary companies or individual bosses since they had fast access to market. By comparison, despite annual price fluctuations, farmers directly benefit from rubber and sugarcane because they can establish a direct connection with the market and thus avoid the 'exploitation' of intermediaries. Obviously, insufficient innovation in pro-poor industrial development has kept areas in deep poverty from relying on their own resources to realise prosperity. Encouraging the intervention of social enterprises, which can drive and cultivate poor entrepreneurs, could effectively help rural areas overcome poverty.

To address deep poverty thus requires comprehensive approaches. Since deep poverty is a long-term deprivation of multi-dimensional welfare, it cannot be quickly eased through basic regular poverty alleviation measures. First, since the 'culture of poverty' will not vanish in the short term or be removed with regular education, developing preschool education and launching child nutrition programmes for areas in deep poverty is most important. Meanwhile, we must realise that quality, rather than quantity, of educational resources in such areas lags far behind. Despite massive input, the problem will remain unsolved if the quality of teachers is not improved. As the World Bank's flagship *World Development Report* argued in 2018, 'schooling is not the same as learning'. Even if access to schools was improved, little would change without meaningful access to good teachers. In many places voluntary teacher programmes are most feasible, and mobilising social organisations for voluntary teaching should be an important measure of targeted poverty alleviation. The best should not be the enemy of the better. Second, medical service centres should also be set up in deeply impoverished villages. Each remote area should be operated by medical staff and volunteers, who should be encouraged to offer regular medical services. Finally, tackling deep poverty should be taken as the top priority in targeted poverty alleviation. Though many anti-poverty resources have been funnelled into areas of deep poverty, a framework for comprehensive governance remains to be put in place. I suggest that we initiate comprehensive poverty reduction plans, integrate resources and provide non-competitive public resources to make up for the absence of direct welfare provision in poor areas while developing pro-poor market mechanisms to boost poor populations' incomes. Assisting rural populations in escaping deep poverty is extremely difficult, but it must happen. Bold approaches, uniting innovative efforts with tried and tested increases of basic opportunities, are necessary wherever pockets of deep poverty will remain.

Preventing the Return to Poverty Is a Priority[4]

China has succeeded in eliminating absolute poverty; a proactive attitude to social services and growth through industry can prevent it from re-emerging.

In the post-Deng Xiaoping era of Socialism with Chinese Characteristics, China has made profound progress in targeted poverty alleviation and elimination. Measured against the 2011 poverty line, the Chinese rural poor population dropped from 98.99 million in late 2012 to 30.46

[4] Published at *The People's Daily* (2018-08-27) at http://theory.gmw.cn/2018-08/26/content_30782890.htm.

million in late 2017, falling 13.7 million annually. The goal, in maintaining this efficiency, was to eradicate rural absolute poverty by 2020; and in February 2021, China's president confirmed that this was indeed achieved. The national goal of lifting all impoverished counties out of poverty by 2020 was also attained. As a 2022 World Bank report notes, the success of the massive poverty reduction campaign is 'historically unprecedented'; in lifting 770 million people out of poverty since 1978, China alone accounted for 75 percent of all poverty reduction globally.

However, the eradication of absolute poverty certainly does not mean that rural poverty will vanish or that fighting poverty is no longer necessary. Poverty is a relative concept, and rural poverty still remains in the form of relative and multi-dimensional poverty. Poverty alleviation will need to continue, to help those who fall back into poverty and save others from sliding back. Of the two options, the second is vastly preferable, for both economic and equity reasons. Poverty reduction must be a sustained effort, and resources and attention must be targeted to the areas at greatest risk of collapsing back below the poverty line. This is a point that has been repeatedly highlighted by China's state leaders. If we cannot prevent rural populations from falling back into poverty, the great success of the recent national battle on poverty will be tarnished.

For an area to permanently shake off poverty, sustainable anti-poverty mechanisms need to be established. When new poverty emerges, or some fall back into poverty, institutional mechanisms can guarantee effective provision for basic needs. This must be proactive and holistic. It is not enough to merely treat the symptoms of a return to poverty: vulnerable areas must be institutionally kept from failing. Education is crucial in this effort. Measures that develop preschool education and improve the quality of compulsory education in extremely poor areas can prevent new poverty and create an environment in which this is less likely. Beyond education, economic growth, the reliable employment that accompanies this, and the development of infrastructure in poor areas are also important conditions for sustainable poverty eradication. In areas that are currently experiencing deep poverty, sustainable poverty alleviation efforts are especially important: local infrastructure and economic development are likely to be backward and to require assistance.

Sustainable poverty elimination requires the sustainable development of industries with a comparative advantage, able to be successful, employ workers and thus reduce local poverty. The sustainability of these industries should be assessed when judging whether an area has genuinely overcome poverty, looking beyond the number of anti-poverty initiatives developed and farmers' short-term income levels. In some areas, poor populations' income rose slowly because their income source was mainly agricultural, and there were few local industries into which they could diversify. The way out of poverty for these areas is to develop multiple local industries to obtain diversified income streams and increase resilience to income shocks that might otherwise send populations back into poverty. A diversity of industries and income streams is important, and local government and development actors should be wary of placing all their eggs in even the most inviting of baskets. In some areas, I have seen the development of large-scale industries supported by development actors, with results of excess supply, a market glut, price drops and attendant problems for workers and poverty alleviation. When attempting to foster industries to support poverty alleviation, efforts should be made to evaluate technical and market risks faced by mainstream anti-poverty industries. Strong risk prevention and disposal measures to prevent failure or loss can prevent areas from blindly following suit in developing industrial projects. Identifying a market's capacity to absorb, and which industries will be sustainable and which should be diversified, is of course easier said than done.

Conversely, other areas have shifted the direction of development by cultivating characteristic industries particular to each village. Despite the small scale of these industries, these can be competitive, enjoy reliable market demand and thus became truly sustainable. Industries that have provided robust solutions for sustainable poverty elimination have included farming and stockbreeding, forestry and protoculture, agricultural product processing, featured handicrafts, leisure agriculture and rural tourism. These endeavours, supported by the state and by development actors, have often significantly raised poor households' income in a deliberate way while also producing marketable and cost-effective speciality goods.

Sustainable poverty elimination requires the engagement of all social forces. Local communities should proactively explore poverty relief mechanisms, led by the government. In doing so, the characteristics of the impoverished population in question, and their particular opportunities and needs, must be carefully considered. Enterprises must also be encouraged to play a role in poverty alleviation. State-owned companies can implement targeted poverty alleviation, and private ones can support poverty alleviation by developing industries, facilitating employment and contributing to charity. Social organisations and volunteers can also play a role, and altruistic efforts to understand the needs of poor populations and provide what is necessary should be supported.

Targeted Poverty Alleviation and Local Governance[5]

> Targeted poverty alleviation has given local government new opportunities and new challenges.

Since the Reform and Opening Up era began in 1978, power in China has been gradually decentralised. By exercising their new authorities and mobilising new resources, local governments drove the country's rapid development within the strategic layout managed by the central government. This has not been a perfect model. We have long been aware that some local governments have risked extreme debts in their desire to invest in development, and in recent years the scale of this problem has started to reveal itself. Despite this, it remains undeniable that local government has been indispensable for China's rapid transformation.

Local governments form an integral part of China's 'developmental state'. In China's particular political conditions, local governments have long played the role of 'agent' in two dimensions: fulfilling tasks set at a higher level, and meeting the demands of the local public. For a long period in the twentieth century, local governments faced the dilemma, typical to their position, of being an agent needing to satisfy two constituencies at two levels. The central government set challenging targets that risked offending local actors; local actors demanded reforms and investments that risked offending the superior levels of government. Local governments were stuck in the difficult position of collecting fees from farmers for rural planning and family planning. As a result of this, relations between officials and the people could sometimes be strained. Prioritising local economic development therefore became the optimal choice for local governments hoping to resolve the 'dual agent dilemma' of satisfying the levels both above and below. Knowledge of the public

[5] Published at www.gmw.cn (2016-02-29) at http://theory.gmw.cn/2016-02/29/content_19093606.htm?utm_source=bshare&utm_campaign=bshare&utm_medium=weixin&bsh_bid=1003412062&from=timeline&isappinstalled=0.

benefits of economic growth helped to incentivise local governments to improve their political behaviours and built a positive image of improved performance while also granting unprecedented authority and resources. At this stage, the image of local government was generally positive.

In the twenty-first century, rural tax and fee reforms, adjustments to the relationship between central and local government and increases in transfer payments from the centre to decentralised actors soon reduced constraints on local governments' activities. The autonomy of local governments surged as their pursuit of economic growth secured greater power and authority. In fact, over the past decade, though local government helped drive China's urbanisation by relying on the land economy, they showed an increasingly obvious pro-capital tendency. The mutual impact of power and economic activities created a massive rent-seeking space. Beyond economic growth, local governments faced other challenges. Public appeals for increased rights were widespread, but some local governments mishandled the appeals. The political ecosystem of local governments soon worsened, and the image of local government started to turn negative.

Driven by an anti-corruption strategy, the local political ecosystem started to change fundamentally. However, cultivating a new political economy of local government under new conditions required new resources. In the twentieth century, resources to boost local governments' performance included funds earmarked for agricultural development, township and village enterprises and promoting investment. At the beginning of the twenty-first century, these resources were expanded to include funds to support urbanisation and innovative development. As the central government strives to transform development modes, local governments require new resources to engage in new areas and to reshape their image. The cross-governmental targeted poverty alleviation campaign, begun in 2013, was introduced at an opportune time to supply the needed resources.

Due to their dependence on and prioritisation of economic growth, local governments found it difficult to change their behaviours to meet requirements for targeted poverty alleviation. Consequently, the central government adopted unconventional institutional approaches, including requesting that Party secretaries at each level of local government take primary responsibility for poverty alleviation, and issuing demands for assessment indicators. The institutional pressure was transmitted level by level and showed noticeable positive political benefits.

I was deeply impressed by the central government's engagement in poverty alleviation while working in Hebian Village. This is not to say that the government had always given Hebian the attention it needed. When I first arrived, villagers there observed to me that they had seldom had the opportunity to meet government officials in the past decade. During the time that I was there, however, they often saw these officials, and were impressed by them. Formerly, visiting officials just took a look and left, but now they stayed to work with the villagers and address their problems together. The Party secretary of the county took the lead, and county-level officials and department heads visited impoverished villages almost every day. The problems that I identified were quickly studied and solved, and issues reported by farmers were also swiftly discussed. This didn't mean that the problems of poverty alleviation were solved, but it did illustrate how a new ecology of local government was forming. Since the launch of the anti-corruption campaigns in the early 2010s, many public voices criticised local governments' inaction, but they required new resources to act effectively. The central government's targeted poverty alleviation campaign responded to the objective need for economic and social development on the one hand and created a platform for local government to engage in new activities on the other. Just as the Reform and Opening Up altered the political ecology of the Chinese government, poverty alleviation, as a political mission, is changing the behaviours of local government.

How is it doing this? First, unlike the approaches of land expropriation and investment promotion aimed for growth that local governments were familiar with, poverty alleviation is an integrated social undertaking centred on people. Though it has always been an important part of work for local government, it has never been prioritised to this degree. Such a change in focus and practises, in which local government becomes obliged to target disadvantaged individuals and households, is bound to foster new institutional paths for local governments. Further, they offer an opportunity for local governments to gain practical experience in comprehensively leading social management rather than economic management. Targeted poverty alleviation will effectively transform local governments from developmental governments pursuing purely economic growth, with little attention given to the poorest, to a new type of government serving comprehensive and inclusive development.

Second, targeted poverty alleviation requires local government leadership to work in impoverished villages. This offers an opportunity for local leadership to fully understand the gaps in economic and social development and objectively shortens their distance from poor populations, creating more opportunities for interactions and revelations. The cultural intimacy and emotional resonance shaped by frequent interaction with poor populations and exposure to their living conditions will be gradually integrated into local governments' political behaviours. Decision-makers' practical experiences and personal feelings will directly inform the local government's political agenda. More interaction with the neediest members of society will embed a people-centred state governance philosophy into local governments' agendas and lay a solid social foundation.

Third, targeted poverty alleviation requires stronger coordination amongst local governments. The central government has explicitly required coordinating various resources for poverty alleviation, but this coordination needs to be carried out by county and township governments. They must work to overcome systemic constraints and find creative ways to practise the policies instructed by the central government. This is a severe challenge for local governments, which are subject to strict regulation. On the one hand, local governments cannot cross the red line of resource use; on the other, they must innovatively integrate resources, leading to further innovations as local governments break bureaucratic restrictions. Like local governments' innovations in the Reform and Opening Up period in the 1980s and 1990s, the challenges of targeted poverty alleviation have created an opportunity for local governments to construct a people-centred government. Innovation under rules and constraints encourages institutional validity and sustainability. For instance, pro-poor funding through different line departments would be subject to different lines of programme regulation, thus falling short of comprehensive poverty reduction effects in a given area. But in the targeted poverty alleviation campaign, some local governments tried to break these bureaucratic constraints and piloted in integrating different sources of funding to maximise its poverty reduction use. Practise of this sort has been further institutionalised for rural revitalisation in the 'post-poverty' era.

On the one hand, targeted poverty alleviation involves intensive, large-scale mobilisation and publicity. On the other hand, it creates pressures that are transmitted level by level. Government at each level must cope with these pressures in various ways. Despite cases of falsification, the implementation of poverty alleviation with strict government accountability and supervision will trigger innovative mechanisms. Moreover, the nature of poverty alleviation requires the government to frequently interact with the poor, which changes governments' administrative and cultural climate. As a community-level official said, 'all the leading officials and all the departments are discussing and working on poverty alleviation now'. Naturally, this cultural atmosphere of directly serving the poor will change previous public perceptions of the government as only serving business. As governments move one step away from capital and one step closer to the poor, the political ecology of local governments will be transformed.

References

1. Dercon, S. (2022). *Gambling on Development: Why Some Countries Win and Others Loose* (pp. 103–124). Hurs t& Company.
2. Sachs, J. D. (2005). *The End of Poverty: Economic Possibilities for Our Time* (pp. 244–265). The Penguin Press.
3. Easterly, W. (2001). *The Elusive Quest for Growth: Economists' Adventures and Misadventures in the Tropics* (p. 165). MIT Press.
4. Addison, T., Hulme, D., & Kanbur, k. (2009). *Poverty Dynamics: Interdisciplinary Perspectives* (p. 20). Oxford University Press.

CHAPTER 5

Why a War on Poverty?

I have already touched on the difficulties of poverty reduction in previous chapters. It is not easy for any single country. And it can be more 'difficult' in a statist country where people tend to count it as a full responsibility of the state and attribute any progress or failure in poverty reduction to the national anti-poverty strategies and policies. In such cases, to formulate a 'good' poverty strategy or policy is extremely important. Since the 'occurrence' and 'disappearance' of poverty is also a product of social and economic changes, policymakers will inevitably need to figure out the causes and dynamics of poverty first. More importantly, poverty policies should be integrated into the grand socio-economic strategies, otherwise 'new' poverty will always occur despite that 'old' poverty is being eradicated.

In China, a targeted national strategy on poverty was first introduced in early 2010s. And in 2015, this national strategy was elevated to a 'war' or 'battle' on poverty. Why was this so? What prompted the changes in policy? What were the challenges faced by this policy? And what were the key elements of this policy? Though today we know that the victory of this 'war' has been announced, it might still be of some interest to dig deeper into these questions.

X. Li, *The End of Poverty and the Taming of Inequality*,
https://doi.org/10.1007/978-981-96-0684-9_5

Why We Needed a War on Poverty?

> In 1980s, an agricultural productivity boosting policy alone would lift tens of thousands of people out of poverty. But in 2012, the problem of poverty was unlikely to be resolved by an increase in agricultural production, or any singular policy.

In 2012 the Chinese government reframed its poverty programme, announcing the start of 'targeted poverty alleviation'. The unstated implication was that earlier anti-poverty practises did not have clear targets. Although this suggestion requires some nuance, it is essentially correct. In the early 1980s, when a few senior officials investigated areas in north-western China, they were shocked by the severity of local poverty. Although 'developed areas' in China at that time were also poor and underdeveloped, the extreme levels of poverty in the north-west (verging on starvation) served to catalyse China's campaign to reduce rural poverty. At the time, this campaign was mainly intended to boost agricultural infrastructure, construction and farmland development, improving the conditions of agricultural production and increasing agricultural development. Within today's development community, we tend to categorise such campaigns as 'regional development'. The strategy lasted until the end of the twentieth century. In 1994, China launched its Seven-year Poverty Alleviation Programme, aiming to meet basic food and clothing needs within the impoverished population. This programme mainly sought to create basic conditions for regional economic development and to develop skills among the poor population and thus help them to escape poverty. It did not directly focus on helping individuals out of poverty.

This campaign to alleviate rural poverty before the end of the twentieth century has been studied by many scholars. One popular view is that regional, development-oriented poverty reduction created better conditions for the poor's development and increased incomes, but it failed to target specific groups. According to this account, poverty alleviation and development worked to the advantage of relatively affluent groups and did not adequately meet the needs of impoverished populations. In the early twenty-first century, the Chinese government began to recognise the seriousness of poverty and the failures of previous measures. Hoping to resolve these problems through new strategies and policies, it attempted to construct feasible mechanisms to target poor populations, developing the first 10-year rural poverty alleviation outline. At that time, I proposed that if impoverished villages could be identified as the basic unit for poverty interventions, anti-poverty strategies could better focus on the population's needs. The assumption was that the poor villages were those where poor populations were more concentrated. With this approach, I hoped to establish an accurate mechanism for identifying and concentrating on impoverished demographics. The proposal was adopted, and in the year 2001, 148,000 villages were identified nationwide as targets for anti-poverty efforts.

Several years later, Professor Wang and his team evaluated village-based poverty alleviation which began in 2001. He found that the programme steered more anti-poverty funds into poor villages and that villagers' average incomes were indeed increased as a result of participation. This indicated that the anti-poverty funds were better allocated and concentrated on the right demographics. Wang also found, however, that richer households benefited more from these funds than poorer households and argued that targeted village-based assistance thus did not necessarily improve the incomes of poor populations. This came to be the general consensus on village-based poverty alleviation measures.

I do not fully agree with this view. First, poor villages are poorer than non-poor ones in general, as long as the income increase in poor villages was significantly higher after receiving the programme's support than that in non-poor villages, one could say that the targeting mechanism had played a role in improving the lives of the poor. Secondly, the disparity between rich and poor had existed everywhere, including in these poor villages, and it didn't make much sense to further divide the village population into 'poor' and 'affluent' since these identified villages in general were poor. Thirdly, if we insisted to divide people in poor villages into 'poor' and 'affluent', the poorest group would usually comprise the elderly, weak, sick and disabled and those who could not work, who were not specifically the target of the poverty alleviation programme but more the target of the rural subsistence allowance programme. Of course, this didn't mean that village-based anti-poverty policies could not have been made more accurate in targeting needy populations, but rather that it was only indirectly aiming at the very poorest. Therefore, technically speaking, before 2012 when China launched its targeted poverty reduction strategy (except for the rural subsistence allowance), China did not have an effective mechanism that could directly aid poor populations.

In 2012, China's rural poverty reduction campaign entered a new stage. By this stage, great changes had occurred in both macro socio-economic development and micro-level development of the poor populations. When measured against the previous low poverty line, income poverty was already eliminated; as discussed, however, China in 2011 identified a new absolute poverty line, leading to the increase of the officially-recognised poor population to 122 million. Although this large number was in fact relatively low when held against the total population, the Chinese government planned to achieve a moderately prosperous society within a tight time-frame, and determined that by 2020 rural absolute poverty should not exist on this scale. Eradicating rural absolute poverty thus became an important objective for China, within which the doctrine of 'leaving no-one behind' also grew in significance. Anti-poverty programmes targeting poverty at the level of the individual thus became an important aspect of government policy.

In pressing ahead with such targeted poverty reduction programmes, those who were engaged in this work found it was necessary to identify not only poor populations, but also the causes of their poverty. While analysing the reasons for poverty and the effects of various poverty reduction policies, researchers and decision-makers realised that the patterns of rural poverty were thoroughly different from 2012 onwards.

First, poor populations came from the bottom of society and were trapped in deep and persistent cycles of poverty. As I argue, they were caught in a poverty trap from which it was difficult to escape. This situation differed from the universal poverty of the 1980s: at that point, an agricultural productivity boosting policy alone would lift tens of thousands of poor people out of poverty. In 2012, the problem of poverty was unlikely to be resolved by an increase in agricultural production, or any singular policy. Second, China's economic structure had completely changed if compared to the 1990s, and economic activities that benefited the poor were becoming fewer and fewer. As society raised the requirements for employees, many poor individuals, including the young and physically strong, found it difficult to engage in mainstream economic activities. For example, when I visited China's largest group meal catering group, the founder introduced me to the workshop of their unicorn company (a privately owned startup company). The workshop was filled with young people busily working on computers. These young people were all college graduates. In the past, it would have been unimaginable that one had to graduate from college to be employed by a catering group. This example vividly showcases the changes within China's economic structure. Thirdly, over the past 20 years, social inequality has intensified and the gap between rich and poor has widened.

In these circumstances, it was very difficult to help individuals to emerge from poverty. General anti-poverty measures were unlikely to be sufficient. In early 2012, many local areas still continued earlier practises of support and assistance, sending a few chicks or pigs to impoverished households; these measures, however, typically did not work. To eradicate poverty, structural factors that hinder the wellbeing of the poor and their escape from poverty must be shattered. This was hard to be put into practise, but efforts had been made. Different government departments had undertaken various development projects: forestry departments converted farmland into forests, agriculture departments transformed slopes into terraces and civil affairs departments mounted subsistence allowance programmes. These could have an impact on poverty reduction, but they did not target the left-behind poor villages and households. In China, only poverty alleviation offices undertook programmes targeting poor villages and households. Fragmented, department-based bureaucratic interests limited the flow of centralised resources to impoverished areas and populations. In this context, without unconventional political mobilisation, it was unlikely that the departmental interests of the bureaucratic system could be overcome.

To eradicate rural absolute poverty by 2020 required massive funds, which would be far from enough if only relying on government input. This goal required resources from many other sources rather than the government. Since it was difficult to mobilise large-scale, social resources through conventional mechanisms, unconventional mechanisms were necessary. One such case was the 10,000 enterprises helping 10,000 poor villages campaign which was co-initiated by government departments and private sector associations in China. The work also faced other challenges. Since there were not enough professionals and human resources available in poor villages to properly execute planned initiatives, some government staff members or SOE youth talents were seconded to targeted villages to develop and implement plans with impoverished local groups, the so-called village first secretary campaign. Such anti-poverty work was a complete change from the previous-stage tactic of helping the poor shake off poverty gradually, over the course of economic development. This represented an unconventional approach. Since 2013 to 2020, as a result, the Chinese leadership had coordinated targeted poverty alleviation work and made unconventional changes to its leadership systems, funding channels and social mobilisation mechanisms, including the inclusion of poverty reduction outcomes in assessment of performance of government officials. With these steps, a mobilised poverty reduction campaign took shape. In execution, the campaign displayed certain characteristics of a 'battle' or a 'war'. This was how China's fight against poverty had turned into a war in the 2010s.

Can Poverty Be Overcome by Developing Industries?

Industrial development is central to poverty reduction. The state can play a role in this by setting industrial policy, but this doesn't always work.

In previous chapters we have considered the nature of poverty and its origins, and I have argued that the commitment of the government to eradicate poverty is a crucial determinant of whether improvement can take place. But what does the government have in its arsenal? Beyond the 'obvious' options, such as education, healthcare and social protection, it can also lift people out of poverty *indirectly*, notably through infrastructure and industrial policy. For many, this will be quite an obvious statement. Any online search for topics related to poverty reduction will yield a flood of successes which have industry-fuelled growth at their heart. Industrial development has an enormous role in overcoming poverty: a rising tide may not quite lift *all* boats, but it will lift most, and growth is quite a rising tide.

The natural question to ask is: How? This is a subject on which many bottles of ink have been spilled. The debate over the role of the central government in the industrial policy of Korea and Japan has been going on for decades and has sparked numerous efforts to copy their success across the developing world. At points, I have been involved personally in industrial policy discussions. Most agree that industrial policy can be transformational for poverty reduction; fewer agree on how to make it a sure thing. Government assistance to developing industries can greatly help, but it always comes with something of a risk. Industrial policy requires 'gambling' on particular sectors [1]. If the bets pay off and the sectors grow successfully, the returns can be large and poverty rates can fall. If the bets are bad, the sectors fail to grow, and money may have been wasted. In the late 1990s, I advised the leadership of Yunnan Province to speedily promote the local flower industry. Sensibly, the Yunnan government sought to learn from how similar efforts had succeeded elsewhere; at the request of the then-vice governor, Liu Jing, I lectured senior officials across the province on the flower industry in the Netherlands. The gamble has paid off. Yunnan now produces over 18 billion stems of fresh-cut flowers annually and exports them to more than forty countries.[1] Today, we have built a city-driven rural revitalisation experiment zone in Kunming, the capital city of Yunnan. Many local villages in this zone are also developing a flower industry. The flower industry has become a pillar of rural poverty reduction in Kunming and has supported the growth of local affluence over the past 20 years. As time passes, similar 'gambles' are being considered in new areas. Over the past few decades, industrial development has provided the strongest impetus for lifting rural areas out of poverty and encouraging prosperity.

Over the past few years, industrial development targeted deliberately for poverty reduction has become one of the most important policies for eradicating absolute rural poverty. With policy support, many poverty reduction projects have been developed. They have often served as good foundations for poor regions to shake off poverty, but not always: in China, we often hear about news of poor sales of oranges, garlic and apples online. This is unsurprising given that, as we know, industrial policy normally involves something of a gamble.

An emergent strategy in the battle against poverty is consumption, as direct government planning has matched poverty reduction projects with developing industries. Recently, I and other local senior officials visited an online live-stream sale of local agricultural products. We marvelled at the high sales records and the ability of e-commerce to connect supply and enormous market demand so effectively, knowing that achieving this is key to alleviating poverty in many rural areas. On the other hand, we couldn't help but ask: is this way of answering market demand sustainable, and is the current industrial policy-focused poverty reduction strategy a sustainable approach to overcome poverty?

Our economic and agricultural structures have changed profoundly compared with the 1980s, 1990s, and even the early twenty-first century.

[1] Data source: This is according to 2022, 2023 statistics, see floral daily. https://www.floraldaily.com/article/9553551/technologies-powering-cut-flower-industry-in-china-s-yunnan/. Note by the translator.

In general, agricultural products are in rich supply, a supply realised through increased production and rising imports. In fact I would go further and argue that some agricultural products are in *excessive* supply. In this context, picking the right industries to build up in order to reduce poverty can be far harder. Some areas only have the capacities for a small range of industries, and these industries may no longer be viable if the goal is poverty reduction. A few years ago I visited a poverty reduction project in a township which was initiated by the township government. I questioned the township leadership on their decision to raise cattle, given the high costs and the fact that neighbouring areas were also investing in livestock. When I visited the place some years later, I found the farmers had sold all the cattle and that the cowsheds were now empty. A gamble on a sector needs to bear comparative advantage in mind; this town overlooked competition, or were over-optimistic. Perhaps also they may have believed that they did not have many other options, and chose to invest and merely hope that the bet would pay off. Whatever their rationale, it did not work.

In China it is not uncommon to see online appeals for customers to buy impoverished farmers' kiwifruits and apples. This reflects the potential awkwardness of the poverty reduction approach through industrial development. If the gamble fails, it is hard to redeem the effort without resorting to a more conventional philanthropic approach.

Whether industrial poverty reduction programmes can eventually increase the poor's incomes depends on various conditions. First, if there is real market demand for the industry's output, it is more likely to be a promising option. Of course, things can still go wrong in terms of logistics, funding, implementation and so on. In agriculture, farmers that develop new products that have not yet been launched in the Chinese market can especially benefit. But the market will catch up with changes very soon. The Fuji apples and kiwis first planted in the 1990s offer a good example of this. Before the 1990s, Chinese people mostly ate Ralls apples, and Fuji apples were something rare and prized. At that time we found these new Fuji apples so big and sweet, but after twenty years of development, Fuji apples have become very common and Ralls apples, ironically, are preferred. The apple market is now oversupplied with Fuji apples, and the need to keep prices competitive has seen Fuji apples become less profitable. Areas that now decide to develop Fuji apples will probably face fierce market competition, and it would no longer be a smart investment. Where the state gets involved in 'picking winners' and setting up subsidy schemes or more, the nimbleness needed to respond to market shifts and adapt might be lost. This does not mean that the state should not intervene, but that we must recognise that there are trade-offs and risks.

Second, the industries to be developed should be sustainable. Agriculture requires relatively heavy upfront investment and a long cycle to generate earnings. Agricultural sectors that offer unstable incomes and unreliable returns can fail to reduce poverty without considerable patience in state support. If the support to the selected industry requires too short a repayment cycle, there might be no poverty reduction effect. In 2015, I saw many areas in the south of Yunnan transform slopes into terraces to grow macadamia nuts with the support of industrial poverty reduction projects. It took four to five years for the plants to bear fruit, and farmers only began to earn money from around 2020. I confirmed the earnings with a few farmers but noticed that local production of macadamia nuts was excessive and wondered if the value of this crop would fall like the now unsellable kiwifruits and Chinese dates. If everyone develops the same product, even with generous state support, no one gets richer. When I exchanged ideas on industrial poverty reduction with the locals, I always encouraged them to develop small-scale, unique industries that could not be easily replicated. If other areas could easily copy their products, their industrial brand would soon be multiplied and faked, eventually crashing the industry.

Third, following the above, industrial projects for poverty reduction is intended to increase incomes *through market mechanism*. Ideally, the government should support firms and industries to supply goods for which there is a market demand. Where this is successful, a demand is met—potentially making other sectors more productive, those firms supported by the state become successful, driving employment and prosperity, and the state receives a return on its investment, either through direct repayment or through fiscal benefits. It goes without saying that this does not always happen. In many circumstances, 'poverty reduction through industrial development' has been driven by government actors quite unqualified to make important choices. Government interventions have often gone beyond providing capital and technical training: it has in some cases set the direction of entire local markets. This is often not for good reasons. I have encountered local industries that have been blindly promoted simply because a few senior local officials heard some information about successes in other areas. Although we heard about successful cases of industrial poverty reduction on TV and online, when we paid field visits to poor areas, we encountered many cases that went wrong because they had deviated from the market mechanism. Government needs to leave opportunities for innovation and market adaptation; attempts to micro-manage firms, especially when government decision-makers have inadequate information, are useless or worse for poverty reduction.

How much hope should we place in government interventions to transform poverty? I would first say that many decision-makers are overly optimistic. They should be looking to eliminate poverty, and then consider how to create prosperity. Instead, the two are often made de facto synonymous, perhaps because politicians are too ambitious. Poverty today has a different meaning from back in the 1980s. Poverty at that time was the product of regional economic underdevelopment, exemplified by Hexi and Dingxi in Gansu and Xihaigu in Ningxia (the 'Sanxi Areas' or three western areas). I was born in these relatively deprived Sanxi Areas. I never took a bath until I moved to another province at the age of eleven. When I spent the summer holidays with my relatives in rural areas, I saw everyone in their family wear the same clothes everyday. This was quite common at the time, and things were not much better in cities. Such universal poverty was caused by under-development. Without developing these areas, there is no way to support such a large population in escaping poverty.

Second, there is plenty of room for hope—but only some of it is attributable to direct state interventions of the sort discussed above. Many of my relatives in northern Shaanxi travel to Beijing to visit my retired mother. When I see them, I love asking about how my home county has changed. When I asked my relatives about the village of cave-houses I had visited, they said it had been left empty, and the villagers had mostly moved away. In this sense, they had all escaped poverty. This was not the result of purposeful support, but of an economic and social transformation. Of the drivers of poverty reduction in China, the most important is industrialisation and urbanisation. Industrial sectors are high-income, and cities are places where incomes are higher. Once people get into these sectors and spaces, their welfare status will change (Of course, moving to a city does not necessarily mean that poor people will be lifted out of poverty. In many developing nations, farmers have ended up in slums after moving to the city.)

Poverty reduction today is intended to ease *relative* poverty, poverty relative to prosperity. Thus, unlike the problem of absolute poverty in the

1980s, contemporary poverty is more about inequality. Inequality-based poverty cannot be addressed solely through socio-economic development and transformation; targeted poverty reduction is still necessary. By nature, pro-poor policy does not aim to help the poor become prosperous: it is a basic action to safeguard social justice, not a social campaign to promote wealth. In this sense, I'm afraid I have to disagree with investing an abundance of funds into poverty reduction projects that develop industries. I believe it is better to name these projects straightforwardly 'industrial development': they can assist capable groups in realising prosperity through access to market competition, but in this sense public services and public resources are used to support the 'non-poor' groups to reduce costs and guard against market risks, which may further widening the gap between the rich and the poor.

Industrial poverty reduction is no panacea. It will first benefit the capable and educated—even among the poor populations. It may help with poverty reduction when the majority of a society are poor. But when the size of the poor population has been reduced, and especially when the majority of the poor are elderly, sick, disabled, or illiterate, this approach can often fail to work, not entirely impossible (a positive case being the innovative anti-poverty workshops that encourage the disabled to work), but to a large extent so. The few left-behind poor can hardly be lifted out of poverty by such industrial development policies.

The Role of Urbanisation

> Village combination has caused many controversies in China, but an important question related in this debate is how to address poverty.

In June 2020, I paid a brief visit to the Jiguan Community in Guandu District, Kunming City, Yunnan. Previously three separate villages, it is now a built-up community, quite modern, in which every household lives in a hundred-square-metre apartment and owns a further two seventy-five-square-metre replacement apartments. Ten years before, I was told, it had only seven brick houses, narrow roads and poor health conditions within the community. The per capita annual income then was below RMB2,000. Looking at the community in 2020, I could hardly imagine how it would have looked ten years ago. Now, the community has hired farmers as cleaners, landscapers, security guards and community managers. The farmers lease their two additional replacement apartments for rent, which alone provided over RMB100,000 for each household annually.

Additionally, they received an annual RMB40,000–50,000 dividend per person from rent from office buildings and residential houses built on the community's collective land. This had become, in other words, a prosperous community. All the households had cars and lived in apartment buildings. While the Jiguan Community was a successful representative of the policy of village combination, the process in which small hamlets are combined to form larger communities, it was also lucky: not all communities enjoyed such good outcomes from this policy. An earlier similar merger in Shandong had sparked heated discussion, since the majority of the community members opposed this change. In Jiguan I could not quite believe that formerly impoverished farmers now lived in this garden-like community, so I visited a few residents at random. The clean and tidy staircases reminded me of my visit to local residential buildings in Tokyo. Except for the less fashionable interior furnishings, everything else here was identical to homes in the affluent cities.

I was further reminded of a community I lived in in the 1990s, Shangdi Dongli, the earliest commercial community in Haidian District, Beijing, when the housing privatisation reform in China just began. It was quite common to see groups of topless men sitting around the community in summer, fanning themselves and chatting. They were the farmers who lived in the Shangdi Village, the place where the new community was built up. Today, the housing prices in Shangdi Dongli are approximately RMB80,000 per square metre, and I would hypothesise that after the village combination Shangdi Village was no longer in poverty. But when I asked one of my students to research the public response to village combination, and they identified similar results to today's opposition to village combination.

The reasons for the controversy around village combination are quite understandable. Merging villages recklessly is very risky, and the process should be undertaken with great care. Even then, it will be impossible for all Chinese villages to change their economic situation this way. However, since populism has increasingly become politically right, any statement on village combination could easily be labelled wrong. Frankly speaking, having visited the Jiguan Community, I believe that a case like this could support village combination. I'm not using a single case to refute those opposed to the concept of village combination; indeed, I agree with some of the opposing opinions, arguing that abruptly moving farmers from their scattered farmhouses to concentrated high-rise apartments would bring not only economic and political interruptions, but also social and cultural ramifications. However, an important question involved in this debate is how to address poverty.

I have mentioned that poverty is relative and that definitions and standards of poverty are developed in the context of modern welfare. If measured by modern poverty standards, rural areas would need to be thoroughly renovated. However, as I mentioned before, many impoverished villages didn't regard themselves as poor. This disparity touches on the very core of development: questions like 'What is development?', and, 'Do we need development at all?' As a developmentalist, I tend to advocate changes, and I am hardly convinced by the ruralist idea that the farmers should maintain the status quo.

In China, the outbreak of COVID-19 in 2020 began in cities, while rural areas experienced limited impacts in the first stage. Consequently, many people pointed out that the countryside was relatively free from the pandemic. I wrote a short article to refute this argument, saying that the pandemic didn't begin in the countryside may be subject to specific conditions, one can not thus extrapolate that the countryside is a safe haven from the virus. In one way, overpopulation in cities provided better conditions for the pandemic to spread, but in the other, the poorer health public service and awareness in rural areas may render the countryside a bigger victim to the deadly communicable disease. In 2021 my students and I visited Hebian Village to assess the influence of COVID-19 and proved that the pandemic did not penetrate into the countryside in the same way as it did in cities. Whereas work in cities was interrupted, and incomes were reduced, villagers in Hebian said they were barely susceptible to COVID-19's consequences. Though incomes from guestrooms dropped for some time, they had a comfortable house to live in and invested more time to agricultural activities to feed the family and make up losses from the guestroom business. This probably explains why many perceive the countryside as a risk buffer. But I have to say, countryside can be a risk buffer in some way doesn't mean it needs to stay where it is; it faces too many risks when it is poor.

I have proposed that agriculture should be one of the main drivers for poverty reduction in Africa. The renowned economist, Professor Paul Collier from the University of Oxford, disagreed, believing it was impossible to reduce poverty through rural mechanisms. He held that the only feasible way to eradicate poverty was industrialisation. He said to me that all countries that had a remarkable record on poverty reduction were highly urbanised: the root cause behind Africa's poverty trap was its low urbanisation rate. In the essentials, I agreed with him. Industrialisation and urbanisation were key to economic growth which were the main driving forces for poverty reduction. I did not mean that poverty reduction solely depended on agriculture or rural development; instead, I suggested that industrialisation and urbanisation should not *skip* agricultural and rural development, since the latter could contribute to poverty reduction in the first place and provide foundations for the former, in particular when it came to countries that had a big rural population.

If measured by modern welfare standards, the residents of the Jiguan Community have long been lifted out of poverty. The community director told me they were extremely poor in the past, making a living merely on rice and migrant work, but now things were different. Urbanisation has completely changed this village. Farmers become urban residents, they live in high-rise buildings, they have stable jobs, they enjoy urban public service and welfare, their children go to city schools. There is no way to turn all poor Chinese communities into urban communities, like what happened in Jiguan. However, if most villages still remain traditional rural communities, it will be challenging to lift them out of poverty by modern welfare standards.

Can Subsistence Allowance Help?[2]

The subsistence allowance supports over 40 million impoverished people. It is costly, and implementation can be challenging; by itself it is not enough.

Rural households considered to be below the state poverty line or living standards receive support through several government transfer programmes. These programmes, including various poverty reduction programmes and the subsistence allowance schemes, have grown considerably in recent years. Eligibility is calculated against an agreed 'poverty line' or minimum living-cost line: households earning less than a given

[2] Published at Narada Insights (2016-10-17) at https://www.aapchina.org.cn/node/84 (the original article has been deleted).

amount in a year, relative to the number of dependents and wider situation, will be given access to grant schemes intended to support them. In the case of subsistence allowance system, people living with extreme difficulties including seniors, minors and those with disabilities who have no capacity or means to support themselves can be beneficiaries. Eligible households are historically, and increasingly, likely to be located in poor rural areas, where there is less opportunity for self-reliance.

Identifying eligible households can be challenging and controversial, especially at the local level, when there are only very minor differences between villagers' living conditions. Given that a lot hangs on identification as an impoverished household, the decision-making processes can become highly locally politicised. The process for eligibility determination introduces power struggles, resulting in village officials and relatively rich groups trying to squeeze into this category to capture the free transferred resources. Even where this problem does not arise, the similarity of village households' living conditions can oblige relatively arbitrary decision-making or force local governments to practise equal allocation, in which the subsistence allowance may be evenly granted to all farmer households, adopting a yearly rotation strategy. This can be a common phenomenon in poor villages. These rare and much-coveted subsistence resources are distributed under complex rural social and political conditions. Because of this, grant schemes do not always succeed in combating poverty: they may instead only succeed in enriching local networks of 'elites', or fail to help the most needed due to the tensions between resource limits and village egalitarianism.

Identifying needy groups requires a rigorous bookkeeping system and reliable income statistics. This is important both practically and politically. The authenticity and validity of this system must be widely recognised by villagers. Otherwise, any method for identifying households eligible for support—and maybe more so, for determining households' exit from support mechanisms—would be highly controversial. Even when households' eligibility and exit are decided by open discussion among villagers, methods of identifying households eligible to receive the subsistence allowance and households categorised as 'in poverty' remained vague.

In the countryside, it is easiest to identify households in extreme poverty or difficulties. Identifying the neediest households among those who have similar poverty situations is considerably harder. Generally, the households in extreme poverty, which indisputably qualify for supports through state grants, are a subset of the larger group of eligible households, most of which are households in poverty to different degrees. Inevitably, there are not sufficient resources to support all the households that could be eligible, and some arguably impoverished households must be excluded. To make these decisions less controversial, participatory practises of open review, in which villages appraise households for their eligibility for transfers, have been introduced. Because of the insufficiency of funds, however, these practises remain a process of formal consensus-building, or rubber-stamping, rather than an authentic investigation of needs. Even after this 'democratic' appraisal, some villagers will still dispute the list of eligible households submitted for subsistence allowance.

Some impoverished farmers who really do urgently need the subsistence allowance will sometimes not be covered after the village appraisal. There are many cases in which those who are not covered are just as poor as those who are covered. In some cases, excluded farmers feel angry and frustrated. They wonder, understandably, why others are considered entitled to aid while they are not. Some will even resort to 'revenge' actions on those who, in their eyes, are responsible for the 'unfair' appraisal result.

In recent years' rising populist wave, government has increased its attention to the plight of the vulnerable; at the same time, it also keeps increasing financial coverage for the vulnerable groups, partly a response to the populist outrage. Despite limited financial resources, the number of qualified households increased, reducing the intensity of support available to individual households. From 2012 to 2021, when prices kept going up, the size of the average rural subsistence allowance had increased by 2.1 times, and over 40 million people came to be supported [2]. In the first six months of 2023, RMB 126.5 billion was provided in subsistence allowances, extreme poverty aid and temporary assistance grants [3]. I question whether the expansion of coverage and grant sizes has been truly effective. In my view, rural subsistence allowance policies have expanded its coverage too fast, risking undermining the effectiveness of support to the poorest and the most needed. I thus suggest government to give priority to improving the identification and exit mechanisms.

Fighting rural poverty remains a complex thing. It also needs professional talents and skills, which the government is often falling short of. The shortage is even bigger for township level government since the lower the administrative level the harder to get competent people, and all rural poverty policies in China will ultimately go to the township level—the basic level for administrative divisions in China—for implementation. In this context, my advice is that the government could purchase anti-poverty services from civil society actors, since there are hundreds of thousands of civil organisations in China. Poverty reduction by social organisations can make up for the government's insufficient organisational and human resources. By sharing the government's political and social responsibilities, this could help mitigate the risk of potential conflicts or tensions between the government and the public.

Is Policy-Driven Poverty Reduction Sustainable?

Targeted, direct, time-capped policies are not equal to sustained support for accessing better opportunities.

How much control do policymakers have over poverty reduction? When can they congratulate themselves, and when must they simply acknowledge that they can not shape the outcomes? I used to use the term 'policy-driven poverty reduction' quite frequently. But to my mind, it is not very accurate. Amid China's economic and social transformation, mitigating and reducing poverty, especially absolute poverty, is never viewed as having happened spontaneously. It always required support from poverty-reducing policies. Since policies were held to drive poverty reduction, the idea of 'policy-driven poverty reduction' was above reproach. However, we must discuss the role of forceful policy-driven poverty reduction when reducing and eradicating absolute poverty becomes a political agenda, and whether this direct policy intervention is really sustainable.

With the Reform and Opening-Up, begun in 1978, the Chinese government embarked on a deliberate process of economic revival intended to allow independent innovation and greater integration with the global economy. In the early days of the reform era, some in the Chinese government realised the state of destitution in some areas. Policies began to be developed aiming to overcome poverty and rescue 'left-behind' populations. In the mid-1990s, the first national 'campaign' on poverty was initiated and called the 'Seven-year Poverty Reduction Programme', which officially concluded in the early twenty-first century. Its goal was to meet basic needs for food and clothing by the end of the twentieth century, satisfying universal needs in rural China through policy-driven poverty reduction projects. In the strategy for rural poverty alleviation and development for 2000–2010, clauses concerning meeting rural needs for food and clothing were re-stipulated. This meant that though hunger-based poverty in rural China had been effectively erased by the end of the twentieth century, the goal of meeting basic needs for food and clothing had not yet been fully attained. Policy-driven poverty reduction was now recognised to be somewhat unstable and hard to maintain: success could be obtained in a given place and for a given period, but there would always be the risk of different populations sliding back into poverty.

In recent years, unparalleled attention has been paid to Chinese rural poverty, and the cause has been elevated to that of a national battle against poverty. The goal of eradicating rural absolute poverty by 2020 was prioritised as the paramount political task, a 'sword of Damocles' hanging over the head of government officials at all levels. 'Policy-driven poverty reduction' was intensified in the following ways.

First, eradicating absolute rural poverty by 2020 became the primary task for the secretary general of the CPC Central Committee and Party secretaries at provincial, city, county, township and village levels. The 'first secretary' led poverty reduction work at all levels. Second, human, material and financial resources of all types were concentrated, and society was mobilised to support the poorest areas and populations. In such a battle, areas and people in poverty gained new access to external support. Third, strict assessment systems were put in place, and government officials' performance evaluations were pegged to assessment results. As a result, people in poverty secured a series of anti-poverty support packages, ranging from focused interventions intended to meet basic needs to broader initiatives increasing income through industrial development, educational assistance, health aid and social security. Over the past few years, the Chinese rural population in absolute poverty plunged from 98.99 million in 2012 by the current standard to 5.51 million by the end of 2019, and to 0 by the end of 2020. I attributed this massive eradication of poverty to policy-driven reasons.

What is the difference between the policy-driven poverty reduction of the twentieth century and that of the twenty-first? First, though rural poverty alleviation started in the early 1980s, coverage was limited, and the basket of anti-poverty policies (including the identification of impoverished households) deployed in the current 'battle' were not available then. In the early stage, poverty policy was merely intended to improve agricultural production conditions in impoverished areas. Even in the later stage until the 2010s, the concept underpinning the poverty policy was still development-centred, i.e., to promote regional development so it can help people get out poverty. In a more strict sense, people shook off poverty on their own feet, they were intrinsically motivated by their desire to escape poverty and become wealthy. They made good use of policies rolled out in the big context of reform and opening-up, in some cases they even pushed for policy changes to happen like what we saw in the Xiaogang Village case back in 1978. In the most recent decade (since 2012, 2013), things have changed. It was not that the poor were not intrinsically motivated to escape poverty, but rather, the state had elevated poverty reduction to an unprecedented high level on its agenda, and various poverty policies targeted at the impoverished households and individuals were introduced, one after another, 'pushing' people to get out of poverty.

Second, new poverty reduction mechanisms emerged since poverty is caused for different reasons in different stages. For a long period after reform and opening up was begun, the poor population in China was huge, and the entire country was in general economically underdeveloped. Poverty then was to a large extent due to lack of development. When pro-growth strategies and policies were carried out, capable but impoverished farmers were the first to benefit. They gradually became more affluent, leaving poverty behind—and often benefited from new opportunities in different ways, as exemplified by farmers in Zhejiang and Jiangsu that left their rural homes to engage in business. Industrialisation and urbanisation, as I argued in previous sections, had become driving forces behind China's massive poverty reduction. Yet by the twenty-first century, the remaining rural population in poverty found it increasingly difficult to escape poverty through migrant work or small business activities. In theory, the higher the economic level and inequality level, the more difficult to overcome poverty through individual efforts. Serious income inequality may contribute to the so-called poverty trap. Under these circumstances, strong policy intervention will become imperative to lift marginal groups from poverty.

Under such conditions, 'policy-driven poverty reduction' faced problems of stability and sustainability. First, with strong policy interventions in place, many impoverished rural groups relied on 'external support', such as paired assistance[3] and pro-poor consumption programmes,[4] which are mainly driven by the state. Poverty was only alleviated while state support was being given; once paired assistance through consumption was suspended, the incomes of the poor would soon be undermined. In the battle against poverty, the outcomes and impacts of infrastructure construction, housing renovation, educational support and health aid were relatively stable, but other anti-poverty policy measures, especially the industrial development ones, can face big sustainability challenge. Second, 'policy-driven poverty reduction' was sensitive to shocks, exemplified by the impact of COVID-19 on farmers in poor areas.

But, for those who have long been mired in the poverty trap, the way out of poverty still depends on policy, and the intensity of interventions has to be high enough to pull them out. It's very interesting if we compare how people fight poverty in Europe and in the United States. The anti-poverty policy interventions are much stronger in Europe than in the United States, and the inequality and poverty rates are far lower in former than in the latter. But the sustainability challenges are bigger in the former than in the latter. Sustainability challenge should be addressed by fostering long-term institutional mechanisms rather than short-term policy campaigns that tend to have short-term, unsustainable effects. On this account, in the post-2020 zero absolute poverty era,[5] China should refocus its efforts on developing long-term mechanisms that help prevent poverty, rather than continue its campaign- and battle-type anti-poverty policies. The latter would consume too much resources and even generate re-poverty problems.

[3] Collaboration and paired assistance between eastern and western regions is a major move to achieve the goal of common prosperity, with the more developed areas helping the less developed areas. Note by the translator.

[4] Pro-poor consumption is an approach for all sectors of society to help the poor through purchasing products and services provided by the poor. In China, government departments, SOEs, even private enterprises rolled out similar pro-poor consumption or procurement programmes that prioritised poor areas as their procurement sources. However, these programmes may to different degrees run counter to the principles of a market economy. The prices of these products and service are often higher, but the quality are not always higher. Note by the translator.

[5] China has announced the victory of the battle against poverty (from 2012 to 2020) that by 2020 it has eradicated all its remaining rural absolute poverty measured by its national poverty line. Note by the translator.

Eyeing Both 'Increment' and 'Stock'[6]

To fight poverty, policies must be both reactive, assisting the impoverished in improving wellbeing and escaping poverty, and proactive, seeking to keep people from falling back into poverty.

Some three, four decades ago, general welfare in China was incomparable to that of today, and China was a low-income country, poverty, however, was not part of the public discourse at the time. This was partly due to relatively low inequality level, and the public's limited information and understanding of poverty and other countries' development levels.

After institutional constraints for economic development are removed and the economy has taken off, an emergent priority for many countries would be how to make growth benefit the poor, especially when the trickle down effect of growth weakens amid rising inequality. China is no exception.

Along with rapid economic growth and urbanisation, regional disparities in development conditions and opportunities widened and income gaps increased, which was particular so in the beginning of the twenty-first century. In this new period of time, the state of poverty in rural China changed. Due to rapid industrialisation and urbanisation, many rural people were left behind the fast train of development, living in what could be characterised as transitional, short-term or interim poverty. Most of them, due to enhanced individual capacities, or improved access to economic opportunities, or expanded social safety net, could escape poverty, sooner or later, by seizing opportunities in development. By contrast, others would be caught in the poverty trap, unable to escape vicious cycles of low earnings, low opportunity and slow state support. These vulnerable demographics were also at risk of falling back into poverty traps even when they escaped. I refer to this as the increment of poverty, a constant teetering population that could with any one of a range of small shocks fall back over the cliff. Second, the intergenerational transmission of poverty and the poverty trap reduced some people to so-called absolute poverty. I refer to this demographic as the stock of

[6] Published at *National Governance Weekly* (2015-10-16) at http://www.rmlt.com.cn/2015/1016/405324.shtml.

poverty: they were at the bottom of the cliff, not teetering, and would only climb up over a long period and with extensive external support.

As those who remained poor were those who remained alienated from the main sectors powering economic growth, the capacity of overall economic growth to reduce poverty lessened. Given that the relative economic value of agriculture (an industry that effectively reduced poverty in rural areas) had declined (agriculture's GDP share in China has dropped from 28% in 1978 to 7% in 2023 according to China's National Bureau of Statistics), conventional small-scale anti-poverty measures based on agricultural development were unlikely to solve the remaining poverty in rural areas.

In recent years, the subject of poverty has again attracted greater and closer attention because the rate of decrease in poverty has slowed. In other words, under current economic and social conditions, the chance for the poor to shake off poverty is slim. It appears that most impoverished people have fallen into a structural poverty trap. The low-hanging fruit has already been picked, and those who remain impoverished are impoverished because of a wider, deeper and more difficult range of problems. This presents a challenge for poverty reduction in the new era.

We cannot allow this situation to persist. Instead, I believe, China must redouble its ambition to assist those who remain trapped in poverty. We must look beyond reactive policies to instead try proactively to prevent transitional poverty from reoccurring. These people, mainly living in central and western areas, are mostly small-holder farmers or migrant workers. Except for some who will fall into absolute poverty, the majority of these people are just vulnerable. They can be kept from the poverty trap by maintaining the pace of economic growth, improving social security, ablocking the intergenerational transmission of poverty and refining human capital. Those who are living in absolute poverty mainly consist of marginal groups, often geographically isolated and with very limited opportunities. These people experience multi-dimensional poverty and find it hard to escape poverty without assistance. In this sense, rural poverty reduction in the new era should focus on reducing both the increment and stock of poverty.

The purpose of reducing the increment of poverty is to prevent vulnerable groups from falling into poverty. The original aspiration of rural poverty reduction policies was to support people limited by various regional and economic conditions and enable them to benefit from national economic growth. On the one hand, these policies targeted demographics who were able to work. On the other hand, these policies supported economic activities centring around agriculture. In areas with transformational challenges, if poverty reduction is always prioritised in economic and social development plans, these policies could play a role in keeping vulnerable groups at least linked to wider economic opportunities.

However, rural poverty reduction policies do not directly offer social security, aside from a small number of relocation and subsidised housing projects. They can create an environment that enables communities to escape poverty, but cannot directly meet the pressing needs of the migrant population and those who were left behind by their migrant families seeking jobs in towns and cities, nor can they directly block the intergenerational transmission of poverty. Except for a few areas endowed with unique resources that can support developing industries, most rural areas are unlikely to avoid falling into the poverty trap simply through small-scale agricultural production. Developing local comparative advantages, and integrating these areas better into the wider Chinese economy, will take time. In the meantime, poverty reduction strategies should aim for a big picture, not only supporting income-increasing economic activities, but also refining social security systems to effectively interrupt the intergenerational transmission of poverty. Poverty can beget poverty, and without support to allow development, the vicious cycles will not be broken.

To gradually reduce the stock of poverty is another priority in the fights against rural poverty. Unlike people in transitional poverty, the demographic that constitutes the 'stock' of poverty are mostly those in long-term poverty. They are poor in multiple dimensions and find it extremely difficult to overcome poverty. Those at the bottom of society need full protection, institutional support and social security because they are seldom in a position to benefit from general development-oriented poverty reduction policies. For them, special development measures that can generate much higher income, together with improved protection of social security, are very much needed.

From Regions to Households[7]

As China's poor become more geographically scattered, poverty reduction programmes must target at the household level.

Since the start of the Reform and Opening Up, China has made tremendous achievements in fighting poverty. Its headcount ratio of poverty fell from 72 percent in 1990 to 0.1 percent in 2019 and 2020 adopting World Bank's most recent extreme poverty line—USD2.15 per day. Rural absolute poverty was declared to be eradicated in 2020 based on China's national standard which is estimated to be a little bit higher than the Bank's extreme poverty line. These achievements were mainly attributable to three factors.

First, rural reform (started with the introduction of household responsibility system in 1979, shortly after the beginning of the Reform and Opening Up) laid an important foundation for rural poverty reduction. Before the rural reform began, farmers primarily engaged in farming and breeding, but the rural reform emancipated productive forces and added value to this primary industry. The agricultural sector maintained an average annual growth rate of 7 percent from 1978 to 1985 [4], and farmers' incomes rose rapidly.

Second, the development of non-agricultural industries provided a strong impetus for rural poverty reduction. Alongside the rapid development of agriculture, township and village enterprises (TVEs) also rose, driving a massive rural labour force to shift from agricultural sectors to non-agricultural industries and significantly elevating the incomes of former farmers, who found themselves in better-paid work, and those who remained farmers, who now had a better market for their goods.

Third, the urbanisation that accompanied industrialisation contributed significantly to rural poverty reduction. Since the 1990s, industrialisation and urbanisation have sped up. The rural labour force has continued to flow into industrial and urban areas, and rural residents have been able to increase their share of non-agricultural income. As rural reform and

[7] Published at *People's Daily* (2015-11-06) at http://rmrbimg2.people.cn/html/items/wap-share-rmrb/#/index/category/8//paper/detail/1629893_paper_1629893/normal.

development were largely inclusive, in addition, the benefits of economic development were soon shared by the large rural population.

In line with economic growth, the size of China's poor population steadily decreased. The nature of poverty itself also changed during this period. This happened for two reasons. First, the proportional economic value of farming and breeding, historically farmers' major sources of income, continued to decline at the national level, while other sectors grew. The share of agriculture in China's GDP dropped from 28.2 present in 1978 to 9.2 percent in 2014; by 2022, the agriculture, forestry and fishing sectors contributed only 7.2 percent of GDP between them.[8] With agriculture contributing less to farmers' income, farmers that relied on farming and breeding were less likely to experience an income rise, and more likely to slip into low-income categories or even poverty. Second, as China's economic structure was transformed and upgraded, people in economically developed, accessible areas could access a dividend of economic development more easily. However, rural populations that were living in economically and socially underdeveloped areas and had little market competitiveness and connectivity found it difficult to continue to share the dividends of economic growth.

Currently, the rural population in absolute poverty mainly consists of three groups: people in extreme poverty without the ability to work, people with heavy family burdens and large educational and medical expenses despite their ability to work, and people in adverse conditions for livelihood improvement despite their ability to work.

In the 1980s, China started to initiate large-scale development-oriented poverty reduction programmes. Since the country was financially struggling at the time, transfer payment programmes to the rural poor were largely skipped. Instead, counties were taken as the main target unit of poverty reduction programmes which were intended to create enabling conditions for impoverished populations to better participate in economic development. This mechanism succeeded in significantly boosting China's poverty reduction. For some years, however, it failed to offer targeted support for impoverished households, leading to a slowed decrease in poverty. As social and economic development proceeds and the poor population becomes increasingly geographically fragmented,

[8] Data source: Statistics from China's National Bureau of Statistics (NBS): https://www.stats.gov.cn. Note by the translator.

poverty eradication increasingly requires targeted approaches that directly aims at poor households.

China initiated its targeted poverty alleviation strategy in 2013, signalling the downgrade of target units from regions to households, and an integration of social security measures with income-increasing developmental measures. These established a basic framework for overcoming rural absolute poverty by the year 2020. By accurately identifying the target of support, arranging projects, using funds, taking measures aiming at households, dispatching teams to villages and ensuring anti-poverty progress, this targeted strategy aimed to maximise the efficiency of anti-poverty efforts, and leave no one behind in the process of building a moderately prosperous society.

'Assets' of the Poor[9]

Without opportunities, asset values stay low; but low assets themselves mean reduced opportunities and continued poverty. Poverty reduction approaches should look to rework processes as well as treat symptoms.

Today, poor populations in underdeveloped areas at the bottom of the income structure find it increasingly difficult to enjoy the benefits of economic growth. On the one hand, since the Reform and Opening-Up policy began in 1978, people are increasingly differentiated into different economic, political and social positions. On the other hand, pillar industries driving economic growth no longer have the same benefits for the poor that they used to, making a real change harder to bring about.

Part of this story concerns the gradual reduction in the share of the economy made up by agriculture. Historically, improvements in agriculture have had powerful poverty-reducing effects. But as the GDP share of agriculture declines, those who rely on farming now have a harder time improving their lives. Conventional low-intensity, small-scale poverty reduction measures based on agricultural development are now unlikely to solve rural poverty, especially deep poverty. Instead, a more comprehensive approach to address poverty is needed, which could include social

[9] Published at Guangming Net (2015-12-31) at http://theory.gmw.cn/2015-12/31/content_18320598.htm?utm_source=bshare&utm_campaign=bshare&utm_medium=weixin&bsh_bid=956759458&from=timeline&isappinstalled=0.

security to provide a safety net, transfers to top up assets and increase their value, diversification of incomes and assistance in utilising natural assets, to name but a few. Among them, it will also be important to seek, in innovative ways, to tap into the untapped resources—'the sleeping assets'—of the poor.

Despite rising incomes among the poor, many have nonetheless stayed poor. There may be two main reasons for this. First, marginal growth in income is insufficient to support the poor population in reaching a threshold level of initial assets, only above which can they start to accumulate [5]. This situation is made worse by the fact that wider economic growth can make education, health, infrastructure and so on, more expensive. Second, despite wider economic growth, pro-poor government transfer payments for education and medical services are not large enough to meet basic needs of the poor. As both the threshold for escaping the poverty trap and the starting point of social security for meeting basic needs are getting higher, limited anti-poverty financial support and small-scale agricultural production cannot be sufficient to lift the poor out of poverty. In this sense, increasing the value of the assets held by the poor could play a role. I have several suggestions in this regard.

Firstly, as the state pro-poor resources transferred to poor areas count as the poor's assets, earnings from these assets should remain in the hands of the poor. This may seem a very obvious point, but it does not always happen. For instance, many local pro-poor projects adopted the 'company plus farmer' approach, under which farmers used their rights to land management as their investment and could thus gain a proportional return. However, government's pro-poor investments on the land (things like infrastructure, agricultural materials, machinery) weren't regarded as the farmers' assets and thus could not turn into returns for farmers. In fact, returns from public resources put into the land usually went, in intangible forms, to external investors like companies. If this type of government assistance for the poor is instead converted into asset shares held by poor farmer participants, their stock of assets will increase by a large margin. Except for direct asset subsidies for housing and infrastructure, anti-poverty project funds allocated to poor households, often for the purpose of enabling development of specific agriculture-related activities, can be converted into asset shares by the poor, thus improving the poor's income-generating assets. This would prevent other groups and market entities from capturing returns, generated by public resources, that were meant for the poor.

Secondly, under new social and economic conditions, emphasis has always been put on supporting the poor's development through direct projects. What is often neglected is the potential economic value of the living and working spaces of the poor. In reality, many areas in deep poverty are mountain and forest zones with an admirable ecological environment. The potential economic value of the land, forest and even farmers' homesteads is usually far from being realised. In many such places, however, external market players have established, for example, a tourism industry to get profits from the poor community's rich natural endowment while the poor, the de facto 'owners' of the endowment, usually had very limited economic benefits. I am not against any market-oriented development that could utilise such natural resources in a sustainable way. As we can see, many of the qualities that have a potential to bring about economic opportunities, for instance, the mountain locations that make them possibly attractive to tourists, are also the causes of poverty—the isolation in areas with few economic opportunities and few connections to markets. To realise any proposed opportunities requires financial capital, human resources and technical capacity which these local communities lack, and which can be provided by external market players. The latter, thus, do deserve a return. But still, the poor local people should benefit in some way. More importantly, their human capital should be improved in the development process instead of just being replaced. In other cases where the state comes in in the first place to invest in these hard-to-tap resources, in the name of 'pro-poor' programmes, the investment on business operation facilities should be counted, at least to some extent, as the assets of the poor communities and their members', letting them benefit primarily, instead of letting the external actors pick the low-hanging fruit and get most of the benefits, just because the latter has the management and marketing capacities which poor farmers don't have. Turning such state investment into assets of the poor can play a critical role in helping people escape poverty, but the mechanism needs to be carefully designed.

Thirdly, China's current eco-compensation mechanism combines the PES (payment for ecosystem service) system with government standardised management. Since at the current stage most of the service is procured by government, the payment is at a low level compared to that in a market mechanism, and compensation is inadequate to make up for the poor's livelihood losses. For instance, government provides a subsidy for forest rangers or game wardens in the needy areas, but the subsidy level is lower than farmers' average income, ranging from RMB800–1500 per month (in 2024 exchange rate it equals to USD100–200 per month) in Yunnan province. I can give another example of the Xishuangbanna rainforest reserve where many impoverished groups plant sugarcane but risk losing 70 percent to 100 percent of their crops due to wild elephants every year. In this case, wildlife-related insurance provided by government only covers a minor part of this loss. Developing a market-based service payment mechanism is therefore necessary, especially when it is related to the livelihood of the poor, who are highly vulnerable to such shocks. However as many areas are rushing to initiate short-term projects for poverty reduction, explorations on market-based long-term mechanisms are simply neglected.

Fourthly, the development of impoverished villages is also controversial because of the constant outflow of the population from rural areas to urban centres. However, even with high out-migration, rural villages will not disappear. They might become smaller, and they might become older, and they might also become richer thanks to the remittances sent back by young migrants; but because their productive and living spaces are often endowed with ecological and cultural value, there will always be many who prefer not to leave. Consequently, targeted poverty reduction programmes in China should view impoverished villages both as target units in a vision of comprehensive poverty reduction approach, and as communities of people with their own dynamics and wider connections, requiring specific and targeted support. Making tailored, long-term and comprehensive anti-poverty plans for impoverished villages and implementing them phase by phase is key to practising targeted poverty reduction in the new era.

Lastly, overcoming poverty is usually understood merely as providing support for the poor, but what is often neglected is that it is also a process of fighting the 'poverty' of anti-poverty thoughts, looking beyond the symptoms to the underlying processes. It seems that the poor may have a mentality to rely on others, but looking further, poverty is almost always the product of uneven economic and social development and inappropriate institutional settings. The past years have seen unprecedented attention given to targeted poverty reduction at both the central and local level in China, but we have seen that implementation requires both innovation and a holistic approach. The poor are the main actors in this endeavour; they should be trusted and supported in making their decisions. Poverty is fundamentally the result of an entrenched lack of opportunity. Changing that can mean thinking outside the box when approaching a small-scale project, but it also means rethinking the processes and systems, to lift up those who have been left behind.

Three Key Points in Targeted Poverty Alleviation[10]

Successful poverty alleviation requires targeting the most vulnerable—but even then, poverty will continue without broader structural advancement.

In any successful poverty alleviation efforts, the process by which resources are targeted at those in greatest need is essential. China is no exception. In the 1980s, China's rural poverty alleviation policies used impoverished counties as the targeting unit; in 2001, the focus was made more granular, instead targeting poor villages; after a decade's time, the poor households or individuals became the targeting unit. Regardless of the administrative level being targeted, the targets and distribution of resources must still be effectively determined. This can be challenging. Since the 'Seven-year Poverty Alleviation Programme' was launched in 1990s, measures for supporting farmers and facilitating poor areas' economic development had persistently faced problems such as inaccurate identification and the loss and misappropriation of anti-poverty resources.

In the past three decades since the introduction of the Reform and Opening Up policies, rapid economic growth has seen China's poor population decrease enormously in size. Alongside this, three economic gaps have emerged: the increasingly wider gap between developed and underdeveloped areas, the gap between urban and rural areas and the gap between rich and poor in the same location. These gaps led to great wealth disparities, and continues to present an obstacle. Poor populations are less likely to benefit from general poverty reduction policies for the following reasons.

First, development-oriented poverty reduction, which is now the prevailing approach, does not have the same goals as protective poverty reduction undertaken through cash transfers. It aims to assist the poor by supporting the development of the socio-economic environment in

[10] Published at *Chengdu Daily* (2015-08-14) at http://news.chengdu.cn/2015/0812/1715659.shtml.

which they are situated, rather than by deliberately targeting them at the individual or household level. Once it's put into operation, relatively rich populations are bound to gain access to anti-poverty resources first. For instance, most development projects aimed at farmers, such as those supporting breeding or processing, required certain conditions: supplementary funds, heavy labour force input and extensive market information. These pro-poor projects were all implemented in poor areas, but field surveys found they predominantly benefited farmers who were relatively more affluent.

Second, the majority of the poor are in a structural poverty trap. To escape the trap requires an accumulation of assets that is unattainable through the general poverty reduction measures available to farmers. Achieving the step-change in assets require to escape the poverty trap is made harder by the fact that most development-oriented rural poverty reduction projects concentrate on traditional agriculture which is usually a long-term, low-return and high-risk business. Even relatively rich farmers with modern equipment and greater economies of scale cannot make very high-incomes through agriculture alone. The poverty reduction impact of income diversification projects—such as support for rural tourism—has proven this point in recent years.

Third, most of the rural poor population experiences multi-dimensional poverty. They cannot easily accumulate assets or engage in new economic activities because educational and medical expenditures consume their income. This is compounded by the fact that, as anti-poverty resources are highly preferential, interest groups and local elites are highly likely to seize these resources and benefits.

In the mid-2010s, the state of the rural poor population had attracted wide attention, but I was sceptical that the central government's target of eradicating poverty by 2020 could be achieved. To my eyes, it was indisputable that the rural poor population was stuck in a near-insurmountable structural poverty trap. Without more forceful and effective measures, I thought, poverty would remain entrenched. From China's success despite this fact, two lessons can be drawn.

First, broader economic development remains an important condition for rural poverty alleviation. This is, in my view, crucial for a direct reason and an indirect one. Directly, economic development creates new employment opportunities and new or expanded markets. This benefits the poor, who have the most need of increased employment opportunities and market growth. For China, expanding international and domestic markets will create new opportunities for the population. If we can manage this, the rural poor population's long-term development outlook will continue to be optimistic despite demographic and economic shifts. Now the second reason, the indirect one: sustainable economic development, entailing real increases in incomes and wealth, will offer powerful opportunities for redistribution, which can allow better social welfare for those at the bottom of the income chart. Without this, the poor cannot escape poverty in the long run.

Second, as the rural poor population is extremely vulnerable, any natural disaster or disease may reduce them to a deeper poverty trap or, if they have already escaped poverty, cause them to slip back. For this reason, rural social security is a crucial safety net, and a major foundation of poverty alleviation. Over the past decade, various forms of social security for poor areas have emerged in China, but they are often not intensive enough to provide for poor populations during major shocks. Our efforts to construct an effective social security system have faced a further challenge: flaws in governance have resulted in massive losses of social security resources. Inevitably, this harms our ability to reduce the prevalence of poverty.

Due to the massive population in rural China living in poverty and at risk of slipping back into poverty, the pure welfare transfer system used in developed countries is not feasible here: the financial burden would be unaffordable. To address poverty in China, we must combine development and protection. This goal is the longstanding focus of targeted poverty reduction strategy. In the previous section, I set out why this is necessary. Now, the question is: how can it be achieved? To implement this targeted strategy, three key points need to be addressed.

First, the targets of poverty reduction measures needs to be accurately identified. As mentioned above, whether the primary unit of aid is defined as poor counties or poor villages, the aiming mechanism of poverty alleviation needs to be refined. Once an administrative level is established, the list of units being targeted should be regularly updated to reflect dynamic changes in their relative situations. In 2005, China started to have poor households registered. In 2014, the central government proposed the targeted poverty alleviation strategy, hoping to accurately identify the poor based on their income, housing, education and health situations. Those registered in the system would get state support. Yet with limited state financial resources the poverty registration system still had to go with a quota. The overall quota for this poverty registration system was determined by poverty headcount ratio based on statistical estimations. The overall quota was broken down on provincial level, then on counties, and further on villages, all based on estimated poverty statistics. Yet in the village, usually poor villages, those who were poor needed to be identified, but the number of which should not exceed the given quota. There was a dilemma between the top-down delegated quota system and the bottom-up targeted identification approach. This created leakage problems, leaving many in poverty unregistered and many registered though they were not poorer compared to their fellow villagers.

Participatory poverty reduction programmes were rolled out nationwide in the first decade of the twenty-first century. During this push a number of effective measures were adopted. One, for example, was the bottom-up ranking of farmer households by wealth: villagers were involved in the identification of the most vulnerable, an innovation that often gave better, and more legitimate, results than conventional development scoping approaches. Another was the posting of public notices to more easily form a consensus on the results of identification. However, once income indicators and additional conditions, beyond those provided through participatory approaches, were also required, the identification of impoverished households needing beneficiary status rapidly became a complex gaming process for political and social resources.

Second, the changing needs of poor populations must be accurately understood. In addition to identifying the poor population, we must also understand what they lack. The anti-poverty measures in our standard 'arsenal', such as industrial development, relocation and credit support, can be effective under certain conditions, but poor populations in different areas can have completely different demands, requiring different measures. For financial management purposes, China currently practises a project-based system of poverty reduction. All planning and auditing is based on projects, with bottom-up applications for funding by project category and top-down arrangement and implementation of approved projects. This system reduces misappropriation and corruption and enhances transparency. However, these sector based projects are subject to policy goals for different sectors, usually determined in the hands of different line ministries or departments, often failing to make a synergy for poverty reduction. Sometimes even poverty reduction projects do not fully respond to the various needs of the needy. Let me just use one case of the Hebian Village where I worked for over ten years. As an identified poor village, it could get state support, but only in specific project forms, including housing renovation subsidies for everyone, additional subsidies only for the identified poor households, and a project for building the main road to get out of village. I have discussed with villagers and local officials and finally came up with a comprehensive plan to turn this village into a tourism and small conference based new economy. But there was no such poverty-reduction project that could provide the money where the village needed. For example, there was no money for renovating the guestroom which I had to raise from other philanthropic projects. It was something worth to mention that, even in 2023, in the post-absolute poverty era, the same old problem still existed. I helped the Hebian Village to apply for a project to beautify its riverside, yet the only project available from the government was a water resource project. Project officers proposed to elevate the village bridge by ten metres and to build high vertical cement dams on the narrow river that flowed through the village. This proposal was based on priority principles of water resource project: to guard against floods. But it would obviously destroy the natural sceneries of the small riverside village: the elevated bridge would block the first sight of any visitor entering the village, and the dam would only add artificiality, a sense that was incompatible to the natural beauty of the mountain village. When I scribble down the story here, I am still helping the village to communicate with local government, to see whether the project design could be altered to respond to village needs without violating project regulations.

Third, the last mile gap of targeted poverty reduction measures must be addressed. Though addressing poverty is primarily a government responsibility and in China the state-ledness is also a main feature of its poverty reduction mechanism, but to effectively organise and implement anti-poverty measures in poor villages remains a challenge. Due to scarce organisational and human resources at and below the county level, higher-level authorities often dispatch pro-poor teams to stay and work in poor villages. These often fail to fully compensate for the lack of capacities in the local administration and community. Non-profit organisations must often step in. For instance, a decade ago, the State Council Leading Group Office of Poverty Alleviation and Development and the Asian Development Bank jointly launched a pilot programme for non-profit organisations to directly participate in village poverty reduction in Jiangxi. Their organisational efficiency made up for the government's insufficient organisational resources. Looking ahead, coherent engagement between the state and civil society will continue to be vital.

From Reduction to Prevention[11]

Subsistence poverty is largely defeated. This requires different approaches: lifting people out of poverty is a different activity to keeping people from falling back in.

At the end of 2012, there were an estimated 98.99 million people living under the national poverty line in China. By the end of 2020, absolute poverty was declared to be over. Does this mean that absolute poverty is now a thing of the past? I would argue that it does not, though statistically it is: the eradication of rural absolute poverty—and that by the current standard, which may in time need to be revised upwards—does not mean the true and permanent elimination of poverty. Eradication of poverty, lifting people out of poverty, is a different activity to prevention of poverty, keeping people from falling back into it.

Even after the success of the 'war' on poverty in the past decade, poverty reduction in rural China remains critical. First, the material baseline for human subsistence gives us a relatively high possibility of a reemergence of objective and absolute poverty. Even the subsistence poverty standard will continue to rise with economic and social development, making it impossible to cease poverty reduction. Secondly, there is still the continuing fact of relative poverty. An essential issue of poverty studies is the fundamentally relative nature of modern poverty [6]. For reasons of social justice, relative poverty must continue to be combated. It also requires us to mainstream poverty *prevention* in broader areas of government and policy: even without slipping back into absolute poverty, relative poverty can increase if the distribution of new opportunities is highly uneven. This is especially the case in rural areas, where relative poverty is reflected by differences in income, public social services, education and medical services between regions, urban and rural areas and different groups. These differences make it necessary to focus on rural poverty reduction policies, and when this is accomplished, undertake proactive poverty prevention policies.

[11] Published at Guangming Net (2019-02-20) at https://baijiahao.baidu.com/s?id=1626064367494135504&wfr=spider&for=pc.

Chinese rural poverty reduction programmes were rolled out *en masse* in the mid-1980s, when economic development was low and impoverished rural areas and populations were large. As I have noted, the scale necessary meant that straightforward transfers were unlikely to adequately reduce poverty. Instead, programmes aiming to support poor populations' ability to participate in economic activities and growing their incomes—what we call development-oriented poverty reduction—became the mainstream anti-poverty strategy. This is not to say that transfer payments, especially at higher administrative levels to support improvements to public social services, have not played an important role in rural poverty reduction. Their role has, however, been largely a subsidiary one. In practise, the implementation of this approach was manifested by changes in identifying and targeting those in need, including a progressive narrowing of targeting scale, from regions down to villages and then to households registered as 'in poverty'.

As the escape from poverty slowed down in early twenty-first century, the central government started to pay attention to factors that contributed to the persistence of poverty. Policies to prevent the occurrence of poverty in various aspects—infrastructure, education, health improvement and rural subsistence allowance—were introduced. Since the battle against poverty was launched, China's rural poverty reduction efforts has, in fact, combined poverty reduction with poverty prevention. However, in terms of master plan and resource allocation, the reduction, rather than prevention of poverty, remained its overall goal.

For the vast majority of the rural populations still at risk of poverty in China, subsistence poverty is no longer a dominant concern. Except for small subsets of populations with difficulties that require direct support from social security policies, rural populations increasingly face the challenge of accessing equal opportunities and welfare as their urban counterparts. In other words, we can now start to re-ascend the scale of administrative targeting granularity. Rural poverty reduction should no longer target registered households in poverty (aside from those small populations in special difficulties): instead, we need to shift from making targeted poverty reduction policies to making our broad spectrum of policies sensitive to poverty. China's master strategy for rural poverty reduction will thus need to continue to be adjusted.

The battle against poverty can only be considered to have been durably won if we can ensure that people lifted out of poverty will not slip back, and that a large 'new poor population' will not emerge. Overcoming these remaining risks depends on an effective poverty prevention mechanism. To this end, it's important to adjust rural poverty reduction strategies and policies in the following areas.

First, the mechanism that addresses poverty should shift its focus from poverty reduction to poverty prevention.

Second, future rural poverty reduction strategies should concentrate on addressing the social mechanisms of poverty. Narrowing regional development gaps, reducing disparities in the public social services available to urban and rural areas, expanding employment opportunities for farmers and cultivating pro-poor market mechanisms are important elements for preventing poverty from happening in the long run.

Third, 'new' poverty in rural China is frequently caused by the 'old': lack of preschool education and low-quality compulsory education can strengthen the poverty cycle instead of breaking it. More village kindergartens in poor areas should be established and quality teacher teams be put in place.

Fourth, medical services of low accessibility and low quality are critical causes of health-related poverty. Less than 30 percent of poor areas are equipped with village clinics, and most are short-staffed, lacking qualified rural medical workers. The shortage of basic rural health facilities and health workers in poor areas severely undermines the effects of existing rural medical and health policies. Quality rural health system should be developed in the future.

Fifth, the rural subsistence allowance plays an important role in preventing poverty. However, it has been expanded too much to accurately target those who are most in need. In the future, instead, only those with extreme subsistence difficulties should be identified to receive support. Its coverage needs to be narrowed, while the intensity of available support needs to be increased to a substantial level.

Methods of Targeting[12]

Targeted policies can use limited resources more effectively and efficiently, but they often require a costly set of identification mechanisms. China has employed diversified approaches to targeting during its fight against poverty which may provide some valuable lessons.

Two concepts are central in discussions of social policy. The concept of universality holds that access to social welfare is a basic right of citizenship, while the concept of targeting indicates that, in a context of limited resources, assistance should be directed to those who have greatest need, identified as eligible based on certain conditions. Both concepts are valuable, but bring tough decisions and trade-offs.

Many social protection policies are universal, because they are meant for a large population if not for all [7]. They carry relatively low management costs, since less attention must be given to assessing the 'deservingness' of policy beneficiaries, but they require huge financial resources and are primarily applicable in developed countries with low inequality. Conversely, targeted policies to serve the poorest populations can use limited resources more effectively and efficiently [8]. In developing countries where money is tighter and the poorest are poorer, policies that prioritise targeting are more necessary. Targeted policies are designed to benefit the very poorest directly, but extensive research in developing countries shows that targeted policies can sometimes fail to do so [9]. A study of cash transfer projects in Latin America, for example, recently found that nearly half the population in poverty is missed by transfer programmes, and that in half the countries studied, 40 percent of transfer beneficiaries were above the poverty line. This is not to say that targeted policies are inherently flawed as a category. We know that many targeted policies can have transformative effects: vaccines distributed to populations at risk of a particular disease, or cash transfers distributed to poor populations at greatest risk of disaster, have allowed major improvements in many contexts. But we can recognise that targeted policies require a costly set of identification mechanisms that require

[12] Published by Professor Tang Lixia from the College of Humanities and Development Studies, China Agricultural University at China Civil Affairs (Issue 5, 2016) at https://mp.weixin.qq.com/s/B332hwbnQfTS4pdMxZrcXQ.

strong management, lest they target those that should not benefit and exclude those that should benefit.

Accurate identification is the prerequisite for targeted policies to have a real effect. It includes rules, standards and methods for identifying qualified beneficiaries of social policies. How can we go about ensuring that poverty programmes actually target the poor? Three methods are in common use today. The first is an automatic exclusion method: designing social policies to have less attractive benefits, attempting to induce richer people to auto-select out of competing for their resources. Examples of minimal benefits include work relief with low pay, petty loans with higher interest rates than bank loans, and low-rent housing in basic accommodation. Many Chinese social policies do not succeed in this regard: their benefits are 'too generous', and they appeal to the 'rich' as well as the poor. For instance, some subsidy policies, especially industrial and housing subsidies, have required beneficiaries to pay first and receive subsidies retroactively: for the poor, who have less access to capital, this is a non-starter. In some areas, industrial subsidy policies requested farmers to raise their own funds for greenhouses, livestock sheds or methane tanks; these projects were only subsidised after being accepted by the relevant authorities. This inevitably excluded farmers with no means to raise money. In other areas, building subsidy policies required farmers to complete a specified amount of construction on their own in a particular time-frame or to build houses in a specified area and manner before any subsidies could be made available. Poor farmers were forced to either give up the subsidy or borrow money to build houses up to the standards specified in the subsidy policy.

Further, although some supportive policies offered limited direct support, they were attached to highly attractive preferential policies and fell prey to 'elite capture'. For example, a subsistence allowance offered a slim monthly cash subsidy to poor households. This was not in itself something exceptional, but in some areas, households on the subsistence allowance could access a full housing subsidy, higher education relief for their children, a full subsidy for new cooperative medical costs, assistance for acute diseases and various other forms of preferential treatment. It was not rare that in some areas, farmers preferred the subsistence allowance title to many cash-transfer programmes. Similar problems emerged in the implementation of other household poverty reduction policies. In the past, farmers didn't care whether they were identified as 'poor households': support and resources were limited, and the benefits of this designation were small. Today, support has been greatly stepped up, and the incentives to compete to be considered eligible for benefits have increased. In some provinces, poor households enjoyed an RMB40,000 subsidy for relocation, while non-poor households only received RMB20,000. Consequently, all households scrambled for the title of 'poor households'. Both rich and poor farmers competed for these appealing resources, and, thus, subsidies and allowances tended to end up supporting the 'rich' rather than the 'poor': the 'rich' have greater access to information, and more time, and thus in the absence of careful screening are more likely to win in the race for assistance.

The second approach to targeting is to determine a population's eligibility for social support by features such as gender, age, geography, ability to work or income level. This is the most common identification methodology for targeted relief policies and is especially frequently used for special groups such as people with disabilities, the elderly, females, children and ethnic minority groups. For instance, China offers a subsidy for rural senior residents, relief for orphans and a subsidy for rural family planning. Methodologically speaking, identifying beneficiaries by social features is less costly if the country has complete and thorough demographic information available. Such policies target particular designated populations according to whether they are perceived to be more likely to need assistance, but they are also inclusive since people in certain social conditions could benefit directly.

In China, the rural subsistence allowance system and support policies for the poor are currently based on income. However, it is very difficult to accurately identify beneficiaries using a means-testing method because of the expense of collection of accurate data, and the fact that incomes fluctuate. In rural areas, it is difficult to carry out income surveys among farmers, and when they are carried out, they are very expensive. Therefore, the means testing method is mostly used in theory and policy, where coarser estimates of incomes are used to estimate and infer the size of an eligible target population in a certain area. In practise, the number of beneficiaries in a village is first determined by the allocation of a quota of support recipients based on statistical estimate of income, before the same number of beneficiaries are identified at the community level.

On the ground, identification methods are more diversified, and indicators are rarely based on income itself. Basic qualifications for being identified as a 'poor' household often include a lack of working age family members, an absence of remittances sent by household migrant workers, being 'burdened' by family members with disabilities or chronic health problems, and having to afford two or more children in school—usually characteristics of families that have a high dependency ratio or low support ratio. Yet we must admit, these non-income characteristics are closely associated with income-generating abilities or, more precisely, income-consuming realities of a family. Some areas adopt other non-income characteristics of the household as qualifications for identification. One category is to exchange the poverty 'entitlements' for implementation of other policies. For example, when some villages had difficulties in implementing other social policies like family planning,[13] poverty quotas were given to households who did well in following birth control programmes. This was to set up examples of 'fewer children and more wealth', promoting the implementation of family planning programmes. In the second category, poverty identification is also part of a trade-off. The quotas are often given to those who support village development or village officials' work. For instance, when public infrastructures like village roads, village reservoirs need to take up some farmers' land, poverty quotas can be filled by these households in order to get their support for using their land. In other cases, farmers who support village committee's work by actively attending village meetings and providing voluntary labour for village development activities are preferentially considered for the quota. The third category is based on requirements for target beneficiaries. Many poverty reduction projects deal with specific industries or have specific goals, targeting farmers who have relevant characteristics: some can only support those who raise livestock; some require target farmers to play an exemplary role, thus only those who are more able or have more skills can be 'identified' (selected) [10]. Though these methods of identifying the poor may be less accurate than means testing, and they do generate externalities when they serve for local actors' self-interest, and can build up consensus more quickly in a rural community and lower the costs of identification, especially when means testing method is not viable.

[13] China's family planning policy involves birth quotas and it evolved along the development of the country. In 1979 China introduced the one-child policy, but it allowed many exceptions: in rural areas, families could have more children, and many ethnic minorities were exempt from the policy. In 2015, China switched to two-child limits and in May 2021, China introduced the three-child policy before it removed all the birth quotas two months later. Note by the translator.

The third approach to targeting is to select the target population by setting benefit conditions. In this approach the target population is identified using conventional approaches, but they must then take certain actions in order to benefit from particular social policies. This is, in other words, a conditional benefit, often distributed as a cash transfer. Conditional transfer payments are prevalent in Latin America and South Asia. The ultimate purpose of this identification method is not only to offer a cash subsidy to the poor but also to improve human capital. This is why conditions related to various other behaviours—in education, health, or nutrition, for example—are set for those collecting benefits. For instance, a beneficiary must ensure their children attend school, have a physical check-up or attend regular health lectures. The attachment of conditions makes the subsidy pertinent and highly targeted. Strict directions regarding the subsidy's use ensure that families spend the subsidy on required and prioritised behaviours rather than other family expenditures. Therefore, the resources gained from social assistance policies are more likely to be used to meet policy goals instead of being spent for other purposes. Some countries even use coupons to replace cash to ensure that funds are earmarked for a specific purpose. For instance, in rural surveys, we often heard about elderly residents paying their grandchildren's tuition with their old-age pension. Rural residents felt this was only reasonable, but it undermined the policy's effects by failing to improve the lives of the elderly. Benefit conditions are also used in China's 'nutrition improvement' programme in rural schools, the student grant programme and vocational education support for rural families.

China rolled out its targeted poverty reduction strategy in the 2010s. This is, in short, an approach that must carefully target its beneficiaries. China does not yet have the capacity to do this as well as we should wish: many theoretically accurate mechanisms actually incur high management costs and require abilities that we cannot yet meet. Each identification method discussed above applies to a particular scope. Without the availability of various inputs they will not work: appropriate policy goals, information availability, governance capacities, distribution of different demographics and so on, will all affect the outcome of targeting approaches. This means that China must use a variety of overlapping approaches, to make sure that no groups either slip through the cracks or take others' resources.

References

1. Dercon, S. (2022). *Gambling on Development: Why Some Countries Win and Others Loose* (p. 44). Hurs t& Company.
2. CGTN. (2022, September 8). *China's Subsistence Allowance Surges in Past Decade.* https://news.cgtn.com/news/2022-09-08/China-s-subsistence-allowance-surges-in-past-decade-1d9I1dpiIUw/index.html
3. China.org.cn. (2023, September 14). *China Allocates RMB126.5 Billion in Social aid in H1.* http://www.china.org.cn/china/2023-09/14/content_116678614.htm
4. Huang, J. (2008). *Zhidu bianqian he kechixu fazhan: Sanshinian Zhongguo nongye yu nongcun [Institutional Change and Sustainable Development: 30 Years of Agriculture and Rural China]* (p. 4). Gezhi Press, Shanghai People's Publishing House.
5. Balboni, C., et al. (2022). Why Do People Stay Poor? *The Quarterly Journal of Economics, 137*(2), 785–844.
6. Fischer, A. M. (2019). *Poverty as Ideology: Rescuing Social Justice from Global Development Agendas* (pp. 8–12). Zed Books.
7. Leite, P. (2014, June). *Effective Targeting for the Poor and Vulnerable.* World Bank Social Protection & Labour Technical Note. https://documents1.worldbanorg/curated/en/747591468125685125/pdf/930590REVISED00SPL0Technical0Note06.pdf
8. Hanlon, J., et al. (2010). *Just Give Money to the Poor: The Development Revolution from the Global South* (p. x). Kumarian Press.
9. Stampini, M., et al. (2023). *Cash Transfers, Poverty, and Inequality in Latin America and the Caribbean* (Inter-American Development Bank Working Paper, No. 01531). https://doi.org/10.18235/0005235
10. Tang, L., et al. (2015). Jingzhun fupin jizhi shishi de zhengce he shijiankunjing [Policy and Practical Dilemmas in the Implementation of the Targeted Poverty Alleviation Mechanism]. *GuiZhou Social Sciences, 05*, 151–156.

CHAPTER 6

How Did a Village Escape Poverty?

At the beginning of 2020, I planned to visit Hebian Village during the Spring Festival. By this point, I had already been working on poverty reduction in the village for some five years: the new guest-room businesses we had helped to develop were doing fairly well, generating income each year mainly through conference-hosting and children's camps. Unexpectedly, I was kept at home in Beijing by the outbreak of COVID-19. I didn't expect the impact of the pandemic to be so profound, but by May, it was undeniable that Hebian's income in 2020 had plunged to the bottom. All the booked meetings and children's camps had been cancelled and, it seemed unlikely to recover that year. Though the top priority of the Hebian poverty reduction programme was to respond to risks and diversify livelihoods, the local villagers were still, after all our work, highly susceptible to shocks. As early as 2020, several villagers text messaged me that they were about to leave home for migrant work.

Hebian Village is fortunate in that it has escaped poverty. It was better prepared for the shock of COVID-19 than other villages in the area. The villagers' living conditions have significantly improved, and the previously poor and shabby village has become a beautiful and attractive tourist destination. Despite the decrease in their guest room income during the years of COVID-19, their actual welfare was still considerably higher than it was at the pre-project baseline. In this chapter, I will share some of my interviews with the press, a few short articles written by members of our poverty reduction team, and several new pieces of articles on what happened after 2020 when China entered a new era of rural revitalisation, to present a

X. Li, *The End of Poverty and the Taming of Inequality*,
https://doi.org/10.1007/978-981-96-0684-9_6

picture of how Hebian and two other villages have changed during the time of our intervention in the broad policy context.

Why Were Hebian Villagers Stuck in Poverty?

In 2015, our surveys showed that Hebian Village's inhabitants suffered from volatile crop prices, high debt, and burdensome healthcare costs. Left to themselves, the cycle of poverty was hard to break.

I first visited Mengla County and its rainforest area in the 1990s. It left a good impression on me. When I returned several years later for further research in villages and saw the area in more detail, I was struck instead by its poverty. Later, when we began our poverty reduction experiment in the Hebian Village in 2015, we set out to better understand the village: its households, its economy, its connectedness with other areas and so on. The village is in the county of Mengla, in the southernmost part of Yunnan, nestled in a curve of border shared with Myanmar and Laos. The region is mountainous, and—as will be seen later to be important—contains several beautiful natural areas preserved in parks.

Let me sketch briefly the state of the village at the start of my engagement, sharing some of the basic details and case studies I and my team compiled in 2015. In that year, Hebian Village was home to 58 households, a small-sized natural village compared to its peers. We ran a survey of these households, although were not able to cover everyone. The heads of two households were married to members of other villages, but their households remained registered in Hebian. The head of another household was a migrant worker beyond the reach of our survey. As a result, the survey covered the remaining fifty-five households, comprising 204 people. There were 112 males and 92 females in the village, with a male-to-female ratio of roughly six to five. Hebian is a relatively 'young' village, with an average age of 28.4 years old at the time. Only ten villagers were aged over sixty, with 21 villagers aged over fifty-one. Women's participation in village development and governance seemed limited. During village meetings and consultations, we saw few speak up or make decisions.

Hebian covers a land area of 782.3 mu.[1] This includes 145.7 mu of paddy fields, 636.6 mu of dry farmland, and 1,382 mu of rubber forest. Per capita, villagers owned 0.7 mu of paddy field and 3.1 mu of dry farmland. Space for paddy fields was limited since the village was in the mountains, and dry farmland was mostly used to grow sugarcane and corn. Only a little land was available for planting 'winter crops'.[2] In 2015, the village's agricultural income was mainly sourced from sugarcane.

Households' levels of income security varied. Many of them received state income top-ups to bring them to the minimum level. One household—of one person—enjoyed the 'five guarantees'[3]; eighteen households (with a total of fifty-five members) received subsistence allowances[4]; and twenty households were registered for targeted poverty alleviation measures. The household receiving five guarantees of support had the lowest income of any household in the village. The household with the 'highest' income belonged to the villager H, who grew sugarcane on 416 mu of rented land. He invested over RMB200,000 in loans in 2015, much higher than the average villager's expenditure. We removed these two extremes from our survey result. From 2015 to 2016, the average annual income of a Hebian household was RMB22,118, with the highest being RMB46,627 and the lowest RMB3,800. Per capita, rural residents had an annual disposable income of RMB5,832, far lower than the national level of RMB11,422 for rural residents and lower than the annual level of RMB8,242 for residents of Yunnan province more widely.

[1] 20 mu is one and a third hectares. Note by the translator.

[2] China has a wide latitude scope from north to south, the Hebian Village, located in the southernmost of Yunnan—a southwestern province, is in the very limited tropical areas of China. Thus, people here can grow many crops, vegetables and fruits that can not be naturally grown in northern China in winter. And they call these winter crops or vegetables. Note by the translator.

[3] '五保', wu bao (Five Guarantees). Households which consist of childless or infirm old people can enjoy the five guarantees, namely five forms of guaranteed support for food, clothing, medical care, housing and burial expenses. Note by the translator.

[4] '低保', di bao (Rural Minimum Living Allowance or Subsistence Allowance). China's Dibao guarantee programme is one of the world's largest social safety net programmes. In 2011, eight percent of all rural inhabitants in China benefited from it. The Dibao programme provides cash transfers to households with earnings below a minimum level. Because the system is decentralised, however, it does not bring recipients above the poverty line. Studies also suggest that local authorities struggle to target the very poorest, leaving many of those who would most benefit unable to access the supplementary funding. Note by the translator.

During 2015 to 2016, villagers' incomes were mainly earned from agricultural activities and government support. Agricultural income accounted for 38 percent of the total village income, wage income—typically related to agriculture—accounted for 25 percent, and income from government transfers accounted for 23 percent. Property income accounted for 6 percent.

Agricultural Income

Hebian villagers' agricultural activities are focused predominantly in crops; livestock is of little significance. In 2016, livestock breeding accounted for only 2 percent of total agricultural income while crops accounted for 98 percent. The farming income was made predominantly by cultivating sugarcane; Fructus amomi[5]; stringless beans; and rubber trees. Sugarcane was the most important of these crops, generating a household average income of around RMB5,800, followed by Fructus amomi, producing an average household income of RMB3,200.

The value of crop yields could fluctuate a lot. In 2016, the income from Fructus amomi was more than four times greater than in 2015 (RMB720). Conversely, income from stringless beans in 2016 was nearly 40 percent lower than in 2015. The average household income from sugarcane in 2014–2015 was roughly RMB5,600; this was less volatile. The dramatic fluctuations in the income earned from Fructus amomi and stringless beans were related to changes in the agricultural market and the regional climate.

The stringless bean market fluctuated particularly violently. During the week of our interviews, the price surged from RMB1.5 per kilogram to RMB6 per kilogram. As farmers could not pick beans quickly enough to take advantage of this price rise, most of them failed to sell beans at the peak price. The cost of the beans for planting (prior to labour costs) was RMB1,000 per mu, and the labour cost was at least RMB3,240 per mu (calculated at RMB80 per worker per day), meaning the beans had to be sold at RMB4,240 per mu to avoid loss. With one ton of beans produced per mu (fifteen tons per hectare), they had to have a sale price of over RMB4.3/kg for cultivation to be sustainable. This was not always attained.

5 '砂仁', sha ren, a traditional Chinese herbal medicine derived from cardamom plants. Note by the translator.

Dried Fructus amomi was priced at RMB300/kg in 2015 and RMB280/kg in 2016, remaining basically stable. However, production was hit by adverse weather in 2015, resulting in poor harvests. It did not significantly improve until 2016, when the weather turned. In Hebian Village, only a few households did not grow Fructus amomi, and the remaining 48 each cultivated an average of 11 mu of Fructus amomi. Since this crop does not require pesticides or weeding and naturally yields fruit after three years (weather permitting), the villagers only needed five or six workers per mu during harvesting. Thus, Fructus amomi was a low-effort, low-labour crop. However, production was highly susceptible to weather and therefore extremely unstable. As local villagers shared, one mu could generally yield 30 kilograms of fruits, but could also often yield nothing if weather conditions were adverse. It was difficult for the farmers to rely on stable income from this crop.

Sugarcane has relatively stable purchasing prices and does not require heavy labour, so it should have been a stable source of income. Yet Hebian Village was located in rainforest nature reserves, and herds of elephants from these reserves often trespassed on cropland, causing severe crop loss. In the past two years, many farmers had no return on their investment and decided to stop growing sugarcane. In 2015, out of the 37 households that grew sugarcane, 22 fell victim to elephants, who ate nearly 60 percent of the village's sugarcane production. Since only RMB700 per mu was offered for compensation, versus a cultivation cost of RMB1,500 per mu, the villagers lost at least RMB800 from each mu of sugarcane. This was a profound constraint on their livelihoods.

The rubber market remained flat in 2014–2015, and few rubber trees were tapped because of the low price. Only five households earned income from rubber. This income barely contributed to household income since the highest income was RMB540 and the lowest was RMB60. Six households planted bananas in 2015; four gained no income from the crop, while the two households that did earned very different returns—RMB400 and RMB4,000.

Wage Income

Wage income in Hebian Village mainly included long-term wage income, income from migrant work and income from odd jobs. Only six villagers received long-term wage income, including one single female who worked at the town post office for an annual wage of RMB19,800, and five villagers who served as 'village officials[6]' for a monthly wage of RMB200. Other waged positions in the village consisted of a loan officer (earning RMB500 monthly) and a forest ranger (earning RMB400 monthly). The positions of loan officer and accountant were held by the same villager, whose annual wage income was RMB7,200—the highest waged income outside the post office. Eleven villagers earned income as migrant workers, picking beans for RMB3,000 monthly or repairing cars for RMB1,650 monthly. The villager receiving the highest income from migrant work was a woodcutter in Laos with an annual income of RMB15,000. Twenty-three households in the village received income from odd jobs, mainly carrying bananas, picking hot peppers and engaging in other local, hourly agricultural jobs in the slack farming season (earning RMB10–20 per hour). The average income from odd jobs was RMB3,600 per household, accounting for only 13 percent of total household income. In Hebian, wage income accounted for a small share of the household income structure. Only five households made higher wage income than non-wage income. Non-wage income derived from farming was considerably more important.

Transfer Income

Transfer income (income derived from government assistance programmes), by contrast, provided a large share of Hebian households' incomes. This averaged 23 percent of households' incomes. The largest subsidy, accounting for half of the village's transfer income, was the subsidy for the production of Huanghuali wood (a rosewood valuable for its use in furniture). It was followed in importance by a subsidy for converting cropland to forests, and a comprehensive and subsistence subsidy. The Huanghuali wood subsidy was introduced in 2015 as part of the management fee subsidy from the Mengla County government and the Ecological Development for Environmental-friendly Rubber

[6] Since late 1980s, China's rural village governance structure has been transformed from a people's commune system to the current village autonomy system. In the village self-governance structure village committee is an executive body that carries out decisions made by the village assembly. Yet it receives guidance and support from China's bottom-level government, the township government. 'Village officials' refer to those who work in the village committee to help with the implementation of policies introduced by government. 'Village officials' are not civil servants but they receive a monthly wage subsidy from government. Note by the translator.

Plantation Programme. Following the government scheme, Huanghuali wood planting was subsidised in Hebian at RMB43.7 per mu and RMB8 per plant. Forty-two households in the village received the subsidy, with an average household subsidy of RMB3,064 and a maximum of RMB11,362. Thirty-nine households received a subsidy for converting cropland to forests, covering a total area of 1,060 mu. The subsidy standard was RMB240 per mu during 2004–2012; this was halved to RMB120 per mu from 2013. In 1999 the villagers struck a deal with a company, leasing converted land for planting oil wood in return for financial support for access to electricity. The company shared half of the village's national land conversion subsidy. In the village, 18 households received subsistence allowances at RMB429 per quarter per person, and one enjoyed five guarantees at RMB440 per quarter. Ten villagers were aged 60 and above, but only four enjoyed a monthly pension of RMB60. According to the village accountant, to get the pension when one turns 60 one has to pay RMB100 per year for at least fifteen years.

Land Rent Income

Land rent income provided a relatively small share of total village income. In 2015, 16 village households received land rent. The land (mostly mountainous) is mainly leased to plant bananas at a rent of RMB500 per mu. The household with the highest land rent income received RMB10,000 yearly, which accounted for 60% of that household's total income. For 16 households, the proportion of land rent income to total household income averaged 14%.

The survey found that household expenditures in Hebian Village mainly concerned day-to-day consumption expenses; medical expenses; educational expenses; and bigger outlays, normally for dwelling construction or renovation. In 2015, 55 households registered a total expenditure of RMB1,667,044, an average of RMB30,310 per household or RMB8,172 per capita. The surprisingly high per capita expenditure is caused by the high outlays of one relatively affluent household, which raises the average but does not reflect the reality for most households. When we were running our analyses of Hebian Village, we removed the highest- and lowest- income households to avoid distorting our results. When we do this, the averages take on a more reasonable appearance: the 53 remaining Hebian Village households share a total cash expenditure of RMB1,385,944, averaged at RMB26,002 per household and

RMB6,755 per capita. In order of magnitude, these costs were for: daily consumption (RMB561,091, 41 percent of the total); agricultural inputs or business operational expenditures (RMB344,789, 25 percent); medical expenses (RMB250,062, 18 percent of the total); educational expenses (RMB153,702, 11 percent); major outlays (RMB76,300); and assorted other costs (RMB7,860).

Daily Consumption

In 2015, the total daily consumption expenditure of farming households in Hebian Village was RMB561,091, an average of RMB10,587 per household and RMB2,791 per capita. Basic consumption occupied the largest share of total expenditure, a category covering food, clothing, housing, household appliances and service fees, daily traffic and communication, cash gifts and other living expenses. In our calculations, the purchase of durables (motorcycles, TV sets, solar water heaters, etc.) and migrant workers' daily consumption were categorised as household appliances and service fees, which explained why this part accounted for a large share (25%) of daily expenditure.

Another large category of daily consumption was unproductive: cigarettes and alcohol accounted for 25% of total consumption costs. Alcohol, preferred by Yao people living in Hebian, was not expensive compared to cigarettes. Almost all men, especially young men, had a smoking habit. Men smoked an average of one pack of cigarettes a day, an addiction that cost RMB8–11 daily, or over RMB3,000 per year. Communication expenses accounted for 18 percent of total daily expenditure (the third-highest cost). The village had no access to landlines and relied on mobile networks, which often had poor signal. All the young villagers aged 15–30 frequently used QQ, WeChat and other instant messaging applications, which they also used to play mobile games and make calls, incurring high monthly data charges. Due to relatively higher call charges, villagers and village officials all chose to communicate with each other via social media applications like Wechat. Hebian villagers travelled to Mengban Town at least once a week, and the rugged village roads resulted in a high fuel expense, approximated at RMB5 for a round trip.

Agricultural Inputs and Business Operational Costs

Village households' operational expenditure totalled RMB584,589 in 2015, averaging RMB10,629 per household or RMB2,866 per capita. Operational expenditure was elevated above normal that year by the fact that villager H contracted over 400 mu of land to grow sugarcane and spent over RMB200,000 on production and operation, far more than the household average. The household receiving five forms of state guaranteed support had lost the ability to work and incurred no operational expenditure throughout the year. To allow analysis that reflected more common experience, we removed these two households. For the rest of the village, total household operational expenditure was RMB344,789, averaged at RMB6,505 per household or RMB1,715 per capita.

Farming and breeding costs accounted for 70 percent of households' operational expenditures. Productive fixed assets cost 17 percent, and fuel purchases and farm tool maintenance cost 13 percent. Farming-related operational expenditure was mainly for growing sugarcane, rice and corn and maintaining rubber forests. As the most important source of income and most widely farmed crop, sugarcane incurred the highest expenditure. Some households reported a high operational expenditure in 2015 because they planted high-cost cash crops such as stringless beans and bananas.

Some households purchased productive fixed assets, typically chain saws for constructing houses; tricycles; and agricultural machinery. Fuel expenses for production and daily life were separated for the purposes of our analysis. Hebian villagers travelled by motorcycle between their homes and the fields because of the long distances involved; during the busy farming season, they could make several round trips in one day. Cash crops also needed to be transported to the nearest distribution market at Naka Village at the foot of the mountain, for which motorcycles were also used. When crop prices were low, transport costs would offset a greater portion of sale values.

Medical Expenses

Household medical expenses totalled RMB250,062 in Hebian Village in 2015. Households spent an average of RMB4,233, or RMB1,141 per capita. This accounted for 18 percent of total expenditure. For some households, this figure was necessarily higher. Sixteen households, roughly 29% of total households, had incurred disease or accident-related inpatient or surgical expenses which shared 37% of the village's total medical expenses. Although the share was not big, these medical expenses were in fact big burdens to the affected families. In 2015, 120 villagers were covered by the New Rural Cooperative Medical System (NCMS).[7] It thus covered 56 percent of villagers, far lower than the 95 percent target proposed by Xishuangbanna Prefecture's government. Local households mostly paid an NCMS premium for chronically sick family members, but not for healthy family members.

Case 1: The highest household medical expense in the village was RMB24,000. We learnt in an interview with household members that C, the 24-year-old head of the household, suffered serious gastritis and regularly purchased costly drugs in Jinghong City (the capital city of the prefecture of Xishuangbanna) that were not covered by medical insurance. RMB2,000 was spent each month on medicines for daily treatment needs. C and his parents did not divide family property, and the two households jointly earned a total income of RMB38,000 from farming and breeding. Against this, they recorded a total household expenditure of RMB61,690. C's mother had severe gynaecological diseases and spent RMB10,000 on hospital stays and drugs in 2015, while C's younger brother spent RMB4,000 annually on medicine for dermatosis. The disease expenses of these three people totalled RMB38,000, accounting for 61.6 percent of household expenditure. The family lived beyond their means for the year and had to live on savings and borrowings.

Medicines and daily disease treatment accounted for 58% of the village's medical expenditure. Most village households suffered from chronic diseases such as gastritis, hypertension, arthritis and gynaecological diseases. In 2015, a total of 78 persons—more than a third of the village population—suffered a condition of one sort or another. Fifteen households registered over RMB5,000 in medical expenses. In our survey, gastritis and gynaecological diseases were most common, with 20 people living with severe gastritis and 14 suffering serious gynaecological ailments. In addition to these conditions, arthritis, pulmonary diseases and intestinal diseases were reported in multiple cases.

[7] The New Rural Cooperative Medical Scheme was introduced in 2002, recognizing the extreme cost of healthcare for many rural households. It departed from the previous community-cooperative model by providing state subsidies for rural medical care. Note by the translator.

In interviews, we learned that many financially strained villagers would not see a doctor until a disease became unbearable. They mainly relied on medication, asking village doctors for herbal medicines to ease the pain. This means that villagers miss the optimal treatment window. Without effective remedies, recurrent attacks of diseases trouble villagers for prolonged periods. Other disease-related expenses refer to accompanying family members for hospital visits and traffic costs. In 2015, such expenses only accounted for 5 percent of the total medical expenses, signalling their limited influence. Nevertheless, because hospitalisation was a heavy financial burden and time in hospital meant time not working, farmers were reluctant to seek inpatient service.

Disease-caused poverty was an important part of multi-dimensional poverty in Hebian Village. Households' income was harmed in two main ways: by labour shortages caused by incapacitation or in-patient hospitalisation and direct medical expenses.

Case 2: 33-year-old F had a wife and three children. Shortly after the birth of his youngest son in 2012, F was diagnosed with acute Guillain–Barre syndrome (a type of hepatitis). Due to financial stress, F first resorted to folk herbal medicines but was later hospitalised. The household spent all their savings, then borrowed to pay medical costs. Because F already owed an RMB50,000 loan to rural credit cooperatives, he was prevented from gaining further loans. In 2013, F borrowed RMB85,000 from relatives and friends for inpatient treatment. The household sold a newly purchased truck to pay off the loans but remained RMB50,000 short. The treatment went ahead, and F asked relatives and friends for another RMB15,000 loan for treatment in 2015.

After continuous treatment, F's health took a turn for the better, and F was able to perform housework and light farm work. However, a thorough cure was still distant. F's condition was particularly concerning to him because he had three young children. During his incapacitation, his wife supported the family by farming. The household had two mu of paddy fields, nine mu of dry farm and 700 rubber trees untended because of the family's labour shortage. In 2015, F's household had a total cash income of only RMB8,300, from which RMB3,800—nearly half—was derived from transfer income. By January 2016, the family had RMB135,000 debt, including RMB70,000 bank loans and interests. It seemed impossible to pay off the debt based on his current income level and ongoing health problem. F had sold most of his productive fixed assets and had to borrow them from relatives if needed. Busy tending their young children, F's wife put most of their land in the hand of F's brother for farming and management. Disease and high treatment costs had crushed F's family's chances of overcoming poverty. With daily medical expenses deducted from annual income, any surplus was used for debt repayment, with no financial source available to improve their situation. F's household was stuck in a poverty trap.

In Hebian Village, few villagers were migrant workers. Labour transfer was nonetheless an effective measure to increase farming households' income and help them to escape poverty. In 2015, only eight young people worked in other areas for more than six months, with most spending their income on personal daily consumption and few sending money home. But D was an exception.

Case 3: D was the eldest son in his family. For three years he took jobs as a migrant worker to help support his family in Hebian Village. In 2015, he worked in Guangdong for ten months, earning RMB3,500 a month, from which he remitted RMB2,000 home. He returned home with RMB7,000 savings in November because his family intended to remodel the house but needed his help to do so. D's mother suffered gastrointestinal diseases and was confined to housework. She was hospitalised for one week at the cost of RMB17,000, for which RMB8,000 was recovered from the New Rural Cooperative Medical System. After she was discharged, she remained on medication, which cost RMB300–400 monthly. D's father lived with hypertension and tremors (for which he did not require medication) and was relatively unable to undertake heavy farm work. D has two younger sisters. The older sister was in high school in the county, which required a monthly living expense of around RMB600, and the younger was in junior high school in town at a monthly expense of RMB100. The annual educational expense of his two sisters was RMB10,200. Thus, the household's monthly fixed expenses for education and medical services were roughly RMB1,350. D also had a 15-year-old younger brother who had dropped out of school. He accidentally consumed pesticides at the end of 2015 and was sent to the hospital for treatment, costing over RMB3,000. In addition to this, the household spent RMB3,600 on a chain saw. The household's 2015 total income of around RMB42,000 was all spent. Although stable migrant work and thrift had significantly increased D's household income, diseases and accidents had completely offset the rise in income. Heavy family responsibility and hard labour had left physical marks on D, and his family's physical state was D's greatest concern.

It is noticeable that a large portion of the money earned by D during his work as a migrant labourer was spent on healthcare expenses—which, as discussed, are onerous for many households. After concluding our household survey of the village, we were left wondering why diseases were so prevalent in Hebian. Two potential factors, we found, were adverse local health conditions and the unhealthy diets of villagers. Before our poverty alleviation programme in Hebian began, only the village secretary had a latrine at home; villagers used grass and the woods as 'natural toilets'. Furthermore, many free-range chickens and pigs roamed the area, and the management of both human and animal faeces urgently needed improvement. Tap water came from deep in the mountains but was not treated or purified at the source, and in hot weather it was common for villagers to drink unboiled water. In the busy farming season, villagers had an irregular diet and consumed large amount of edible wild herbs, which can easily cause gastritis. Few villagers had regular physical check-ups. Most villagers sought herbal medicines to ease symptoms when feeling unwell, but when disease became more acute, higher medical expenses would be incurred.

Poor health was a major factor limiting villagers' ability to escape poverty. In 2015 only ten villagers were aged over 60—just 5 percent of the total population—but most suffered from some form of disease. Children also suffered from ill health. In 2015 three children were already diagnosed with pulmonary diseases and had weak immune systems, frequently catching colds and fevers. We thus see a form of poverty cycle: disease made poverty more likely, and poverty reduced the ability to avoid disease, even at young ages. To improve the local health environment and cut the intergenerational transmission of poor health was an integral part of the comprehensive poverty alleviation programme in Hebian Village.

Education-Related Costs

Twenty-eight households in Hebian Village paid for education in 2015, about half of the total. The village's total educational expenditure was RMB153,702, averaged at RMB5,489 per household and RMB4,270 per student. Tuition, incidental expenses and board and lodging accounted for 37 percent of the costs. 'Pocket money' took up a large proportion of total educational expenditure at 52 percent, for the reason that local students mostly had breakfast away from school and the breakfast fee was regarded as a part of pocket money. Travel expenses for school differed by location, its share in total educational expenditure was not high, only at 11 percent.

There were 37 school-age children in the village, one of whom had dropped out of school. Nineteen students went to primary school, thirteen attended junior middle school and four attended high school. The high school students reported the highest educational expenditure: four households spent over RMB10,000 on education, of which all had children in high school. Of the four high school students, one was at school in Mengla County, and three attended a school in the prefecture capital city of Jinghong, incurring high board, lodging and daily living expenses. Due to distance they seldom returned home, thus limiting travel expenses. Board, lodging, and travel expenses were generally RMB1,200–1,400 per year for a primary school student and RMB1,600 per year for a junior middle school student. Currently, all the village's primary school students attend Hope Primary School in the nearby village of Naka, and all the junior middle school students attend Mengban Middle School. We estimated that travel expenses of primary and junior middle school students for one year were RMB560 and RMB800, respectively. Households' financial status determined students' pocket money allowances and was an important factor in educational expenditure decisions.

The educational expenditure of the 28 households accounted for an average of 19.4 percent of their total household expenditure. The household with the highest percentage (64 percent) was headed by a single mother who rarely engaged in agricultural production and relied on short-term jobs and transfer subsidies to support her family. The household's income was almost fully used for education and daily expenses. Eight households spent over 20 percent of their total expenditure on education, which showed that households with school-age children faced heavy education-related costs, intensifying as children moved on to higher studies. In the survey, many parents and villagers stated that higher levels of education incurred higher expenses. This had some negative consequences for education: students aware of their parents' financial stress burdens also found it difficult to focus on their studies.

Among the ten households with the highest educational expenditure, only two reported a considerable surplus when educational expenses were taken from net household income. The highest negative balance was reported by villager H, who had a negative net household income because of heavy losses in 2015. For the remaining seven households, educational expenditure evidently consumed their income, with four relying on savings or borrowings to get by and three achieving a slim surplus.

Major Outlays

Major outlays were mainly made for house construction. These were typically made within the plan established for the pilot comprehensive poverty alleviation programme. The programme created a detailed timetable according to which each household would build houses. These planned houses would be brick-wood structures, recycling timber from old houses and chopped wood purchased from collective forests. Material costs include purchasing timber; oil for use in chain saws; and labour and transport costs (including meals).

Debt

In 2015, a total of 30 households in Hebian Village had borrowed from relatives and friends, banks and credit cooperatives. The village in total borrowed RMB518,900 (RMB9,435 per household and RMB2,544 per capita) that year. The lowest household borrowing figure was RMB300, and the highest was RMB270,000. Loans were mainly used to build houses, treat diseases, pay for education and cover daily living expenses. The household with the highest debt earned a much higher income than other households. This was the 'affluent' household of H, who had planted sugarcane with RMB270,000 loans in 2015 but suffered a heavy loss after wild elephants trespassed on his sugarcane. He failed to repay his debts in 2014 and 2015. Since his debt was disproportionately high compared with other households, we removed this data to more accurately assess village debts levels. Removing H's household leaves the village with total debts of RMB248,900 in 2015, averaged at RMB8,583 per household.

11 households had not borrowed in 2015, but were still in debt. After H's household, the next highest debt amount was RMB135,000. In this case, the householder was sick and had high annual medical costs. He had borrowed from banks, credit cooperatives and relatives multiple times over the previous decade and could not pay interest as his debts kept growing. The village's total unpaid debts stood at RMB1,217,800, averaged at RMB22,142 per household and RMB5,970 per capita.

In general, Hebian villagers were under heavy debts. Even if the villagers' per capita net income in 2016 surpassed the national poverty line of RMB2,760, it was still insufficient to pay off their debts. Poverty alleviation policies that intended to simply increase incomes by a marginal amount could not fundamentally address the deep poverty in which Hebian Village was then sunk. Villagers also had few options for escaping it themselves: their large debts placed them in a credit crisis, and few households could apply for more loans. Even if villagers found productive investment opportunities, those in the deepest poverty, with the highest debts, would thus have had great difficulty in obtaining funding from banks or credit cooperatives. The comprehensive poverty alleviation programme's focus on house-building and renovating thus could not depend on loans being taken out by individual villagers. Government credit guarantees provided an alternative approach. This was only possible thanks to outside help and connections, however: left to themselves, the poverty trap would almost certainly have continued to be perpetuated in unhappy cycles.

Why Did We Build Yao Guestrooms?[8]

Hebian's villagers faced an annual income deficit and spiralling debt. Escaping this poverty trap required an entirely new approach; we chose to chase the tourist dollar.

In 2014–2015, per capita expenditure in Hebian Village was over RMB7,000. This was a big problem: per capita income was only RMB3,000. Each villager, therefore, had a debt mounting by RMB4,000 annually. In 2015–2016 incomes and expenditures remained roughly constant, and the average debt was on track to rise to a total of RMB8,000. The improvements offered by conventional, moderate, development interventions were therefore wholly inadequate. Even if the average villager's income grew to RMB7,000—an increase of over one hundred percent—they would still be on the hook for the debt from the previous year. To pay off the previous year's debt but maintain the same expenditure, the average income had to climb to RMB11,000. Even

[8] Published at xiaoyunzhupin (2017-04-23) at https://mp.weixin.qq.com/s/XRFE8qrEWlOV795Wz0XVzQ.

after these vertigo-inducing bounds, however, this income level would see villagers pay off their debts but not enjoy an improvement in overall welfare. This is a head-scratching poverty trap: poverty, compounded by local shocks, leading to a spiral of debt merely in order to tread water. For Hebian to escape the poverty trap, per capita income had to rise by nearly four times.

This was of course extremely challenging. When we founded Action Against Poverty,[9] we took some time and care in considering how we might crack this nut. We intended to propose to provide external support to assist the villagers in increasing their incomes and of course needed to pick the right core industries that might help bring the village out of the poverty trap in which it was caught. We quickly realised that traditional agriculture alone, no matter how effectively managed, was unlikely to increase Hebian's income substantially. After a systemic analysis of local resources, therefore, we decided that conventional agriculture would only be used as the foundation. It would provide a steady base for a transition into a new sector: unique, high-end tourism, focused on meetings and leisure. Hebian has a lovely local climate, beautiful natural landscape and distinctive cultural resources: we proposed to leverage these innate advantages for development.

The idea was well received. As a major target for relocation programmes in Yunnan Province, Hebian Village was granted generous policy support. Each household enjoyed 20-year RMB60,000 interest-free loans; a RMB10,000 subsidy, and an RMB7,000 subsidy for house renovation. Moreover, each household registered in poverty was entitled to a RMB40,000 housing subsidy. These state transfers were foundational to the programme, and greatly improved villagers' housing conditions.

Although the state-provided transfers solved the need for a housing improvement programme, they did not offer a sustainable method of poverty reduction: they did not, in themselves, create a new source of income. If the government inputs were a blood transfusion, we wanted to help the patient to generate her own blood. We therefore had to

[9] Action Against Poverty is an NGO founded by the author Professor Li Xiaoyun in Mengla County where Hebian Village is located, in an attempt to conduct poverty reduction experiment in the Hebian Village through programmes and projects funded by governments and various social actors. It is also part of Li's experiment on bringing philanthropic resources to remote areas. In China most of the philanthropic resources are concentrated in big better-off cities where most NGOs are established or registered. Note by the translator.

make sure that the transfers were used for innovation and growth, to generate incomes that could support welfare improvements. Of course, this decision was not ours to make. The organisation therefore engaged extensively with the villagers, preparing unified plans for the entire village. The money would be used to develop wooden structures with Yao characteristics, and each building would have a Yao guestroom embedded in it in which to receive paying guests.

The state transfers alone would not be enough to accomplish this. To avoid increasing farmers' debt, Action Against Poverty raised funds through 99 Giving Day (a donation platform on Tencent, China's largest social media provider) in 2015 and 2016. These funds, and donations from other channels, were mainly used for landscaping the village, constructing demonstration buildings and guestrooms, and subsidising decoration materials for the Yao Guestrooms.

By early 2017, 11 guestrooms in Hebian Village had been completed, and the second batch of 16 guestrooms was being decorated. New roads to the village were under construction, and the prospect of real change was growing. To all intents and purposes this was a strong step in the right direction: a careful collaboration between villagers, an expert NGO, and the local government. With the strong support of the county and township government, Action Against Poverty had assisted Hebian Village in developing a new core industry. For the likes of myself, who takes pride in contributing to development, this was greatly satisfying; for the villagers, it was tremendously exciting, a door to a better future.

The Varied Visions on a Pleasant Village Home[10]

> When I discussed with villagers how they wanted to have their houses improved, I discovered that almost all wished for modern buildings of brick and concrete.

My history with Mengla County can be traced back to 1993. I had just returned from abroad and travelled with an anthropologist on a local knowledge survey across tropical rainforests for days. I was impressed by the ethnic minority culture in this southern Yunnan county, its wooden

[10] Published at xiaoyunzhupin (2017-03-03) at https://mp.weixin.qq.com/s/9nXJn5RMTPU75VlgT20ptQ.

stilt structures and women walking with bamboo baskets on their backs. I was new to the county, and couldn't yet distinguish the customs of the different ethnic minority groups from one another, but recognised that I found something special in them. I lingered on the thought of Mengla's unsophisticated style, and, over two decades later, I decided to pay a visit and conduct a survey on poverty. When I arrived, I found the place had changed profoundly, just like other areas in China.

Director Deng from the county poverty alleviation office brought me to Mengban Township, and it was him who brought me to Hebian Village. On the way from the county to the township and the village, I kept spotting shabby stilt houses and brick-concrete modern houses. During the survey in Hebian, it occurred to me that I could settle down here and put my theories of poverty reduction to the test, committing myself to trying to help these villagers. Consequently, I registered a small public-interest organisation in Mengla County and started my anti-poverty work in Hebian Village. This was the origin of the NGO: Action Against Poverty.

From discussions with government officials and local villagers, I discovered that housing was their most significant concern for villagers. Except for the brick and tile village office, the fifty-seven Yao households of Hebian had lived in small wooden stilt structures for decades. These wooden houses were windowless and dilapidated, and they let in air and rain. When I discussed with villagers how they wanted to have their houses improved, I discovered that almost all wished for modern buildings of brick and concrete. I found this a great 'shame'. The characteristic Yao architecture is beautiful and unique, and it seemed to me a tragedy that poverty should lead to its replacement by soulless brick accommodation. Surely, I thought, there had to be a third way. I tried to persuade them to modify and improve their wooden houses, but they responded: 'Professor Li, we've lived in such houses for generations and get tired of them. Our children don't want to live here. Girls are all married elsewhere'.

I could understand this response. In the eyes of some the houses were 'backward', and to be sure, no one would want to live in a dark house with a leaking roof. The villagers quite reasonably sought a dry and pleasant home. The government had identified the village as a major target for poverty reduction policies, and it would be receiving significant state transfers. In neighbouring villages, I had witnessed an improvement in living standards and government support, but I had also witnessed the introduction of standardised brick accommodation. I feared that this unique Yao mountain village would slowly turn into a place of bricks and cement. There would be none of their distinctive ethnic roof decorations, and this very visible display of the value of cultural diversity would be lost.

I decided to stay in the village to investigate its housing problems. Before long, I found that I agreed with the villagers: their houses were quite inconvenient. With no toilets and no way to take a bath, you might run into a dog, cat, or pig on your way to the toilet outside. You could feel the cold wind blowing through the house in the winter, even while in bed. The villagers' demand for better housing conditions was reasonable. But I also knew that new-build brick and concrete houses were not inherently warmer than a wooden structure in winter: they could be just as cold, and sometimes even less comfortable. I joked with the villagers, 'How come you would rather live in such houses than wooden structures? They seem even colder!' The villagers said it was because they were not ventilated. My perspective might have been ignorant—and coloured by my outsider's love for their architecture—but the villagers' vision of the brick houses was also rose-tinted. Another Mr Deng, this one the village accountant, said to me: 'Brick and concrete houses represent cities and a better life. You all live in those houses, and we want that, too!' Some villagers, although not many, took my side. One older villager spoke in favour of the traditional architecture, noting that the new houses were cold in winter, but hot in summer.

At the same time, I also had qualms. Brick and concrete houses had their flaws, but I did wonder whether the damp, unventilated houses would negatively impact the villagers' health in their rainy and tropical climate. There was in fact no brick or cement available in the mountain village, and any new houses would have to be constructed at great effort and with a lot of organisation. If we could avoid this outcome, the wooden houses should also undoubtedly be adapted to local climate conditions. I asked myself how I could communicate with the villagers, and how I could develop and persuade them of a good plan. The Hebian villagers badly wanted to improve their housing, and so did I, but it would take thought and patience.

I visited each household with village Party secretary Mr Li and accountant Mr Deng. We discussed how to find a solution that could meet local demand for improved housing while also preserving the culture of the Yao village. As a scholar, I often conducted surveys on the primary level and often amused myself with writing, but I had no experience in housing.

I had expected the work of poverty reduction to be dominated by the usual tasks, helping farmers raise pigs and plant crops to increase their income, but I soon realised that to help Hebian Village I would need to learn a lot more about houses. After repeated discussion and field observations, I came to the conclusion that the key to meeting local housing demand while still preserving the village's culture lay in fundamentally changing the functions and form of currently available houses. If the wooden stilt houses in Hebian had broad windows and bathrooms, were reasonably divided for living and catering and were generally improved and modernised, would their inhabitants persist in wanting brick-concrete structures? I discussed the question with the man who was then head of the township. He was a member of the Dai ethnic group and had long experience and abundant knowledge of the local areas. He explained to me the advantages of stilt buildings and agreed that while cuboid brick houses appeared superficially better in some respects, they in fact did not meet the needs of the area. Having agreed on this, we discussed how the existing dwelling could be improved, while still retaining their original structure and advantages. He fully supported the idea and offered his help in our plans.

Starting in 2015, the government began to invest in infrastructure in Hebian. As per the plan, village roads and retaining walls were constructed and improved. We benefited from the cooperation and commitment of the government of Mengban Township, and Mengla Country. Officials came to village to spot and address problems on the site over time, we conducted a series of housing projects.

The new plan prioritised reconstruction and renovation in situ, without movement of households. We found, however, that some adjustments were necessary, and that some families' dwellings did have to be relocated within the village. I and my team had a range of factors with which we were concerned in considering where a house should be located: connections to water; risk of flooding; waste management; and so on. Our technocratic concerns were legitimate, but we also realised that the villagers had their own priorities, and that we had to take these into account. Due to the tradition of 'feng shui', changing a house's position would inevitably lead to conflicts and friction. We had hoped to move two houses at the entrance to the village to make space for a small central square, but one of the house owners was so unwilling to move that we had to give up on this plan. We didn't force the household to move because the house was so important to them.

We also found that not everyone was as convinced of the project as we would have liked. Mr Deng, the village accountant, was always ready to help others in improving their houses, but he kept putting off constructing his own house. He was quite frank about his reasons: he thought wooden houses were simply no good. 'Professor Li', he told me, 'I don't want to build a wooden house. I would already have built one if I had wanted to. My family don't agree [with your plan] because they are tired of living in such houses'. I told him that anyone living in such houses as they were now would get tired of them, but that he would be pleased to live in the house we had designed for him. He later went to the town Party secretary, insisting on building a brick-concrete house. Since his homestead adjoined the main village road and a brick-concrete house would mar the village landscape, the Party secretary didn't approve his request. Instead, in fact, Mr Deng was rebuked, and the Party secretary reminded him of his role as a village cadre and asked him to take the lead in following the plan.

We worked hard for a year. As this first year was drawing to a close, I realised that solving the housing problem was becoming a crucial question of morale. The farmers had laboured for nearly twelve months and longed for nothing more than a satisfactory house of their own. If this desire was not met, I feared, the farmers would soon show little interest in anything else. In April 2016 we started a morale-boosting exercise, hurrying to finish one house to have a proof of concept. We hired technicians, selected one household to be supported in completing a model house and purchased tools for the villagers to assist in its construction. Due to the technicians' high contracting costs, we decided to set up a construction work team that learnt skills while working with the technicians' guidance. Since the farmers had basic construction skills, we used site construction of the model house to demonstrate how high-quality timber should be processed and how to maintain safety during construction.

Building the model house took a little over a month. It was brand-new, a beautiful and modern house which still retained the distinctive Hebian architectural style. The villagers were pleased with the broad windows, new roof, and flat and seamless floor.

What does this tell us about the management of development projects? To my mind, as I look back, this short account holds three key lessons. Firstly, those seeking to improve a community's standard of living must above all consider the needs, desires and perceptions of the community itself. This is not a new point in this book and may (I hope) seem obvious, but is still overlooked startlingly often. The villagers wanted houses; we would not have got very far if we ignored this fact. They also wanted houses of a particular quality; we wanted to introduce other factors, namely the retention of the traditional architectural style in order to boost tourism in the future, but if we had prioritised our vision over their quality demands, the project again would not have succeeded. Secondly, a development project requires local political support. We received much of the funding we needed from higher levels of government, but we also received political commitment at the local level. Had the township Party secretary caved to Mr Deng's demands for a solitary brick house, faith in the development project would have been lost, and I doubt we could have continued. The Party secretary's support for our vision and willingness to stand by it meant a lot. Finally, development over the longer term needs encouragement and morale. Many projects can take a considerable time to come to fruition. For those struggling to stay afloat, keeping faith in a very gradual process for future rewards that may not materialise is a big thing to ask. In Hebian, the construction of the 'model house' served as a lighthouse for the rest of our work. It encouraged the villagers who were still waiting for their own leak-free houses and gave them something to hope for. Development is ultimately a human endeavour, and human factors matter just as much as the numbers in the economist's datasets.

The Primary Player in Poverty Reduction[11]

Poverty reduction is a matter of removing barriers to opportunity. It needs an enabling environment for development, which the state and society can provide—but also the engagement and participation of beneficiaries.

[11] Published on the WeChat official account xiaoyunzhupin (2016-02-21) by Zhang Ping (former director of Action Against Poverty in Mengla), Gao Ming (doctoral candidate admitted in 2015, majored in rural development and management at the College of Humanities and Development Studies, China Agricultural University) and Xiao Jin (doctoral candidate admitted in 2015, majored in rural development and management at the College of Humanities and Development Studies, China Agricultural University) at https://mp.weixin.qq.com/s/lIadj4Ar5Gv-0OMIRthN8A.

In a previous section, I wrote about the identity of the key actors in poverty reduction projects. Who is it that is responsible for poverty reduction? Is it the poor themselves, whose hard work actually transforms, slow moment by slow moment, their lives? Is it the state and its representatives, which creates an enabling environment for their hard work, provides services and diverts money towards supporting projects? Is it the NGOs and organisers like myself, who identify problems and try to rally society to fix them? This question is of more than merely conceptual importance: it creates tension when organising events, when attributing credit, when preparing communications and speeches and when trying to set expectations among beneficiaries.

Everyone has their own goals, and their own perceptions of their obligations. In Mengla Province, the Party secretary and some county government department heads have frequently visited poor villages and provided various resources. These resources have sometimes been transformative, and without steady support from the local government, poverty reduction is very hard. However, such support has also tended to cause misunderstandings amongst villagers: they have sometimes believed that the government and society were set on bringing them an affluent life, and that accordingly they could look forward to relative relaxation. The expectation was not wholly wrong, because the government and civil society actors were indeed trying their best to lift them out of poverty. Nevertheless, this perspective risked overlooking the fact that poverty reduction primarily occurs as a result of the activities of the poor themselves. Somewhat surprisingly, those eager to minimise the contribution of the poor to poverty reduction are comprised firstly of the poor themselves. This attitude is not rare in any state-led intervention programme, and we had to be careful in trying not to raise expectations too high. Poverty reduction will not happen unless the work and initiative of the poor themselves is mobilised—with government and social support, of course.

The local political context was highly important. The comprehensive actions against poverty undertaken in Hebian Village relied on the leadership of the county and township governments which provided enormous financial and technical support. Again, this support was vital, but did somewhat shape the attitudes of Hebian villagers. I mentioned earlier in the book that the Chinese government encourages villagers not to 'wait for, rely on, and ask for, assistance': instead, those in poverty should be energetic in seeking out opportunities. I myself am very wary of allowing complacency to set in, and was keen to make sure that villagers' intrinsic motivation for developing their own homes did not become suppressed by the sudden flood of outside support. This, I always felt, was critical to sustainable, comprehensive poverty reduction in Hebian. At one of the earliest village mobilisation meeting, I said in a speech—and thank a graduate student for transcribing this—'It's up to you whether the future of Hebian Village will be the way we have planned. The county and township governments and Action Against Poverty are sparing no effort to support you, but we cannot replace you. You are wrong to think that building houses, roads, and other infrastructure is the government's responsibility. We can never replace you, because this is your home'.

If overcoming poverty is fundamentally about supporting the poor in accessing and embracing opportunities, a key part of any intervention must be to map bottlenecks in this process and to work to reduce them. Early in the Hebian Village programme, Action Against Poverty and the government drew up comprehensive plans to address development constraints, increase farmers' income and improve welfare. This plan was ambitious. We hoped to help Hebian sustainably shake off poverty by enhancing community organisation; nurturing new industry that could help raising farmers' incomes substantially; expanding channels for return on assets and so on. Of course, these goals were not attainable with the input of government and social resources alone. Hebian villagers are the key to overcoming poverty in the village. Therefore, Action Against Poverty supported the village to set up a local 'Youth Start-up Group' and established a 'Development Work Team' led by village officials. These two teams played a critical role in mobilising and organising villagers to join and own the village's poverty reduction programme.

We believed that rural community organisations had paid attention to the function of governance, but less attention to organisation for economic development. Community-building efforts had created formal processes in a range of areas, but had overlooked mechanisms for promoting development. If this continued, we felt, we risked falling into the trap of developing 'parallel systems', in which the new development efforts were run by outsiders from the government or NGOs without much leadership and commitment from the villagers themselves. This is bad in several respects: it risks creating a relationship of dependence between villagers and project organisers; it makes the project less likely to be sustainable, because villagers aren't properly involved in the systems being established; and it makes the outcome less likely to be successful, because villagers have less of a voice in organising actions and identifying potential problems. These are lessons painfully learnt in many other contexts. We tried instead to promote organisational innovation in Hebian, relying on existing village-level political and administrative systems to embed autonomous development functions. The two development teams both relied on and grew out of the existing village committee. When volunteers working on the poverty project created construction blueprints for village houses, we transferred them to the village's Development Work Team and Start-Up Group. We supported them in remaking their village with their own resources, and using their own designs. This process showed the value of villagers' wisdom and initiative from the very beginning.

If Hebian villagers proceed the way they started, Hebian is bound to be a beautiful home of their own in the future. I once said: 'We'd like to go back to our rural hometown but can not bear the backwardness of it; we desire development but can not stand the problems that come with it'. As a scholar I am opposed to fundamentalist and populist participation and I am cautious about the problems that could emerge in the development process. I am a moderate developmentalist, doing a prudent poverty experiment in Hebian. I work to support government's actions in fighting poverty, I always take some precautions against big capital, and my biggest ambition is that the poor population could become active players in development, where they could effectively utilise external support. Maybe I am naive, but I will keep trying.

Demonstration and Mutual Aid of Villagers[12]

Even before we arrived, Hebian was notable for its customs of mutual aid. These customs were notable and important during our house-building project: commitment and collaboration are crucial.

In Hebian Village, January to March is the busiest season. Sugarcane is harvested in these months, and this cash crop determines the fortunes of

[12] Published at xiaoyunzhupin (2017-03-28) by Gao Ming, doctoral candidate admitted in 2015 majored in rural development and management at College of Humanities and Development Studies, China Agricultural University, at https://mp.weixin.qq.com/s/LPA110ECgRwhEXtSHnyLmg.

the villagers. What happens in January might set a household's fortunes for the entire year. The entire village knows this. They also know that, just as there is a chance of a large harvest that allows greater breathing space, there is also a great risk of a failed harvest that tightens a family's range of options. This is especially the case given the exposure of the sugarcane harvest to destruction by elephants. Over the years, dozens of wild elephants have broken into sugar plantations from the rainforest, and cutting the fields is therefore known to be a race against time. If each individual villager harvested their own patch of land by themselves, the harvest would take longer and the window of vulnerability would be larger. Instead, sugarcane growers organise themselves to cut one plot of sugarcane at a time, significantly improving their efficiency and saving more sugarcane from being trampled by elephants. Contributions were not limited to those with an immediate stake in the sugarcane harvest: hardworking people were entitled to a higher labour subsidy, and thus even farmers who had not planted sugarcane could earn some income. When I first encountered Hebian Village, I had an impression of poverty, but also of strong solidarity and mutual aid. I thought at the time that, while the villagers' lives must be hard, this mutual support must make things much more bearable.

When our poverty reduction project started, and building new houses became a theme in everyone's lives, we found that the villagers' collaborative approach to cutting sugarcane continued in their approach to house-building. Wherever we went, we saw people in camouflage overalls shuttling between plank structures. Except for one or two hired carpenters, most were Hebian villagers. In fact, in addition to putting up houses, village efforts drove the entire process of preparing and constructing wooden stilt buildings. Every house was a credit to their initiative and mutual aid.

When they decided to build wooden houses, preparation of the necessary materials became a regular part of villagers' daily labour. Looking for and modifying timber took at least six months, during which time they cut, sawed and shaped the wood according to each household's plan and need.[13] Many people had to carry the sawn wood from high in the

[13] At the time villagers were allowed to cut trees from their collective forests but it needed to be approved by local forests authorities and was subject to strict quota. Note by the translator.

steep surrounding mountains to places where it could be loaded into vehicles. This wood, mainly for support pillars, was priced at a market rate of RMB1,000 per piece. Obtaining and preparing the wood by themselves saved villagers more than half of their houses' cost.

The villagers' wood and the planks purchased at the market or obtained from mountains needed to be processed, polished and cut before use. The villagers finished almost all of this work themselves. Villagers bought electric saws and chainsaws (separately or in cooperation) to modify the timber, meeting their construction needs while accumulating more assets for production. The modification was technical, but most villagers had dealt with wood in their lives, and this did not pose a problem. Since the village was located in a tropical rainforest, cutting and preparing wood was once a main income source for the village.[14] Villagers made division planks for guestrooms and even wardrobes, tables and chairs by hand.

Once the foundations of a house were complete, frameworks were put up. This was an important local event because it marked the accomplishment of the most important step in house-building, and was a powerful reflection of the villagers' mutual aid and collaboration. Before putting up the frameworks, the host household would tell other villagers to get ready. Villagers helping on the day would arrive early in the morning and more would be called upon via phone or broadcast if the work was shorthanded. In general, each house required around forty volunteers. The frameworks were normally set up by the men, while women would cook. The volunteers did not ask for pay, but the host family would provide cigarettes, alcohol and two hearty meals. After the framework was put up, house construction could officially start.

Construction expenses would begin to mount once this most basic work was complete. This was in part because of the cost of hiring technicians: these could be up to RMB30,000–40,000, twice that an average Hebian household could earn in that year (2017). Initially, because villagers didn't know how to build houses, we hired carpenters to build the first batch of wooden structures, including model houses. Some villagers helped with the work while learning the necessary skills. They showed an incredible capacity to learn. Later, the Hebian villagers could finish all of the building by themselves, except for placing tiles'.

[14] But with introduction of policies that intend to protect rainforest, logging is increasing being banned in Xishuangbanna, a villager in Hebian even received prison sentence due to logging. Note by the translator.

Prices went up when relocation projects money came in. The average labour costs of building walls reached RMB80 per square metre, RMB700 for an average bathroom on one floor, and RMB1,500 for that of two floors. We offered villagers free bricks to build kitchens and bathrooms that avoided wooden structures' possible weakness and hidden risks in damp environment. After the example of the demo houses and opportunities for learning, some of the villagers could independently finish building walls and cementing the bathrooms.

Learning to build houses saved the villagers money and enabled them to master construction skills for stilt-style wooden buildings, a potential new income source. For instance, Li Ming, a diligent and energetic member of the Youth Start-up Group in Hebian Village, learned housing construction skills. He was planning to build other houses in the village and work in neighbouring villages for income.

By 2017 nearly fifty households in Hebian had put up new houses. Rates of progress varied, but the village plan had started to take shape. Every visitor would comment, 'How Hebian has changed!' More importantly, visitors could see that the villagers' spiritual outlook had also changed. Although the houses and furniture they have had built were not yet tidy and elegant, and though they faced many challenges, the farmers' proactive participation in house-building helped realise our initial goal of participatory development.

For me, this proves wrong those who say that areas in poverty lack a culture of self-development, and who believe that villagers are backward and self-interested. Our practise indicated that commitment and collaboration were critical for Hebian's development. The entire village showed enormous initiative, from collectively cutting sugarcane to building houses in mutual aid. In our opinion, poverty does not result from inaction of the 'poor', but from a lack of opportunity and appropriate support.

A Developmentalist's Experiment in Hebian

Development is fundamentally about improving lives. But how do we do that while safeguarding what people value? There are always enormous questions that we must pose ourselves.

My children and my students grew up in an era of reform and opening-up, with increasingly abundant material goods in an increasingly open society. They have received a good education. I disagree with them on a lot of things. Most of them are cynical do-gooders. For example, if I say somewhere is developing rapidly, it's quite likely that they would counter: 'There are people living in poverty there. You should not ignore that'.

When I was a child growing up in a small county in northwestern China, we got by with a few essentials and most people were conservative. Every year, I had only one suit of winter clothes and one suit of summer clothes. I don't remember having many baths when I was a child. During my university years, as China gradually opened up its economy, I began to have a better understanding of the world. I learned that people in western countries had more plentiful material possessions and showered and ate meat every day. This was possible because they lived in developed countries. Learning from the West and pursuing development became ingrained in my mind.

On many occasions, I have defined myself as a developmentalist. Though I agree, development can bring in its train health issues, environmental problems, inequality and other issues, my views of critique on development are sceptical rather than cautious. To be more specific, I'm a social evolutionist, I believe in development. Without development there is no difference between the past, the present and the future, in essential terms. Only with development, today can be better than yesterday, but i am not denying the problems of today. One question I can pose to those who always resist development is that: why are few people willing to return to primitive society? In a conversation with Professor Emma Mawdsley at the University of Cambridge, I said, 'British scholars have contributed too much to postcolonialism. It even makes them appear a little hypocritical. They regard development as the colonisation of a single value'. She said: 'Xiaoyun, I also think we went a bit too far'. Pluralism, especially multiculturalism, is undoubtedly one of the facets of human progress. My thinking, however, has continued, and I now find myself asking: although progress is a relative concept, when cultural diversity is emphasised, don't we find ourselves obliged to make value judgments on things? It is true that I use this thought to defend my developmental propositions and actions. I haven't delved too deeply into this topic, but I did frequently visit rural areas in China and Africa and put developmentalism into practise. When I was in the countryside, I asked many villagers: 'Do you want to live in a city?' Almost everyone answered, 'We want to, but we can't'. In rural Tanzania, I asked local villagers the same question and they gave me the same answer. The gaps between urban and rural areas are a common problem in developing countries. On the one hand, most of the rural population are attracted by cities' material wealth and colourful culture; on the other hand, due to lack of skills, insufficient education and other reasons, the rural population cannot really enjoy the benefits of living in a city. Many call this 'the illusion of city life'. However, this does not mean that the rural population should not pursue their urban dreams; and furthermore, this is not a problem of development. On the contrary, it is precisely a problem of underdevelopment.

Even among my students, very few who come from the countryside say that they wish to return after their graduation. I have talked about similar topics with villagers whose children are studying in cities. They told me: 'We spend our hard-earned money on the education of our children. We hope that they will have a good future and do not come back to the countryside'. During these discussions, I kept asking myself, 'how can we make the countryside a place that people want to return to and that urban people want to visit?' I believe the answer lies in development.

I feel that I fall into the category of persons who are criticised for being 'brainwashed by the hegemony and ideology of developmentalism'. I fully understand the seriousness of these critics' concerns and I appreciate their persistent commitment to critical thinking. I am not ignoring the problems of development, but the question I want to ask is: 'Can the problems caused by development be solved through development?' This does not seem logically sound. How can the cause of a problem be the solution to it? But if development cannot solve the problem, how can we solve it?

In the 1990s, I travelled to Europe for a study programme. I was shocked by the fact that even the bathrooms in Europe were better than many Chinese homes. I visited a village in Germany and lived in a farmer's house. The landlady cleaned the bathroom and the kitchen every day. After cleaning, she would put a small bouquet of flowers in the bathroom. She also watered the flowers in the garden. She made her home look like a garden. These things left a deep impression on me.

After returning to China, the first thing I did was to renovate the public toilets in the building of the College where I worked. After the renovation, my German colleague sighed happily: 'Finally, the toilet in our workplace doesn't smell anymore!' In the past 20 years, our office building has been renovated several times. We now have a toilet as clean and beautiful as the one in my landlady's home in Germany. There are flowers on the washstands and beautiful landscape paintings on the tiled walls. This has been appreciated by our students, faculty and guests.

Sometimes I laugh at myself. Can't dirtiness and messiness be a part of a culture? Do all civilised societies need to keep bathrooms and kitchens clean and tidy like Europeans do? But then, if my behaviour is a product of Europe's cultural colonialism, why would people who have never been to Europe like our workplace toilet so much? Of course, we can say it is because Chinese civilisation was infiltrated by Western values, leading to the reshaping of our values. Yet I still believe that progress and what we often find ourselves calling 'a civilised way of life' are universal pursuits. A scholar's perspective is that the expansion of modernity brings in the expansion of the lifestyles and values of a certain culture. It is obvious that globalisation mainly means the propagation of modern Western culture. Despite my nationalistic tendencies, I still think that there are some universal values in this world.

In January 2015, I visited Hebian Village. Seeing the muddy roads and dilapidated houses in this poor little village, I came up with the idea: I would stay and make some difference here. In the past, the 57 households of Hebian Village made a living mainly from growing sugarcane, picking Wurfbainia villosa (a plant in the ginger family), or doing local odd jobs. In 2015, the per capita income of Hebian Village was RMB4,303, and the per capita expenditure was RMB5,098. About 80% of households had incurred debts that they could not repay. Most lived in dilapidated houses raised on stilts, without toilets, kitchens or windows (for me, the absence of toilets was the biggest challenge). Many villagers lived in these houses together with their farm animals. There were no paved roads in or near the village, so it was extremely difficult to travel in the rainy season. No one cared for preschool-aged children in the village. The dropout rate at the secondary school level was over 50%. Generally speaking, Hebian Village was a village that had been trapped in poverty for a long time.

I spent some time reflecting on how to modernise this community of ethnic minority. Most villagers, as I said, made a living from picking Wurfbainia villosa or growing sugarcane. However, the output and price of Wurfbainia villosa were very unstable; the income that a village household made from the sale of Wurfbainia villosa might range from RMB2,000 to a little over RMB10,000. Although sugarcane was a more stable source of income, wild elephants could destroy the crop, and the compensation for every mu[15] of destroyed sugarcane was only RMB700 at the time. Under these circumstances, most villagers were unable to make enough money to cover everyday expenses. After much discussion with the villagers and the government, I finally proposed an experimental programme: we planned to make full use of the natural rainforests and local Yao culture to transform Hebian Village into a destination for leisure tourism and convention economy. If more city-dwellers visited this village, there would be more chances for the villagers to come into contact with modern ideas, values and skills. At the same time, tourists could enjoy the nature and local culture. Isn't this an effective way to integrate tradition and modernity?

By 2019, I had worked in Hebian for four years. Me and my team worked with relevant government departments to gain funds for Hebian. We helped villagers renovate their stilt houses and transform them into Yao culture-themed homestays with modern bathrooms and kitchens that are as clean and tidy as those in cities. We also built a small conference centre with modern facilities and improved sanitation and environment in the village. With strong support from the government at all levels, Hebian Village underwent remarkable changes. New stilt houses were built. The magnitude of the change was far beyond my expectations.

We tried our best to ensure that the villagers benefited from the programme process as we were advancing it. Since I was introducing a set of 'modern/urban' ideas to a traditional rural village through much-criticised development intervention, I attached great importance to the participatory approach: engaging with the villagers and government and repeatedly sought their opinions and advice. Without the villagers' participation and governmental support, this programme would definitely have failed.

At the same time, I had to acknowledge the interventionalist touch of the programme. Sometimes, even my students criticised me for being too persistent in my own ideas. For example, the villagers had never had windowed houses, but I insisted that in their new homes, windows should be large, in some proper places even French windows could be used. I said to the villagers, before, you didn't have chances to know how it felt to have the sunlight shining in your homes, but now you would! My colleagues kindly reminded me to respect the local culture and not to impose my own opinions on others.

[15] 20 *mu* equals one and a third hectares. Note by the translator.

There is no doubt that I am a development interventionist, but my interventions have brought tangible benefits to the villagers. From 2017 to 2018, Hebian's income from hosting conferences, winter and summer camps, and other activities exceeded RMB800,000. During the four-year housing construction period, the villagers learned much from professional construction workers and some became very proficient in building houses. They began to work in pairs to build stilt houses for other villages. Their wage income has increased from RMB100–150 a day to RMB250–300. If we take their income from construction work into account, the income of Hebian Village in 2017–2018 definitely exceeded RMB1,000,000.

To help a poor group of people pull themselves out of poverty, we have to not only help them to solve their current problems but also focus on future needs. We placed a great emphasis on preschool education. Hebian Village was affected by the so-called 'culture of poverty'. This culture of poverty is continuously transmitted from generation to generation and between groups, giving rise to a social mechanism of the reproduction of poverty. When I first came to the village, few villagers spoke Mandarin, and the children ran away when they saw strangers. School-age children had to go to a boarding school in a town more than ten kilometres away and came back to the village once a week.

We therefore built a children's activity centre in the village, and with the assistance of the Yunnan Provincial Department of Education we sent a girl who had completed lower secondary education to Kunming to receive training to work with children. She has become a child counsellor at Hebian Village's activity centre. In November 2018, when I returned to the village, I met some students from the activity centre. They greeted me warmly, 'Good morning, grandpa!' It was my first time being called a grandpa. I felt sad and happy at the same time, sad for being old, and happy for seeing the future.

I suddenly realised that the dream of development that had accompanied me throughout my childhood, adolescence, and youth was what had made me a developmentalist. However, being a developmentalist is, sometimes, painful. To advance the poverty reduction programme in Hebian, I registered a small non-profit organisation (Action Against Poverty) in Mengla County. We had been working in the village for four years. As an outside group working in Hebian, we avoided any discriminatory language that implied that poverty was caused by laziness. We believed that this deeply impoverished village had been stuck in the poverty trap due to structural failings. Only through external interventions enabling villagers to connect with modern values and skills could they get out of this poverty trap. However, we inevitably carried some urban-oriented modern values, discourses and mindsets. The villagers were sometimes overwhelmed by the unfamiliarity of modern ways of life and gradually became dependent on our interventions. For example, my colleague Song Haiyan worked and lived in the village for two years. During her stay, she visited everyone's house every day and asked them to clean and tidy up their houses, including the guest rooms. I reflected on the potential risks that we, as external interventionalists, might bring to this village.

On the 23rd of January, 2019, we held a village meeting where the Hebian Cooperative was officially launched, marking the end of the externally-driven development stage and the beginning of a new explorational stage of independent management and sustainable development by farmers themselves. I have been thinking about how to help this village catch up with China's rapid train of development. My approach is to seek solutions to problems amidst development.

Objectively speaking, my approach cannot stand up to theoretical scrutiny. I sometimes think that my persistence is due to a lack of reading; I seldom ponder problems from the theoretical point of view. Enthusiasm has been the main driver for my perseverance. Many academic thoughts and theories are difficult to put into practise. They may even make us have cold feet and hesitate to move forward. Therefore, I said on many occasions: 'I am not a scholar. Scholars rely on their brains. They read and write articles. On the contrary, I like travelling, and I rely on my legs. I have visited a lot of places, from China to Africa. I learned quite a few folk songs and ballads in different languages. At best, I am a practitioner of development. You could say that I'm a doer and an optimist'.

Nevertheless, my work in Hebian Village has been supported by the government, quite a few colleagues and friends. Recently, many people approached me and said, 'Professor Li, come and help us do something in our village'. Speaking with them, I couldn't say no. But in fact, I knew very well that it would be impossible to replicate the Hebian programme elsewhere.

I call the poverty programme in Hebian Village a 'developmentalist's experiment'. Certain conditions were essential to this experiment's achievements. The secretary of the county-level party committee had an interesting response to my initial plan. He said, 'Professor Li, it's done!' I said, 'It's too early to say that'. Whenever the Hebian programme encountered a problem, I called him, and he would try best to offer help without hesitation. Great changes have taken place in Hebian Village, but it is too early to say whether the experiment will be successful in the end. I could not rashly launch another similar experiment nor would I encourage any of my colleagues or students to do so.

I still don't have an answer to the question of whether the problems that arise in development can be solved through development.

Are the Achievements of Poverty Reduction in Hebian Sustainable?

The projects in Hebian have seen striking success, but COVID-19 has nonetheless forced villagers to diversify.

When diagnosing the reasons for Hebian Village's impoverishment in 2015, my team and I hypothesised that Hebian was in a poverty trap resulting from an extreme shortage of materials and human resources. This affected the choices we made when trying to improve its conditions.

We put the hypothesis forward for the following reasons. For a start, the local villagers had no safe housing. When we examined the village in 2015, the minimum cost for building safe housing in the village was RMB150,000, and Hebian faced a low growth rate of per capita income. It was almost unlikely that the villagers could quickly improve their basic living conditions.

Next, almost all Hebian households were burdened with debts, which at the time surprised me. How could they fall into debt, I initially wondered, since they lived a simple life and could provide for themselves by farming their land? Later, after moving to the location and taking the chance to ask more questions, I discovered that their living expenses had kept increasing, while their incomes had remained static. To sell their produce where it was needed villagers increasingly had to travel to the local region's market; this required a motorcycle, which itself needed petrol and regular maintenance. Those who had school-age children had to send them to a boarding school outside the village due to absence of primary or secondary education in this small natural village, which demanded a boarding expense and even more petrol and maintenance costs. The villagers' main sources of income, however, were their harvests of sugar cane and fructus amomi; in the absence of improvements to the efficiency of their production or increases to the market price of these products, their incomes could not rise to meet needs. Faced with the difficulty of obtaining stable cash flows needed to satisfy the rising costs of basic needs, the villagers had begun borrowing money by various means, which they were often then unable to pay back completely. For several years, we saw quite often workers from the rural credit cooperative[16] go to the villagers' homes to collect repayments to loans. In this way, the farmers had fallen into a cyclical poverty trap.

Finally, the village lacked human capital. When I visited the village for the first time in 2015, I found that most villagers had only received primary school education, a few received junior high school education, and a mere handful had been to senior high school.

In the early days after I arrived in Hebian, I found a man driving a car. Later, I learned from the villagers that the driver was the 'richest man' in the village, and the car itself had been given to him by a debtor unable to pay off a debt owed to him. Nonetheless, the 'richest man' was himself also burdened with debts. According to my findings during the first visit to the village, no one was 'rich' in a way that would match definitions outside the village, judging from their housing conditions. No villager had been able to carve out a path to wealth, which added to the scarcity of human assets in the village: all the villagers were struggling merely to continue, and none were sufficiently wealthy to offer investments and some stability.

Based on our hypothesis, we formulated a poverty reduction plan to increase the comprehensive assets of farmers in Hebian Village. It is hard for local villagers to escape the poverty trap without external support. Therefore, after negotiating with the government, the state relocation-based pro-poor project funding was integrated into the comprehensive Hebian poverty reduction programme which supported villagers to build safe housing while equipping each house with a Yao mother's guest room, thus providing villagers with a durable income stream. With the help of philanthropic organisations, we installed facilities to accommodate small meetings, nature education, and leisure and tourism in Hebian Village, including a newly built conference room and public toilet, bars and convenience stores using villager's housing space. These new business activities were coordinated by a newly established village cooperative

[16] A rural credit cooperative is a cooperative or credit union sanctioned by China's central bank the People's Bank of China to provide credit in the rural areas of China. Note by the translator.

but ran on different modes. Conference, children's camps and newly-built guest rooms were run by the cooperative, while guest rooms and restaurants embedded in villagers' houses were mainly operated by the householders but marketed and coordinated by the cooperative. Since the cooperative was held by village households through their guest room shares, each household not only got income from cooperation with the cooperative, but also could obtain 'returns' from the profits from the cooperative account if there was any. In Hebian's case, the village cooperative shouldered some of the village's collective responsibility, paying teachers' subsidies for the Hebian children's centre, maintaining village roads, scenery and public areas, to name but a few. This was counted as returns for the cooperative's shareholders—the village households. The funding from government projects and from various social and philanthropic channels were thus used to both enhance the assets level for local farmers and to develop new business forms to help farmers escape the poverty trap.

On top of this, we provided training programmes for farmers, especially women, to develop new skills, such as cleaning guest rooms, receiving guests, providing various services and making handicrafts with distinctive ethnic Yao features, thereby improving the quality of human capital in the village. In this way, both the farmers' individual human capital and the village's collective human capital were improved, thereby ensuring that the villagers are the main beneficiaries of the new forms of business in Hebian.

In 2019, Hebian Village was officially lifted out of poverty, as measured by the government's criteria. As our plan had been designed to benefit the farmers by constructing new housing in the project's first phase, some villagers' incomes began to increase in 2017, and most local households had risen out of poverty by 2018. The average household income in Hebian Village increased from about RMB10,000 in 2016 to over RMB30,000 in 2018. During the process, we helped the village cooperative to carefully 'allocate' guests to every household and supported those who lacked guest room service skills in receiving guests, so that even the poorest households can benefit to some extent. Although the income generated from guest rooms were different among households, depending on quality of facilities, decoration and service, the variation was minor.

By 2019, over 60 percent of local households' income came from new forms of business. These new business streams were not limited to the guesthouse project. If small agricultural households in Hebian Village must rely upon a single source of income, they will be exposed to market risks that could see them fall back into poverty. Recognising this, we began to plan a pilot initiative to showcase new comprehensive approaches to revenue-building, implementing demonstration projects in pig breeding, beekeeping, and wine-making. In particular, we encouraged farmers to grow 'winter vegetables'.[17] By the end of 2019, great changes had occurred in the village, and the villagers' living standards had improved significantly. We could say with confidence that Hebian Village had got rid of poverty.

For years afterwards, many people asked me whether the results of our poverty reduction project in Hebian Village were solid and sustainable. These were very reasonable and sensible questions and indeed must be asked of any lauded development project. In 2020, our efforts were put to the test when the village was hit by the first wave of the COVID-19 pandemic. During our visit to the village at the beginning of 2021, we found that the villagers' income had increased rather than declined. To my surprise, the average household income in Hebian Village in 2020 was higher than in 2019. Many villagers had their own cars—a tremendous leap forward given that they had previously struggled to run even motorcycles. Analysis showed that the initial effects of anti-pandemic had basically eased by June 2020, allowing the resumption of many activities. The village therefore did not suffer a severe blow from the early wave of the pandemic.

Since I didn't visit the village that year, I didn't see the pandemic's impact on the village in person. My own eyes and ears were supplemented, however, by those of my students. According to the annual data that they collected, the villagers' incomes did not drop, and the pandemic continued to only intermittently impact the village's economic security. Compared with 2019, the villagers' income from the guest rooms was lower in 2020 and 2021, but their income from agriculture was

[17] Since Hebian Village is located in tropical area, vegetables can be grown throughout the year, but in northern China where temperature is much lower, crops and vegetables cannot be grown in winter unless with greenhouse facilities. Vegetables grown in southern China in winter times are thus called winter vegetables. They are usually in short supply in winter times and are therefore sold at good prices. Note by the translator.

higher. It showed that our programme for diversifying the villagers' livelihood options, launched in 2018, had both significantly boosted the local economy, and had made it considerably more resilient.

We knew at the start of 2022 that if the pandemic situation was similar to that in the previous two years-without any long-term lockdown, Hebian Village would not fall back into poverty. However, Mengla County—given that it is on the China-Laos border—was listed in 2021 as a border port area under the pandemic prevention and control policy, and the relatively fixed flow of tourists to Hebian Village over the previous years was ultimately severely disrupted. We expected that should the lockdown continue, it would negatively impact the villagers' livelihood in Hebian Village. Many people, out of concern, asked me about the situation in the village. I explained to them that since every household in Hebian Village already has a safe house and farmland, the probability of them falling into poverty was minor, but that there was still an arduous and long way to go for the villagers to obtain the modern life to which they aspired.

Some Hebian villagers have jokingly asked me, 'Professor Li, since you've helped us get out of poverty, are you going to help us get rich?' I could hardly turn down their kind request and could only reply by saying 'I would try'. Actually, when people asked me whether the achievements of our poverty reduction projects in Hebian Village were sustainable, I wondered about the future of many villages like Hebian. At one point during the lockdowns two of my students stationed in the village told me they had run short of vegetables after a positive COVID-19 case was reported, and they went to the mountain to gather wild vegetables with the villagers. The villagers grow very few vegetables and usually travel beyond the mountain to buy vegetables in the town, so the lockdown restricted their access to vegetables. It has struck me that if villagers become dependent on external sources of income to the point that they abandon their previous practises, they are highly vulnerable to forces beyond their control. Instead of placing all of our eggs in the basket of tourism, I and my colleagues agreed, we had to support a broad diversification of revenue streams.

Part of this requires ensuring that Hebian has a good stock of intelligent young people, who are supported in beginning their own enterprises and continuing the ones we have catalysed. Hebian has, like other rural villagers, increasingly been able to send young people to university. In recent years, however, few college graduates have returned to their hometown in Hebian Village; even if they return during vacations, they are always eager to leave. I learned from conversations with them that returning home was their last option. Several students from the village have married elsewhere after graduating from college, and bachelors in Hebian Village, old or young, have no opportunities to get a wife from outside the village. Even with a stable income and a scenic rural landscape, the village pales compared to other noisy, bustling counties. That prompted me to think: How can we judge whether the achievements of our poverty reduction projects will be sustainable? A city measures its success according to whether it grows; should we apply the same test to Hebian?

At the end of 2021, the Yulin Yaojia Cooperative in Hebian Village underwent restructuring after a majority of the managers expressed their intention to quit. My colleagues told me the cooperative had run out of funds for internet fees and salaries. The situation made me think of my previous work in Africa. Back then, we built learning centres in two villages in Tanzania, with furniture and equipment shipped from China. Then, one day, when I saw the pictures of my Tanzanian friends at a meeting in the decayed learning centre, I felt mixed feelings in my heart.

In recent years, while discussing modernisation, I have often quoted the case of Hebian Village to explain the integration of tradition and modernity. In fact, the essence of both poverty reduction and rural revitalisation lies in modernisation. For rural China, modernisation means transforming the economy, society and people. The poverty alleviation project in Hebian Village has attempted to bring in modernised elements, from a window, a house, to a new industry and its management. Whether these elements can take root and develop in such a traditional village is the key to sustaining the achievements of our poverty reduction projects in Hebian. There's no lack of young people in the village. The junior high school students I met when I first visited the village seven years ago in 2015 have now grown into adults. They idle around the village on motorcycles and lie in hammocks playing on their phones to kill time when it's too hot at noon.

The mother of a student of mine runs a business in Guangdong. After hearing about the young people in Hebian Village, she wanted to offer them work but was rejected by many. In recent years, some young people (those who do not have a college degree) left the village for work but returned a few days later because of the different dining habits and heavy workload of town life. Under such circumstances, whether the achievements of poverty reduction in Hebian will be stable and sustainable does not depend on the village's income levels, but rather, it depends on whether the village has been put onto a track of modernisation. In another word, to what extent the villagers' daily practise has entered the modern world really matters.

I have mentioned that the external definitions of poverty in Hebian, made for example by visiting researchers from the China Agricultural University, do not always align with villagers' own understandings of their situations. This certainly does not mean that local villagers thought they were rich: they were aware that they were not wealthy compared even to inhabitants of the regional town, and that they lacked basic services. When I first visited, the villagers yearned simply for a road leading up to the village. This, through the work of the villagers, multiple levels of government, and NGOs, has been addressed. After a fashion, however, improvements to basic services are really fairly simple. Now that Hebian is becoming more developed the goal is to reduce local relative poverty, and this is more complex.

Poverty, defined by visiting researchers, is a concept with both material and cultural implications. Getting out of poverty means entering a state of modernisation which is closely associated with urbanisation, industrialisation, modern consumption, and modern way of life. In this sense, the sustainability of poverty reduction in Hebian Village means completely transforming the village from a traditional and 'backward' one into a modern place. In fact, such a transformation has already occurred, as evidenced by the growing car ownership of rural households. Despite limited car use, they regarded car ownership as an important goal of a better life.

At the core of maintaining the achievements of poverty reduction lies the relationship between traditionality and modernity, a problem that has perplexed us for a long time. While working in Hebian Village, I thought I found a way to integrate traditionality with modernity despite the lack of theoretical support. It's difficult for traditionality and modernity to accommodate each other. Therefore, I have no answer about the future of Hebian Village. However, judging from the material and cultural perspectives, the villagers seem to be moving further away from a past with prominent community characteristics.

Shared Apartments in Hebian

Improving the context for investment, enabling external money to enter impoverished rural areas, can be a catalyst for development.

In 2021, the residents of Hebian Village found a well-decorated modern wooden building standing over their village. Similar renovation works in another three wooden buildings were also ongoing. These structures are part of an early project for the renewal of the village and the upgrade of the guest room business.

The poverty reduction programme in Hebian Village was largely financed by state relocation project, supported by philanthropic projects initiated by Action Against Poverty and various other social organisations and fund-raising channels. As I have explained, the Hebian programme is centred on the 'Yao Mother's Guestroom', a new composite business model that promotes conference economy, leisure tourism and nature education. With pooled funding from government, society, philanthropic organisations and Hebian villagers themselves, Hebian has been turned into a new village with Yao stylish homestays, conference and catering facilities.

With construction and renovation work completed in 2017 and 2018, Hebian has been pushed onto a new track of development: the fledgling conference economy, nature education projects and various other tourism-based new business dramatically increased Hebian villagers' income-average household income in 2018 tripled that of the 2016. It was officially documented that the entire village shook off poverty in 2018. In 2019 alone, the guest room-centred new business yielded nearly one million yuan income to the village. Yao Mama Guestroom has become both the village's calling card and a tentpole of Xishuangbanna Prefecture[18]'s poverty reduction efforts. This project is deemed meaningful in many ways, such as developing new rural industries, allowing women to get paid jobs without leaving their homes, preserving traditional villages and ethnic cultures, and integrating alternative livelihoods with rainforest protection.

[18] According to vertical administrative jurisdiction, Hebian Village is in Mengban Township, Mengla County, Xishuangbanna Prefecture, Yunnan Province, China. Note by the translator.

It is also good for those visiting, who are typically city-dwellers in need of repose and time in nature. In May 2020, my entrepreneur friend Mr Li vacationed in the village. He was trained as a doctor and later established his own business. He travels frequently. After staying in Hebian Village for a few days, he said to me, 'Xiaoyun, this place is really nice. It's an oxygen bar. I slept so well here. It is a good place for the healthcare industry'. Many people—myself included—feel the same.

From many perspectives, the Hebian programme has been a great success. At the same time, we know that there are still improvements to be made—even at the quite small-scale level. In the days of construction, the use of poverty reduction funds was subject to strict project restrictions, so the guestrooms were not very well-equipped. The partition walls and floorboards were all one-layered, resulting in poor insulation. One could hear loud footsteps from other rooms. Although the new buildings are much better than their predecessors and look nice and elegant at first glimpse, minor problems do exist.

Hebian is located in a tropical area but is at a higher altitude—800 metres above the sea level. Around the Spring Festival, at the end of winter, it can be cold in the mornings and nights. These well-ventilated buildings are poorly insulated, guests can feel a little bit cold, even with air conditioning. Therefore, it is fair to say that these guestrooms do not tap efficiently the potential of this rainforest village's natural and cultural resources as well as they could do in time.

Mr Li stayed in Zhou Zhixue's home and asked me whether there was any support he could offer to the household. I told him he could help build an apartment building, 'the shared apartments'. We agreed that Li would fund a renovation project to rebuild half of Zhou's home into a three-storied apartment building. This upgraded version of the Yao Mama's guestroom had three bedrooms, two living rooms, three bathrooms and one spacious kitchen and dinning room. Li would not be the property owner but would have the right to use. Li would pay Zhou RMB 6,000 per year in management fees to cover the water, electricity and sanitation bills as well as some maintenance costs, and Zhou could rent the property to other people when Li does not use it, and all the income would go to Zhou and the village cooperative. Thus, the apartment building was built after over half a year of construction.

In the spring of 2021, Li came to Hebian Village with some friends and stayed in the shared apartments. My colleague Song Haiyan helped Zhou

Zhixue develop the Rain Forest Set Menu so Li could enjoy three home-cooked forest-themed meals every day during his stay. The Rain Forest Set Menu is another philanthropic experiment centred on nutrition, initiated in cooperation with the Vanke Foundation and incorporated as part of the shared apartments project. The menu is carefully designed, integrating locally sourced food and ingredients to ensure the freshness, tastes and nutrition of the meals. Rice, pork, chicken, fish, bamboo shoots, papaya and banana leaves are all from the village.

The shared apartments began operating in the summer for a trial period. The special price was RMB1,500 per night, half the anticipated price of RMB3,000. The eight-day trial brought in RMB18,000 for Zhou Zhixue, nearly three times that of the average household's guestroom income that year. Without the impact of COVID-19, the project should have generated an income of several tens of thousands yuan per year. Following this example, I invited a few other friends to support building similar shared apartments in the village, and four such buildings were completed in 2022.

Building a society of common prosperity is not easy, and it is harder when we approach the task with a blinkered perspective. When we pursue common prosperity, we usually think about the second or third distribution: the reallocation of resources from the rich to the poor, through deliberate and direct interventions by the state. However, the reality is that we can also support rural areas in accessing what you might ultimately call 'indirect distribution', by making them attractive places for investment and by supporting them in selling products that richer inhabitants are willing to buy. In saying this, we must recognise that poor and rural areas face specific obstacles in their path to this improved state. For agricultural areas, our pursuit of common prosperity means increasing farmers' income—and this means improving their relationship to the wider economy, increasing the inflow of resources from other areas to areas dominated by poorer rural populations. We have attempted to do this through our Hebian Village project.

This is not to say that China's approach is unsound. Over the past years, the increase in the incomes of impoverished rural households has come mainly from deliberate transfers. Strategically, this is the right approach (while it would not have been decades previously). There are fewer farmers, and much fewer impoverished farmers, now than there used to be. There is now the opportunity to provide direct, higher-value transfers to the more limited number of people in need. Yet, at the same time, we should also be aware that production, the creation of value-added, as a sort of primary distribution, can play an important role in increasing farmers' income and changing the overall income structure of rural households. More opportunities must be made available to farmers to obtain greater incomes.

I recently published a book in which I cited the words of Mr Xu Yongguang, a prominent NGO leader in China: 'philanthropy is not just giving. It is about searching solutions to real problems in society'. This is indeed the underlying principle of my friend Mr Li and my colleagues' philanthropy. They did not merely give. They initiated a durable and profitable project, which benefits both the local community and investing stakeholders, and which sets the stage for further, similar investments. When the investors have time, they fly to Xishuangbanna to, as Mr Li put it, 'lie in the rain forest and sing, breathing in fresh air'. Li benefits from what he gave out, while Zhou, the recipient, also obtained assets to help him increase his income. It is not the case that all rural villages' fortunes can be reversed through investments in real estate development and increased access to tourism. Most, however, will have some kind of comparative advantage—as Hebian is fortunate to have in its architecture, environment, and rural charm—which can, with support, be made attractive investment opportunities for outside actors. As part of a wider poverty reduction programme, this can be effective.

Zaoqin and Her Walnut Oil

> To grow their incomes, rural farmers must now start to capture more of the value chain.

Many rural areas in China rely disproportionately on individual sectors or products. Even in these sectors, however, there are often significant inefficiencies and missed opportunities. Among other reasons, this can be because of inadequate access to particular equipment; lack of capital to buy this equipment, if farmers do know of it; lack of knowledge, either of possible opportunities or of how to take them; lack of time and qualified labour; or lack of access to markets in which additional products could be sold, if they were produced. These gaps in key local industries present both a challenge, making it harder to foster development, and an opportunity: with support, existing industries could offer still more revenue and employment, allowing investment and improved quality of life. I'll illustrate this with an example.

In November 2021 the President of China Agricultural University (CAU) Professor Qixin Sun visited Ms Zaoqin Li's Walnut Processing Workshop in Luoboshan, a village in the southwestern province Yunnan (on the border with Myanmar), with leaders of the province's Rural Revitalisation Bureau. While witnessing the processing on-site, Sun found that the walnut skins and walnuts were not separated after the oil was squeezed. Subsequently, Sun turned to China Agricultural University professors specialising in food processing for help and ultimately provided the workshop with peeling equipment.

In April 2022, the National Academy for the Rural Revitalisation at CAU convened a meeting on rural revitalisation. President Sun, who is heading the Academy, and deans of relevant departments and colleges in the university also attended the meeting. As the executive deputy dean of the Academy, I attended the meeting as well. Before the meeting, I showed the attendees a well-packaged bottle of walnut oil, and told them it was processed by the farmers of Luoboshan Village. I handed these bottles out as gifts. Sun was amazed and asked, 'Have they produced it already?' Many attendees at the meeting were interested in Li's walnut processing project. We were, after all, there to discuss the modernisation of small rural households: the walnut processing project gave a good example of how this could be done quite rapidly. More precisely, Li's walnut processing demonstrates how small rural households' incomes can be increased by integration of the three industries (primary, secondary and tertiary industries)—which are, in the case of Luoboshan, those relating to the production, processing and marketing of walnuts.

Mountainous areas constitute a large part of Lincang City, the district within which Luoboshan is situated. Previously, local farmers made a living mainly by felling trees and opening up terraced land for the cultivation of upland rice and maize. Most of the farmers there were smallholders in a real sense. After forests reclaiming policies were implemented, the original terraced fields were planted with walnut trees and tea trees. During the same period, the quality of life in this area has improved significantly. Thanks to a raft of policies supporting poverty alleviation and rural development over the past decades, the villages now have convenient access to transportation, and the formerly impoverished villagers have built new houses, leaving only a handful of dilapidated ancient houses to tell of the tough life of the past.

How do local farmers make a living now? Luoboshan Village in Lincang City is home to 126 households. Each household farms a mountainous area of 5–20 *mu*.[19] Instead of growing upland rice and maize, the village has developed a multi-dimensional farming system focusing on cash crops such as walnuts, tea and cherries. Currently, a dozen walnut trees are planted on every *mu* of land. In the past, the walnut was sold at RMB6–10 per kilo, and a *mu* yields an output of 500kg—thus giving a revenue of RMB6,000–10,000 per *mu*. However, the price has dropped in recent years, down to RMB1.4–1.6 per kilo in 2019. Since labourers must sort the walnuts and daily labour costs about RMB100, the labour cost for sorting out walnuts produced on one *mu* of land could reach RMB400–500. Since the walnuts produced on one *mu* of land could be sold for about RMB400–500, this leaves hardly any profit for the farmers. Under these circumstances, farmers have stopped selling walnuts which are mostly left untouched on the tree.

This is not a unique situation. The experience in Luoboshan is similar to that of the walnut industry in the neighbouring Nujiang Prefecture located in the northwest of Yunnan Province. According to people in Nujiang, the main explanation is that the growing area of walnut trees had excessively expanded year by year. Today, Nujiang's Lushui county alone has planted 600,000 *mu* of walnut trees. As a result, unsellable walnuts have become a dilemma for local industrial development. Apart from walnut trees, Luoboshan Village farmers also planted tea trees, with a tea forest of 5–20 *mu* for each household. Assuming a price of RMB40 per kilo and an output of 100kg per *mu*, the farmers could earn about RMB 4,000 from each *mu* of tea tree. Apart from walnut and tea trees, the villagers also grow cherry trees, with about 20 trees on each *mu* of land. Assuming an output of 25 kilos per *mu* at RMB20 per kilo, the farmers could earn about RMB5,000 from each *mu* of cherry trees.

In addition, farmers in Luoboshan Village plant radishes. The name Luoboshan Village literally translates to Radish Mountain Village, originating from its long history of planting radishes. The radish output of this village could hit 1,000kg per *mu*. If sold at RMB1.2–2 per kilo, the farmers could earn RMB1,200–2,000 per *mu*. The villagers thus maintain their livelihoods through multi-dimensional farming on limited mountain land. Assuming a land of 5 *mu* for each household, they could obtain

[19] 20 *mu* is one and a third hectares.

an annual gross income of over RMB50,000 from crop farming alone. Some households also raise pigs, cattle, chickens and bees, which can also yield a handsome income. Furthermore, nearly all households have family members who travel to cities for work, increasing their household income by RMB30,000–40,000 annually. According to our estimate, the average household income in Luoboshan Village ranges between RMB50,000 and RMB100,000. The per capita disposable income of the villagers has reached or surpassed the national average among farmers.

The above cases show that over the past two decades, the original poverty-stricken village has undergone fundamental changes thanks to multi-dimensional planting, the development of high-value forest crops, and the combination of agriculture and animal husbandry. This has been the main economic development model for most villages, especially in mountainous areas in southwest China. Technically speaking, smallholder farmers are on the track to development.

However, judging from its appearance and overall socio-economic development, Luoboshan Village remains miles away from being prosperous. While the current agricultural system has helped them maintain and improve their livelihoods, further analysis suggests that its upgraded livelihood system and improved quality of life have materialised against the backdrop of rapid national economic growth over the past decades. That is to say, the villagers' better life are largely due to the broader national economic development. Without economic growth, urbanisation and a huge market demand, Luoboshan Village wouldn't have achieved such development. Nearly all the tea leaves, cherries, walnuts and radishes produced in the village are sold to the local and national market. Over the past few decades, the self-sufficient economy in Luoboshan Village has shifted to a commercialised economic system fully integrated into the external market. Such transformation has greatly enhanced farmers' income and living standards, but at the same time also integrated the local economy into a wider market system entailing new risks.

Thriving business constitutes an important part of rural revitalisation. People will propose new industries to boost business development. However, in the case of Luoboshan—a typical mountainous village—the crux of thriving businesses lies in sustained market demand, the key to which lies in overall economic development and the advancement of urbanisation. Without a domestic consumer group that keeps expanding its capacity to purchase, the agricultural products in the village will be in excess demand. In this regard, thriving business relies not only on farmers' production but also on developing the local and national economy, and pursuing urbanisation. Rural revitalisation therefore involves not only rural areas and residents but, indirectly, the entire urban consumer class. In this sense, agrarianism does not help much with rural revitalisation.

This does not mean that rural construction and growth can be ignored. Rural areas have great potential for thriving businesses, albeit needing improvement in production. The multi-dimensional farming and animal husbandry in Luoboshan Village is a good case of successful production-side reform. Yet this is not enough. My team worked with the Linxiang District government in Lincang City to explore the household-based three-industry (first industry, second industry and tertiary industry) integration model that was related to the radish, tea, cherries and walnuts industries. By developing a special product for each household and a unique brand for each village and combining agriculture with processing and tourism, the industrial structure in Luoboshan was expanded. We employed household-based processing, village and household brand development, and radish-themed agro-tourism to enlarge the space for added value in the village's industrial development.

Take tea as an example. The farmers' price for tea leaves is RMB 40 per kilo, while the purchasing enterprises can sell the tea after rough processing at a price of RMB280 per kilo (about 4–4.5 kilograms of fresh leaves can be made into 1 kilogram of dry tea leaves). The same tea leaves can then, be sold in shops for up to RMB2,000 per kilo. Obviously, there's a huge gap between the farmers' price and the market price. The price gap for radishes is relatively narrow, but the market price almost doubles the farmers' sale price. Therefore, a substantial proportion of the profits are taken by the intermediary sales companies due to their capacity in processing, packaging, branding or marketing. The solution to this problem is usually proposed to be the development of rural cooperatives. In fact, however, most cooperatives develop into organisations that then themselves gain high profits by monopolising sales channels between individual companies and intermediaries. Developing an effective organisational structure to reliably fulfil farmers' interests is difficult. Given that this is the case, and that previous experiments have not always succeeded, how can we develop a cooperative mechanism that truly serves farmers and ensures that they gain most of the agro-industrial profits? This is a practical challenge for rural revitalisation.

Despite the great emphasis on production-side reform, the core role of market demand cannot be ignored. According to officials in the Nujiang area, a great many agricultural products have been sold through poverty reduction programmes or platforms[20] over the past few years, but what should we do after the fight against poverty has been won? Many places have turned to live-streaming commerce, a marketing approach in which viewers can instantly buy products seen in an online live video. This has indeed boosted the sales of agricultural products to a certain extent. However, an organisational mechanism that truly benefits farmers and effectively connects them with the market has yet to be developed. The supply and marketing cooperatives in Lincang City are exploring innovations to expand sales channels for local agricultural products by developing brands, formulating standards and connecting farmers to the market. The rich variety of agricultural products is a boon for connecting farmers to the market through branded and standardised development since products in insufficient supply are easy to sell but hard to standardise.

The success of businesses in rural areas in future requires branded development and quality control. Brand development is needed to increase awareness of farmers' products beyond their locale; online marketing, such as through the widely-used livestreams, can assist in this. Rigorous quality control is needed to ensure that there is consumer trust in farmers' products. In many rural areas, farmers have moved, or are moving, away from efforts to *increase* the supply of agricultural products, and towards efforts to *improve* the supply. For many, the knowledge of marketing and distribution that this requires is currently not available, and they must either receive support in developing it, or rely on third party actors who, as I have noted, take too great a slice of the total value.

All of this is, of course, useless without effective wider support for market demand. More than ever, the livelihoods of smallholder farmers in rural areas fundamentally rely on continuing broad market strength, as well as the ability to stimulate robust product-specific demand through the supply of higher-quality agricultural products. Under a sluggish national economy, farmers' incomes will hardly increase, and rural revitalisation will run into trouble. This is also why rural revitalisation cannot

[20] Consumption-based poverty reduction programmes usually encourage government organisations, state-owned enterprises and even private companies to procure goods made in poor areas or service provided by poor farmers. Note by the translator.

be viewed separately from broader economic development and urbanisation. The modernisation of smallholder farmers requires not only high land productivity but also high labour productivity. Both depend on a system that protects farmers' interests and promotes the integration of urban and rural areas.

While I'm writing these words, Li's workshop has succeeded in its experiments with processing walnut oil. However, this walnut oil cannot be sold on the market yet due to the lack of a permit for market entry issued by the food regulation department. Obtaining this permit requires compliance with rigorous requirements on the production scale, factory size and others imposed by the food regulation department. These requirements target large modern processing companies. It's hard for household farmers engaging in secondary processing to meet these production scale and factory size requirements. Therefore, there's still a lack of institutional foundation for developing smallholder farmers' production systems.

In China, smallholder farmers are here to stay. Nonetheless, they cannot merely rely on farming a few acres of land for living. They need to develop industrialised agricultural businesses, such as in the processing sector, and even in the service sector to preserve their farming livelihoods while increasing their income. Therefore, we need to think about innovative ways to make the modern scale-favouring market system also favour those smallholder farmers.

Café in Damiao Village[21]

> 'Development by tourism' works outside Hebian: the tourist's marginal dollar can be guided to where it will have the highest impact.

[21] Damiao Village is in Luozehe Township, Yiliang County, Zhaotong City, Yunnan Province, it is located in the Wumeng Mountain area, one of the most impoverished regions in China. This area was an important target for China's national campaingn on ending extreme poverty in the 2010s and it continues to receive policy support in the new era of rural revitalisation. The author and his team went on to have rural revitalisation experiments in more villages across the Yunnan Province, after his first poverty reduction experiment in Hebian Village. Note by the translator.

At a meeting to draw up a plan for the development of Damiao Village in 2021, I proposed to transform an abandoned pigsty into a café. With no land available in the village, we could only focus on idle assets-empty houses. The officials from the county and township didn't reject my proposal outright, but their facial expressions as they sat in the meeting allowed me to read their objections. Sometime later an official from the county government explained to me, 'Professor Li, at the meeting that day, I was wondering who would come to a mountain village for coffee'. The plan I proposed was therefore quite despised by the village officials. Ultimately, however, the café would grow into the most profitable small business in the village. In its first year after opening, the café generated a total revenue of over RMB160,000, with daily earnings ranging from RMB500–600 to RMB2,000. Today, the café has become a popular must-see destination in the area. Surprisingly, I found that the café in this mountain village was packed with young people every day, just like the café next to my university.

For sure, the revitalisation of the village has not rested solely on the café. From 2021 to 2022, we used many of the village's and farmers' idle assets into guesthouses, cafeterias, multifunctional meeting rooms and other facilities that could generate an income. More importantly, we started a new experiment of recruiting and fostering village CEOs to run these business for the village. At the same time, village infrastructure and environment were improved. During 2022 the revenue of Damiao Village exceeded RMB 2.5 million which surprised even me, the 'designer' of this project. A poverty-stricken mountain village has become a popular place for leisure and tourism. In the village, I met tourists from the neighbouring Sichuan Province who were attracted by the village's beautiful red-brick architecture. The 'scarcity' of rurality is increasing. As I had observed in the Damiao Village, such scarcity is creating new values that constitute a driving force for rural revitalisation.

In Yunnan Province, many people may disagree with the idea of developing a tourist economy in Zhaotong City. Historically, Zhaotong has not contributed much to Yunnan's tourist economy. However, the past few decades have witnessed a rapid development of tourism in Yunnan Province more broadly. For the province, this is easily understood. Cultural relics and natural landscapes usually underpin the tourist economy, and tourism grows into an important pillar of the local economy in places endowed with distinctive cultural sites and beautiful landscapes; Cities like Dali and Lijiang have both. Zhaotong City, by contrast, has long been held not to have such advantages. However, as the concept of the tourist economy continues to expand, the tourism industry in Zhaotong has begun to show unique potential.

Zhaotong is nestled within the northeast corner of Yunnan province and in the hinterland of the Wumeng Mountains, bordering Guizhou and Sichuan. Located in an elevated transition zone from the Sichuan Basin to the Yunnan-Guizhou Plateau, Zhaotong enjoys cool summers. In summer, the temperature ranges from 14 °C to 24 °C, or below 20 °C on average, making Zhaotong a summer paradise: it is cool while other areas are swelteringly hot. Contrary to the widespread assumption that Zhaotong lacks natural beauty, there are in fact vast and marvellous plateau grasslands, dozens of rarely seen waterfalls, superb canyon hot springs, as well as diverse ethnic cultures. In the past, due to poor transportation links to this hinterland of the Wumeng Mountains, Zhaotong's potential as a tourist destination was not unlocked. Nowadays, with its socio-economic development, especially the implementation of poverty alleviation projects, transportation has been fundamentally improved, and people have begun to turn their eyes to the potential of tourism.

According to my friends in Zhaotong, the city's tourist economy is now doing very well. Hotel rooms quickly sell out in the summer. Many people from Sichuan and Chongqing visit the city by bus and can be seen dancing in the public square. Some even buy a house in Zhaotong, which has raised the local housing prices to a certain extent. I've not conducted systematic studies into the situation. In recent years, though, tourism in the downtown areas and counties of Zhaotong has been booming, as evidenced by an abundance of small and medium-sized hotels. Obviously, summer tourism has become the highlight of Zhaotong's tourist economy.

Over the past few years I have spent a great deal of time on rural development, broadly related to rural tourism. In fact, I am neither an expert on tourism research nor a practitioner in the tourist industry. My work has focused on bringing growth drivers from urban to rural areas to boost rural development. In the mid-1990s, when I went to Zhaotong to work on poverty alleviation, its poor transportation links and the decay of its countryside left a deep impression on me. During my visits to Zhaotong in the past two years, however, I found tremendous changes in its rural areas, and I was particularly amazed by the apple orchards all over the mountains and the development of the local potato industry. I cannot help wondering whether the large-scale homogeneous agricultural industry will lead to a surplus of agricultural supplies and whether Zhaotong's overreliance on the agricultural industry incurs the hidden risk of constraining rural development. Zhaotong is not conditioned to develop large-scale industries, but relying on a single agricultural industry has both advantages and hidden risks.

Another important feature of the rural economy in Zhaotong is that the farmers' income mainly comes from migrant work in other cities. The earnings of migrant workers constitute the largest contribution to the rural economy in Zhaotong. Take a close look, and you may find that, instead of enhancing the strength of the indigenous economy, the large-scale agricultural industry that has developed in recent years has mostly increased profits for external companies. This is good for the development of the agro-industry but has failed to play a role in increasing the farmers' income.

My survey of the countryside of several counties in Zhaotong shows that as villagers go out for work year after year, their income has also been increasing yearly and has been used to build houses in the village. Local people in Zhaotong said jokingly, 'Those of us who work in cities live in the basement like mice; we return to build large houses in our hometowns, and we provide homes for mice!' I saw lines of spacious and luxurious houses in the village, but most were vacant. The local people built their houses in the same style as those in the cities where they worked. When new housing styles emerge in the city, locals rebuild their houses in the village accordingly. This is the case with most migrant workers in the village, who spend most of their hard-earned money on building houses they rarely occupy. Such investment is unlikely to create new capital.

While talking with local people in Zhaotong, I told them I'm engaged in rural revitalisation and I am against urban-bias. I hoped Zhaotong could avoid the traditional path of developing an urban tourist economy. In other words, instead of building large hotels, parks and squares in cities, we could think of building tourism facilities in rural areas to develop rural tourism in Zhaotong.

The past few years have witnessed fundamental transportation improvements in rural areas of Zhaotong, linking all counties with expressways and all villages with highways. With better tourism infrastructure, rural areas' scenic landscapes, mountains and grasslands, magnificent waterfalls and vast orchards could all serve as appealing natural tourism resources. Since the houses built by local farmers after the Wenchuan earthquake in

2008 are all of good quality, their redundant rooms could be converted into quality rural family hotels. In this way, urban purchasing power could be brought to the countryside. With greater investment in rural tourism resources, such assets could boost rural revitalisation. More importantly, the farmers' idle assets could be transformed to into assets capital that could generate returns.

In 2021, I led a team to start work in Zhaotong. Government helped us select three poor villages in Zhaoyang District, Ludian County and Yiliang County under the jurisdiction of the City. This project explored how urban growth drivers (including financial capital, purchasing power and human capital) could be channelled to rural areas, piloting using cross-provincial and cross-regional urban resources. Rural tourism will expand the space for developing the tourist economy in Zhaotong. Given the limited space of urban areas in Zhaotong, the development potential of urban tourism is small. More importantly, the development of the rural tourist economy in Zhaotong holds great significance for sustaining the achievements of poverty reduction in the previous stage, upgrading rural economic structures and protecting resources and the environment.

In discussion with local officials, I pointed out that developing the rural tourist economy could expand Zhaotong's economy in three aspects: economic structure, economic growth drivers and farmers' income sources. With the Chongqing-Kunming high-speed railway under construction, Zhaotong will become a pivot station for the one-hour commuting circle between the major cities of Chengdu, Kunming and Chongqing. The arrival of these high-speed rail links will present a huge opportunity for the development of Zhaotong's tourism approach—and with it, associated rural revitalisation programmes.

The manufacturer's authorised representative in the EU is Springer Nature Customer Service Centre GmbH, Europaplatz 3, 69115 Heidelberg, Germany. If you have any concerns regarding our products, please contact ProductSafety@springernature.com

Printed and bound by CPI Group (UK) Ltd, Croydon, CR0 4YY
01/10/2026
02225924-0004